HIKING WASHINGTON'S HISTORY

HIKING
WASHINGTON'S
HISTORY

JUDY BENTLEY

A Samuel and Althea Stroum Book

UNIVERSITY OF WASHINGTON PRESS
Seattle and London

This book is published with the assistance of a grant from the
Samuel and Althea Stroum Endowed Book Fund.

UNIVERSITY OF WASHINGTON PRESS
P.O. Box 50096, Seattle, WA 98145, U.S.A.
www.washington.edu/uwpress

LIBRARY OF CONGRESS
CATALOGING-IN-PUBLICATION DATA
Bentley, Judy.
Hiking Washington's history / Judy Bentley.
p. cm.
Includes bibliographical references and index.
ISBN 978-0-295-99063-7 (paper : alk. paper)
1. Hiking—Washington (State)—Guide-
books. 2. Trails—Washington (State)—
Guidebooks. 3. Historic sites—Washington
(State)—Guidebooks. 4. Washington
(State)—Guidebooks. 5. Washington
(State)—History, Local. I. Title.
GV199.42.W2B46 2011
917.97—dc22   2010019717

Printed and bound in the United States
of America

Designed by Ashley Saleeba

Composed in Adobe Garamond, Whitney,
and Helvetica Neue Condensed

All photographs by Judy Bentley
unless otherwise indicated.

Maps by Matt Stevenson of CORE-GIS.

COVER: Looking south toward Cape
Disappointment from the North Head
Lighthouse. Photograph © 2008 by Andrew
Gorohoff. BACK COVER: Jack Kerouac
spent the summer of 1956 at this lookout
cabin atop Desolation Peak. FRONTISPIECE:
Mount St. Helens from the Truman
Trail after the 1980 eruption. P. 266: The
Columbia River at Wallula Gap.

This book is dedicated to Allen Bentley and Bill Hines,

who both gave me heart as a hiker.

Contents

Legend

- ● Trailheads
- ▲ Destinations
- – – Featured Trails
- ○ Distance Markers
- ▴ Peaks
- • Cities and Towns
- ••• Historic Trails and Roads
- ⁄⸝⸝⸝ Other Trails
- ■ Waypoints
- 🛡5 Highway Markers
- 〜 Highways
- ⌒ Lakes
- 〰 Rivers

Historic Sites and Other Features

- ■ Campsite
- ✝✝ Cemetery
- ☠ Headland
- ■ Historic Site
- 🗼 Lighthouse
- 🔭 Lookout
- ■ Museum
- ➡ Petroglyphs
- 🚹🏠 Ranger Station
- 🏛 Tunnel
- ░ Waterfall

Preface

History lies close to the surface in Washington. We are a young state, only a few generations removed from Indian trails over mountain passes, grand exploring expeditions, and rutted wagon roads. When I moved to the state in 1981, my first hike was only a mile from home, at Cougar Mountain Wildland Park. I tromped through woods that seemed to my urban eyes like wilderness until a guide revealed mine openings and slag heaps, signs of coal mining in the old town of Newcastle. I was amazed that this mountain, edging fast-growing communities, had a vibrant but hidden history underfoot.

Washington's history is easily obscured. Densely settled regions feel like historical wastelands, filled with urban condominiums and suburban tracts that have uprooted trees, rerouted creeks, and paved trails. Dams have flooded the pictograph and petroglyph records of ancient people. Public utilities, office parks, and shopping malls have interrupted trails. Such change supports more people but obliterates the ways the land sustained life in the past.

Even recreation muddies the past, bringing crowds and riding toys to distant mountain meadows. One third of the people living in Washington identify themselves as hikers, backpackers, trail runners, or climbers, and for many the hike is more than exercise, more than recreation or escape. We hike out of curiosity: Who went this way before? Where were they going?

In his book *Winter Brothers*, Ivan Doig writes of his kinship to James Swan, who lived more than a century before him. Reading Swan's diaries, Doig finds himself "in a community of time as well as of people." Doig watches gulls sail across his line of sight much as Swan saw them. "Resonance of this rare sort," he says, "we had better learn to prize like breath."[1] Hiking historic trails connects us to the people on the land before us and to a landscape constant across centuries.

Acknowledgments

Who can resist a summer jaunt through history and nature? Many friends joined me in my usually faithful 1989 Toyota Camry station wagon to explore the vast state of Washington. First there were students in my classes at South Seattle Community College, such as Jan Pollard, and teaching colleagues, such as Dolores Mirabella, Tim Walsh, Esther Sunde (with me when the brakes failed), and Amy McKendry. On Tuesdays, the Trekkers tested directions: Helen Anderson, Sharon Bond, Susan Christie, Kimiko Dickey, Ginger Fulton, Lynn Hall, Sherry Katsuhisa, Arlyn Kerr, Joy Neuzil, Linda Paros, Marlee Richards, and Diane Sengstock. Grand Canyon hikers Debbie Anderson, Sylvia Odom, and Jody Sweet morphed into Northwest backpackers. Thanks to my hiking friends Darel Grothaus, Vicki Mau, Kristin Tregillus, Nancy Valaas, Leona Vittum-Jones, Connie Wentzel, Kristi and Tom Weir, Eli Davis, Dave Stokes, Daniel McKendry-Stokes, and Lynn and Kay Youngblood.

Writers groups over the years heard many variations of the text. Thanks to Vivian Bowden, Deborah Davis, Janine Brodine, Susan Starbuck, Kate Willette, Terri Miller, Christine Castigliano, and Mary Wright.

Historians such as Clay Eals, Andrea Mercado, Chuck Richards, Lorraine McConaghy, Jacqueline Williams, John Daughters, Cathy Lykes, Tim Eckert, Robert Kuhlken, and Paul Spitzer provided support, as did Washington Trails Association editor Andrew Engelson; history writers and naturalists Jack Nisbet, Joan Burton, Austin and Roberta Post, Ruth Kirk, and William Sullivan; local historians Gladys Para, Yvonne Prater, and Kelly McAllister; trails advocates Ruth Itner and Harvey Manning; longtime Oregon Butte lookouts Charlie and Bev Heebner; Mary Johnson; Forest Service archaeologists Rick McClure, Susan Carter, and Jacilee Wray; and Nisqually National Wildlife Refuge manager Jean Takekawa. Members of the Northwest chapter of the Oregon-California Trails Association—Tuck and Kay Forsythe, Chuck and Suzanne Hornbuckle, Don Popejoy, and Lethene Parks—introduced me to the comforts of four-wheel drive. Mark Borleske shared his comprehensive knowledge of the Milwaukee Road.

When the book was just an idea with notes, Joan Gregory offered encouragement. Years further down the trail, Beth Fuget at the University of Washington Press kept the manuscript alive, and Marianne Keddington-Lang and Kerrie Maynes shepherded it to publication. Jan Koutsky and Peter Bentley helped early on with the maps when my writing group clamored to "see the trails." Matt Stevenson of CORE-GIS provided the cartographic art.

Thanks to my daughter Anne Bentley, who hiked and provided technical expertise along the publication route; my son Peter Bentley, who hiked and provided artistic advice. First and last thanks to my husband Allen Bentley, who would always hike one more day, climb to just one more lookout, and scale one more mountain pass long after others had politely declined.

Introduction

People have moved across Washington's landscape for thousands of years. Paths led to places of value: to meadows full of berries and roots, to trade emporiums on the rivers, to forests of old-growth trees, to prairies for homesteads and towns, to grass for grazing, to gold mines and coal.

First there were game trails, trampled grass or hoof prints in the dirt, the spore that marked where elk, deer, bear, or coyote had gone. Early people traveled the ridges and crossed mountain passes, camped in the meadows and along the rivers. Rock shelters, pictographs, and fishing artifacts reveal what life on the water was like, from Ozette to Kettle Falls.

When Europeans and Americans came to the Pacific Northwest, they recorded their travels in journals and ships' logs. From the west, they sailed or paddled from the Strait of Juan de Fuca into Puget Sound and up the Columbia River from the Pacific Ocean. From the north, they canoed down the Columbia from the fur-rich Canadian mountains. From the east, they crossed the mountains and followed the rivers to the coast.

Through government reports and the publication of books, word of their discoveries reached Americans back east. Missionaries and settlers came, veering off the Oregon Trail at Waiilatpu or The Dalles. After rafting down the dangerous Columbia, they went up the Cowlitz River and overland to Puget Sound. Major military and scientific expeditions led by Wilkes, McClellan, and Symons crossed the state. Painters, writers, botanists, ethnographers, archaeologists and geologists followed in their wake. The most remote, least hospitable, and least accessible regions—the North Cascades, the Methow, the Olympics, the Columbia Plateau—were settled last, and a very few places were never disturbed.

Each generation learned from earlier travelers, and the trails changed. Native Americans advised fur traders about the best passes through the mountains. Emigrants drove wagons on any path wide enough to follow. Railroad surveyors staked out the best routes east to west and along the Puget Sound waterfront. Travois ruts became wagon ruts, became dirt roads, became railroads or highways.

Some of the busiest trails in the state can no longer be followed on foot. The Cowlitz Trail, an extension of the Oregon Trail to Puget Sound, has been superseded in most places by I-5. The Cariboo Trail, a cattle drive trail to the Cariboo mining region in Canada, is Highway 97. The Snoqualmie Trail through Snoqualmie Pass has become I-90. Lewis and Clark rafted the Snake and Columbia rivers now harnessed by dams and dominated by barges.

Yet a remarkable number of historic trails remain. Some trails, like the Iron Goat Trail on an old railroad grade, have been fully restored and interpreted by thousands of volunteers. Others, like the Naches Pass wagon trail over the Cascades, have been abused by off-road vehicles but survive in parts. Some are easily accessible, like the Duwamish River Trail in Seattle and Spokane Centennial Trail. Others, such as Chief Joseph's Summer Trail in the Blue Mountains, require a half-day just to reach the trailhead from the nearest town.

This book is organized by regions, roughly west to east. We'll begin on the Olympic Peninsula, at the very edge of the continent. From the Pacific Ocean, we'll move east across Puget Sound lowlands, the Cascades, central Washington meadows and deserts, to the Idaho boundary, south and west along the Snake River and then back to the coast where Lewis and Clark first saw the ocean from the Columbia's mouth. Each chapter begins with a brief overview of the region's history followed by individual trail narratives, with historical highlights. I'll tell you how to get there, what to expect, and what to look for as well as who was here before you and why they came.

If you choose one of several backpacking trails in the book, be sure to bring a more detailed map and hiking guide. Also, Forest Service roads wash out often, so check road conditions online or at ranger stations.

Let's begin at the northwest tip of the state where the ocean roars in on Cape Flattery, where the Makah people first saw a ship with sails enter their traditional whaling waters.

HIKING WASHINGTON'S HISTORY

CHAPTER ONE

The Olympic Peninsula

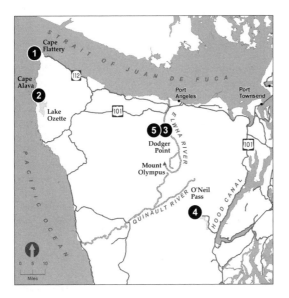

For centuries, the Olympic Peninsula has been the wild edge of the continent, a rugged, remote thumb reaching west into the wider world. Native American tribes cluster along the rivers and coasts, from the Quinault people along the Quinault River at the base of the thumb; north to the Hoh, Queets, and Quileute; on to the Makah at Cape Flattery; and east to the S'Klallam and the Suquamish. Just thirty-three miles in from the coast, Mount Olympus rises almost 8,000 feet. Mountain ranges stretch north to south and east to west, walling off the interior of the peninsula. Port Townsend and Port Angeles anchor commerce along the Strait of Juan de Fuca in the north; the deep fjord of Hood Canal seals off the peninsula from the east.

On this far northwestern coast, Europeans, Americans, Asians, and Native Americans first encountered one another. From the high cliffs of Cape Flattery and Tatoosh Island, the whale-hunting Makah saw the ships of explorers in the late 1700s; they called the ships "houses on the water" and carved the images in stone. From the deck of his ship in 1788, British captain John Meares saw the island, which appeared to be a barren rock, almost inaccessible, "But the surface of it, as far as we could see, was covered with inhabitants, who were gazing at the ship." The Europeans were astounded not only by the people but also by the land. "The appearance of the land was wild in the extreme—immense forests covered the whole of it within our sight, down to the very beach, which was lofty and cragged, and against which the sea dashed with fearful rage," Meares marveled.

Astonishment gave way to commerce. On his third trip around the world, in 1778, English captain James Cook sailed along the same rocky coast and traded for sea otter pelts, which his crew sold in Canton at high prices. Within a few years, a procession of Spanish-, British-, and American-flagged schooners rounded Cape Flattery, looking for trade and safe harbors. The Spanish and British competed at Nootka Sound on Vancouver Island. A U.S. customs post opened at Port Townsend in 1851, halfway between the ocean and Puget Sound, on the Strait of Juan de Fuca.

As trade increased on the coast, the mountains of the peninsula remained little known. From a safe distance offshore, Meares had named Mount Olympus an appropriate home for the New World's gods, not suitable for casual travel. Coastal Indians warned of convulsions of nature in the interior. Still, in the late 1800s, two exploring expeditions braved the remote valleys and peaks and put trails on the maps. A few homesteaders established lonely outposts between the mountains and the sea. For about ten years in the 1890s and early 1900s, Scandinavian immigrants logged and farmed the forests and prairies around Lake Ozette, until logging and a national forest reserve crowded them out.

Archaeological digs on the coast turned up a piece of bamboo, evidence of the peninsula's relative closeness to Asia. During World War II this proximity aroused alarm when a Japanese submarine lurked off of the Strait of Juan de Fuca. Patrols walked the beaches, and lookouts stationed on Olympic peaks scanned the skies for foreign planes. After the war, the peninsula returned to relative obscurity, except for loggers and national park visitors, until the Makah attracted worldwide attention by reviving their whale hunting in 1999.

What remains of this peninsula's history to beckon hikers? Petroglyphs, a small replicated longhouse at Ozette, a sign on a remote mountain pass, images of goblins and sounds of imaginary geysers, abandoned prairies, and a boarded-up lookout cabin. We'll begin at the far northwestern tip in the 1700s. We'll visit the site of Ozette village and walk from the coast inland to the Scandinavian settlements near Lake Ozette. We'll follow the bootprints of nineteenth-century expeditions across mountain passes. Finally, we'll climb to the World War II lookout post at Dodger Point to take a deep breath of moist Olympic air and gaze full circle to the widening horizon.

1

Cape Flattery

GETTING THERE: Take Highway 112 to and through Neah Bay. Purchase a ten-dollar recreation permit at the Makah Marina, Washburn's General Store, the Makah Tribal Center, the Makah Museum, Neah Bay Charter and Tackle, Makah Fuel Company, or the Makah Smoke Shop. Follow the

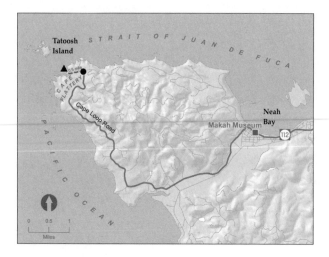

sharp corner that turns left, then take a right at the Indian Health Service Clinic on the right. Go one block, then turn left and follow the signs to the Tribal Center, 2.2 miles. Continue past the center on the paved road for 4.5 miles to a parking lot, facilities, and signs for the trail.

DISTANCE: .5 mile one way

LEVEL OF DIFFICULTY: easy

HISTORICAL HIGHLIGHTS: viewpoint at Cape Flattery; Tatoosh Island

On a cold, rainy night in April, my family set up camp at Lake Crescent on the northern edge of the Olympic Peninsula. It was our first spring vacation in Washington, and we expected spring weather. After a night spent warming our hands under the restroom's blowdryer, we renewed our mission to reach the northwestern-most point in the continental United States. Along Highway 112, we picked up a hitchhiker, Skip Green, who was returning to the Makah reservation after years working in logging and high-rise construction. He delighted our eight-year-old daughter by sketching an eagle.

After dropping Green off just outside of Neah Bay, we warmed ourselves again in a longhouse at the Makah Museum—appreciating the ingenuity of using conical cedar hats to deflect the rain—and then continued west. At the Cape Flattery trailhead a sign read, "Rugged cliffs, extremely dangerous." A rain forest of fir, hemlock, spruce, and cedar blocked our view of the ocean, and the dense salal undergrowth separated our four-year-old son from the cliffs. As we hiked through mud, the roar of the Pacific grew louder.

The hike to the very tip of the country is short, but the history is ancient. The Makah have lived here for more than 2,000 years. When John Meares sailed past Cape Flattery and Tatoosh Island in 1788, he saw many Makah on the island but "could by no means reconcile the appearance of the place, with such a flourishing state of population." According to Makah estimates, between 2,000 and 4,000 people were living in five villages along the coast at that time. Flourish they did, on clams, mussels, octopus, crabs, and even barnacles. Launching canoes from Ozette village, south of Cape Flattery, and the more sheltered base of Neah Bay, they hunted whales, sea lions, and fur seals. They fished halibut and salmon from the seas and rivers, gathered roots and berries, and hunted elk and deer. By trading whale oil and seal oil to vessels, the Makah established a reputation as international traders.

This bountiful life changed when Europeans arrived. Smallpox epidemics ravaged the coastal villages in the late 1700s, and half a century later the Makah were decimated by the smallpox brought by a San Francisco trading ship. By 1854 their population had dwindled to only 150. The next year they signed the Treaty of Neah Bay with new territorial governor Isaac Stevens, who represented the United States. The treaty preserved Makah fishing rights but consigned the tribe to a reservation around Neah Bay of forty-four square miles and to a smaller reservation at Ozette village. United States government policy tried to turn the Makah from fishing to agriculture, but they had no heart for it. Seeds rotted in the moist ground—there was too much rain for farming.

As most white settlement and commerce moved east toward Puget

Sound, Neah Bay remained isolated until 1931, when state Highway 112 was completed. Archaeological excavations at the Ozette village site in the 1960s and 1970s attracted thousands of visitors, and the discoveries led to the opening of the Makah Cultural and Research Center in 1979. By the 1980s there were over 1,400 tribal members. In 1999 the Makah launched their first successful whale hunt in ninety years, and tasted blubber again. Under the glare of publicity brought on by the hunt, the tribe renewed their welcome to visitors by improving the trail to Cape Flattery.

On Memorial Day weekend 2000, my adult family returned to the cliffs of Cape Flattery. The mild, clear day dispelled any foreboding that lingered from our first visit. The Makah have fashioned a groomed earthen trail with a cedar boardwalk crossing the muddy spots. Again we heard the ocean but could not see it. Then, at the end of a half-mile trail, the ocean and Tatoosh Island grandly emerge. Waves pound the high cliffs, cedar decks and guardrails secure four observation perches, and signs interpret the cape's history.

Although the Makah canoed the waters around Cape Flattery with confidence, sailing ships found the tip forbidding. Captain James Cook approached from the south in 1778 and saw a small opening "which flattered us with the hopes of finding an harbour." "On this account," he continued, "I called the point of land to the north of it Cape Flattery."[1] Unable to find a safe harbor, Cook sailed on to Nootka Sound.

American captain Robert Gray came within a pistol shot of foundering on the rocks beneath the cliffs in 1791, in "foggy disagreeable weather." An offshore breeze saved the ship. The next day was just as perilous. "Heard the roaring of Breaker, foggy[,] haul'd more offshore. At 3 PM saw a rock about stone's throw distant, and narrowly excaped being dash'd upon itt. Damn nonsense to keep beating about among rocks in foggy weather," wrote the young clerk John Boit in the ship's log.

The Makah used these rocks to their advantage. Hunters in

Native Americans gather at Tatoosh Island. Courtesy of the Clallam County Historical Society.

whaling canoes would drive herds of seal and sea otter toward the cliffs. Harpooners stationed on rocks inside caves under the cliffs would spear the seals and otters who sought shelter there.

To the west is Tatoosh Island, where 150 inches of rain fall each year. The island was originally named Chadi by the Makah; Meares called it Tatoosh, after the chief whose canoes came out to meet his ship. Tatoosh Island was a seal-hunting and fishing camp as well as a burial ground for the Makah. From this ancient vantage point, the Makah watched for the annual migrations of the whales. They also raised dogs on the island, shearing off solid mats of brushy brown or white fur with a mussel-shell knife and using the coats to make blankets.

A lighthouse was installed in 1857 to shine its light twenty miles into the ocean, guiding ships entering the Strait of Juan de Fuca. It was built over the opposition of the Makah, who said the light scared away the whales. James Swan, a census taker, customs agent, schoolteacher, and early anthropologist, saw the lighthouse as a beacon of civilization. In 1859 he spent five days trying to enter the

Strait of Juan de Fuca during an adverse wind. "But every night we were cheered by the light on Tatoosh Island, which, shining like a bright star amid the primeval gloom, seemed to us not only a beacon to the mariner, but as an evidence of civilization, and a proof that the 'star of Empire' had made its way westward." The light at the lighthouse is now automated and its buildings unoccupied.

When we returned to Cape Flattery a third time, in 2008, foghorns sounded and Tatoosh Island was invisible. The new interpretive panels at the trailhead were funded by the legal settlement from an oil spill during a similar heavy fog in July 1991. The Japanese fishing vessel *Tenyo Maru* had collided with the Chinese freighter *Tuo Hai* northwest of Cape Flattery, spilling 475,000 gallons of oil and fuel and killing thousands of seabirds.

Despite its location at the end of a serpentine road on a treacherous coast, this northwestern tip remains an intersection of cultures. Thirteen thousand vessels pass this point each year. The Makah say they live not on the edge of the world but at "the beginning of the world."

2

Lake Ozette to Cape Alava

GETTING THERE: Take Highway 101 west to 112, then north to Seiku. At 2.3 miles beyond Sekiu, turn south on the Hoko/Ozette Road. Drive 21 miles on a paved road to the Ozette Ranger Station and beginning of the trail.

DISTANCE: 9.3-mile loop

LEVEL OF DIFFICULTY: easy; pay attention to the tides

HISTORICAL HIGHLIGHTS: Wedding Rock petroglyphs; Ozette village site; Ahlstrom Prairie

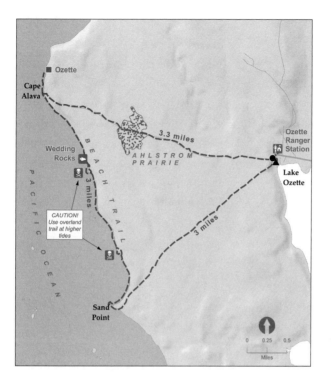

A few miles south of Cape Flattery, Cape Alava juts out as the westernmost tip of land in the contiguous United States. Migrating sea animals mass as they swim around the cape, making it the perfect spot for ocean fishing. For hundreds of years, the Ozette people braved the waves to hunt. Here offshore islands and a reef calm the waters, making it safe to land canoes. The Ozette split cedar logs into planks and built houses as big as seventy feet long by thirty feet wide. Then, 300 years ago, something—probably an earthquake—loosened the eroded clay bank above the houses. The village of Ozette was buried in a mudslide.

Inland from Cape Alava, Scandinavians settled the prairies around Ka'houk, the Makah name for Lake Ozette, the third-largest natural lake in the state. In the late 1890s, immigrants from countries like Finland and Sweden were attracted by homestead acts that offered land. They hoped that the Northern Pacific Railroad would extend to Port Townsend and carry their produce and timber to market. In 1895 homesteaders Anders and Britta Nylund hired Indians to transport them and their three young daughters and goods from Neah Bay, around Cape Flattery, to Cape Alava. Then they walked three miles inland to the north end of Lake Ozette, where Anders claimed a 160-acre homestead and Britta 40 acres of timber.

The new Americans and the surviving Ozette people used, and sometimes shared, the same resources. Settlers bought canoes from the Indians; these were useful for moving on the large lake and on the Ozette River. Hulda Nylund, a daughter of Anders and Britta, remembers that the Ozette canoed up the river and through the north end of the lake to Eagle Point to catch, dry, and smoke salmon, a harvest they celebrated with potlatches, drumming, and singing.

Indians and early settlers used the same method to fell trees: they bored two holes in the tree, poured in hot coals, and kept the fire burning until the tree was ready to fall. The western red cedar provided housing and clothing for the Ozette and a possible cash crop for the settlers, but neither the Scandinavians nor the Ozette would be able to sustain their way of life here.

The remoteness that doomed the Lake Ozette settlement is both the charm and the challenge of getting to the trailhead. At the end of the Hoko-Ozette Road, which was completed in 1935, a triangular trail leads west to the historic site of a warehouse at Sand Point, north to Cape Alava and the site of Ozette village, then east through homesteaded prairies back to Lake Ozette.

The trail begins at the Lake Ozette Ranger Station, where the headquarters building claims part of the site of the Nylund homestead. The first trail segment, from the ranger station to Sand Point, was built by members of the Nylund family in 1927, following a compass course. The stretch of trail closest to the beach was built on top of logs that washed in. Boardwalks carry hikers over the bogs for most of the three miles to the coast, where campsites huddle back from the high-tide mark. Climbing Sand Point itself provides a view south, toward the site of placer mining for gold at Yellow Banks.

A small warehouse at Sand Point stored supplies for Lake Ozette settlers, items they could not grow, such as nails, matches, pipe tobacco, flour, sugar, and coffee beans. The Nylunds would haul their supplies by sled to the lake, paddle them by canoe or boat to the landing at the lake's north end, and load them onto horse and sled for the final slog to their house, a two-day round-trip.

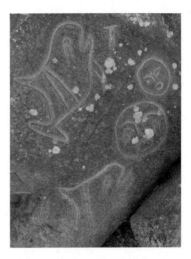

The Ozette carved whale petroglyphs south of Cape Alava. Photograph © 2006 by Andrew Gorohoff.

Later, surplus cream, butter, and quarters of beef and pork from Lake Ozette homesteads were shipped out from the same warehouse, which is now long gone.

From Sand Point, follow the beach north, watching for danger points where waves beat the rocky shore at high tide. At the second danger point, after crossing a cobbly beach and a creek, look on the shore side of the dark volcanic rocks for the Wedding Rock petroglyphs. There are more than thirty petroglyphs of whales, birds, and a mask here that are about 300 years old. On the higher rocks are carvings of sailing ships, records of early encounters with European and American mariners. On a rock face along the trail high on the bank is a carved image of a fish. Imagine "Do Not Touch" signs and appreciate these carvings visually.

At Cape Alava, named for a Spanish naval brigadier, sea lions bark from the offshore islands. Here the beach widens below grassy bluffs, inviting exploration. At low tide, it is possible to walk to

Tskawahyah (also called Cannonball Island for its cannonball-like concretions of sandstone), but climbing or hiking is prohibited. As with Tatoosh to the north, the Makah may have used this island as a retreat. A midden at the top revealed that the tribe had carried baskets of clams, fish, and fur seal meat up the bluff. The remains of an abandoned World War II coast guard cabin are also on top.

The causeway to Tskawahyah creates quiet waters on the south side. Paths cleared between large rocks were canoe dragways leading to the water from the village. The Ozette people, who were related to the Makah, left their homes in 1897 when the federal government required their children to go to school at Neah Bay, fifteen miles away. By 1923 a population of about 800 had dwindled to three, and Ozette became an occasional fishing camp.

On a rainy day in 1947, an archaeology student named Richard Daugherty surveyed this same coast for signs of ancient habitation; he found the site of Ozette and realized that it had been a large village. Twenty years later, then a professor at Washington State University, Daugherty returned with students. They excavated a 200-foot-long trench, cross-sectioning beach terraces, and found evidence that people had lived at the site for at least 2,000 years. In the winter of 1970, severe winter storms uncovered something new and significant. Ed Claplanhoo, Makah tribal chairman, heard rumors that hikers were "pot hunting" at the site and walking away with artifacts, the belongings of families who had lived at Ozette. He and a friend boated from Neah Bay, around Cape Flattery, and down to the village site to take a look. Then he called Daugherty.

Daugherty drove for ten hours from Pullman, Washington, napped at the end of the road at Lake Ozette, and the next day hiked the three miles to the sea. What he saw were the partially exposed remains of a longhouse, buried in mud that had preserved the house and its contents for 300 years. For the next ten years, archaeologists, working with the Makah tribe, excavated four of six longhouses and recovered a rich trove of artifacts—more than 55,000—including a bow and arrow, a club, a basket, a harpoon head, a bailer (for bailing water out of a canoe), a paddle, hats, rope, a carved wooden bowl, a cedar hat, bone fish hooks, shell knives, the bones of many whales and fur seals, and shuttlecock paddles. Many of the artifacts were remembered by Makah elders and are now housed and displayed in the Makah Cultural and Research Center and the Makah Museum at the east end of Neah Bay. The artifacts revealed the ingenuity and richness of the Ozette coastal way of life.

At the height of the archaeological dig, thousands of people hiked through the muddy forest and along the beach to visit Ozette. The excavation is covered and closed now, but a small longhouse on a bank above the beach shelters an evolving memorial to the people who lived here. A plaque, whale vertebrae, carvings, and shell necklaces are all carefully arranged on the dirt floor, walls, and cedar plank benches.

On the northern return leg to the lake, the country is more open. James Swan, the first white man to see Lake Ozette, made the same trip with a Makah companion in 1864 and recorded in his diary, "The trail commences a short distance south of the village and runs up to the top of the hill or bluff which is rather steep and about sixty feet high. From the summit we proceeded in an easterly direction through a very thick forest half a mile and reached an open prairie which is dry and covered with fern, dwarf sallal and some red top grass, with open timber around the sides." Other excerpts from Swan's diary are found in Ivan Doig's *Winter Brothers*.

The Ozette used fire to clear forests and produce ideal hunting grounds for deer. Settlers found these same prairies good grazing for cattle. Ahlstrom Prairie was the homestead of Lars Kristopher Ahlstrom, who laid most of the original puncheon planks on the trail. Ahlstrom was the westernmost white resident of the United States for most of the years between 1902 and 1958. A bachelor Swede, he played his accordion at social gatherings and hiked to Lake Ozette twice weekly for mail, supplies, and companionship.

For a decade or so, the Lake Ozette community seemed promising. About 130 homesteaders cleared land and planted orchards. The Pederson store supplied essentials, and a Lutheran preacher held services at his house on Preacher Point, but a school was hard to maintain, as teachers found the area too isolated and remote. Then, in 1897, the federal government created the Olympic Forest Reserve, which included Lake Ozette, and closed it to both logging and farming. Many settlers left. When timber companies successfully lobbied Congress to reopen the Lake Ozette section of the reserve, timber companies with claims rushed in, and the remaining homesteaders gave up on farming. Ahlstrom was one of the few who hung on, working in the mills or logging camps in the fall and winter. At the age of eighty-six, he cut his foot while chopping wood and moved to Port Angeles.

The coastal strip of Olympic National Park was added in 1953 to preserve the coast and the lake. Left to grow unchallenged, trees are encroaching on the prairies. As thousands of hikers make this popular trek each year, history remains in the place names, artifacts, memories, and the carvings of whales on ancient rock.

3

Press Expedition, Elwha River

GETTING THERE: Take Highway 101 southwest of Port Angeles to the Elwha entrance to Olympic National Park. Beyond the entrance, take the road to the Whiskey Bend trailhead, 5 miles.

DISTANCE: Whiskey Bend to Low Divide, 28 miles; Whiskey Bend to Lake Quinault, 44 miles.

LEVEL OF DIFFICULTY: difficult

HISTORICAL HIGHLIGHTS: Goblin Gates; Michaels Cabin; Difficulty Hill; Press Valley

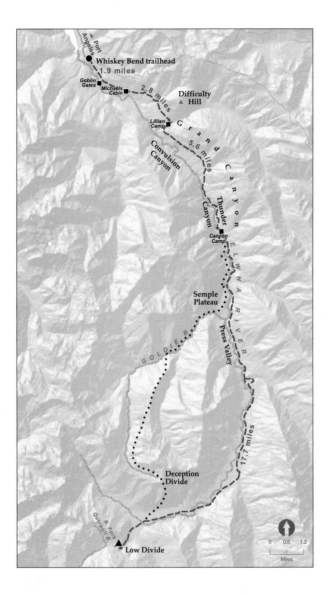

In the 1880s, the rugged interior of the Olympic Peninsula remained a mystery. Native American oral tradition told of a "convulsion of nature" that had overtaken the last gathering of tribes in a once-happy valley amid the mountains. Territorial governor Eugene Semple, who could look out his office window in Olympia at "this grand wilderness," speculated that "nature had designed to shut up this spot for her safe retreat forever."

As the population of Washington Territory grew and the wilderness contracted, a lingering sense of adventure lured explorers to this shut-up spot. Inspired by newspaper reports of Sir Henry Stanley's explorations in Africa, the *Seattle Press* advertised for "men of vim and vigor" to undertake a crossing of the backbone of the Olympics. Six men, four dogs, and two mules answered the call in December 1889.

The Olympic Mountains stretch north to south, and sometimes slant east to west, in several ranges separated by deep river valleys. The Elwha River drains north into the Strait of Juan de Fuca; the Bogachiel, the Hoh, and the Queets drain west into the Pacific Ocean; the Quinault, south into Lake Quinault and on to the

The Press Expedition poses, December 6, 1889. University of Washington Libraries, Special Collections, La Roche 10018.

ocean; the North Fork Skokomish, southeast into Lake Cushman; and the Dosewallips and Duckabush, east to Hood Canal. To go from one river drainage to another, explorers had to cross divides, and usually not just one but several. The Press Expedition chose to start from the north and follow the ridge dividing the Elwha drainage, which flows north, from the Quinault drainage, which flows southwest. In the next six months, they blazed a forty-four-mile route, the only trail that still goes completely through the Olympic Mountains from north to south.

The trail now leaves from Whiskey Bend in the canyon of the Elwha River. The expedition spent two and a half months just getting to this point from Port Angeles, and their whiskey was "well nigh exhausted," wrote James H. Christie, their leader. Bad weather caused the delay, along with a frustrating attempt to use a boat, Gertie, to haul their gear up the river. Once they gave up Gertie and transferred her burden to mules, progress was better but still very slow. In an increasingly severe winter, the expedition tramped through snow that was sometimes frozen and sometimes slush and crossed the Elwha many times in water that froze their chests. Through March and half of April, they slogged to Low Divide, some twenty-eight miles.

The Elwha is still a dangerous river to cross without a bridge, and the trail today stays on one side. Three female explorers came with me to follow the Press Expedition route as far as our summer vacations allowed. After a three-hour drive from Seattle, we arrived at Whiskey Bend and set out on a well-trod fisherman's trail along the east side of the Elwha. In four days of trekking, we saw scenery that had changed only in name and ease of travel, leaving plenty of time for reading about the men's travails.

Feeling fresh the first day, at 1.2 miles we opted for a side trip to Goblin Gates, which was named by expedition member Charles A. Barnes. Barnes thought he saw goblins in the rock walls above this beautiful blue-green turn in the river. At 1.9 miles from Whiskey

Bend, the trail passes Michaels Cabin above Geyser Valley. Here expedition members heard "low, rumbling noises" they thought were geysers. "The sounds lasted exactly eight seconds," wrote Barnes, "beginning slowly like the clicking of a ratchet on a cogwheel, gradually increasing in rapidity, and at the end becoming too rapid for the ear to distinguish, and ceasing abruptly at the end of a few seconds." The name stuck when the sounds of the wind reminded Addison "Doc" Ludden of geysers too, and he opened a trailside inn, Geyser House. E. O. Michaels, a cougar hunter and trail guide, lived in the cabin after Ludden, hence the name Michaels cabin. No geysers have ever been found here; the mysterious rumblings were more likely the drumming of grouse.

Above this valley, the trail follows the lower contours of a steep mountainside that the Press Expedition called Difficulty Hill and reaches Lillian Camp on the Lillian River. The men carried a lump of sourdough from camp to camp, shot bear and elk (eating the livers first), and made fires to warm themselves. Contemporary hikers bring freeze-dried dinners, backpacking stoves, and warm sleeping bags—no fires, and no guns.

The expedition crossed the Lillian in knee-deep cold water and clambered up an elk trail on the opposite side with "much labor and shortness of breath." On the snow-free trail, the leaders made "one little discovery" they knew "would gladden the hearts of the boys in camp." They found kinnikinnick, whose dried leaves substituted for their dwindling tobacco supply; it still grows along the side of the trail.

With sound effects from the Elwha, the trail climbs above Convulsion Canyon and Thunder Canyon, names superseded by Grand Canyon. Convulsion Canyon provides evidence of a landslide that supports the Native American report of an earthquake in the interior. At Canyon Camp, just above Thunder Canyon, about five and a half miles beyond the Lillian River, the expedition crossed the Elwha and climbed to a small bench on the west side they named

The Press Expedition followed the Elwha River into the mountains.

Semple Plateau, after the governor. Barnes thought that they had found evidence of an old Indian village—tree blazes made by axes, an unnatural-looking mound, and a scarcity of trees indicating they may have been cut down for fuel. The fact there was no water nearby was not a problem, Barnes thought, "for the labor of fetching devolves on the squaw." Robert Wood, author of a definitive account of the expedition, discounts their evidence of a village.

Just south of Semple Plateau, where the Goldie River flows into the Elwha from the west, the expedition made a crucial mistake. Thinking that the western path would take them to the Quinault, they veered west when they should have stayed east. They followed the Goldie River and climbed along the sides of treacherous ridges to a point they later called Deception Divide because it had deceived them: instead of looking down on the Quinault running south, they were rather surprised to see a river running north through the same valley they had left—the Elwha again. In twelve days of hard work, the men had traveled over twenty miles "of the roughest country and through the most rugged canyon in the mountains," only to find themselves at the other horn of this crescent-shaped valley. "We might have made the journey on snowshoes in a couple of days' easy traveling," wrote Barnes. This disagreeable discovery "gave rise to sundry hard expressions not usually found in Webster," Christie acknowledged.

The modern trail forgoes the wrong turn and climbs above the Elwha into the tranquil Press Valley, named after the route the expedition should have taken. It was May when the expedition finally came down from Deception Divide, recrossed the Elwha, and climbed up from the south end of Press Valley to Low Divide, the central divide of the Olympics that separates north- and south-flowing streams. Pausing only briefly, they headed down and picked up the North Fork of the Quinault River, homeward bound. On the way they shot a bear, which stemmed their hunger after a diet of flour and water.

As they passed through the mountains, the expedition named several peaks no one else had put on the map: the Bailey Range, which they named after *Seattle Press* owner William E. Bailey, and Mount Christie and Mount Barnes, after the two narrators of the expedition. As they continued down the Quinault on a makeshift raft, a logjam dumped two of the men, the dogs, and their baggage into the swift-flowing river. Barnes emerged clutching the backpack of records in one hand and grasping a log with the other. "We are indebted to his grit and pluck for preserving the records of our winter's work within the charmed circle of Olympus," wrote Christie. So are we.

Five and a half months after they started, five men and three dogs emerged at Lake Quinault.[2] The men were in rags, with only their ammunition belts intact. One of the expedition members proposed to hide in the woods while the others negotiated a trade with a clothing merchant—which they found in Aberdeen, along with a barber. Accounts of the expedition's journey were published in the newspaper in July 1890. As explorers with an "abundance of grit and manly vim," the men struck heroic poses in the photos taken before they set out and when they returned.

As soon as a trail was blazed, the curious followed. Homesteaders such as Ludden, Michaels, and the Humes brothers found a life along the lower Elwha, and the creation of a national park preserved Governor Semple's "safe retreat." Enough mystery remains, however, to entice others of vim and vigor. After lolling along the river in the Press Valley on a sunny afternoon, we four explorers returned to Whiskey Bend the next day, sobered by the news heard from a ranger on the trail that a hiker had drowned fording the Elwha just the week before. The river's waters had been swollen by a week of rain, a potent reminder that happy valleys and convulsions of nature still coincide.

4

O'Neil Pass

GETTING THERE: Drive to the Staircase Ranger Station west of Hoodsport.

DISTANCE: 20 miles from the Ranger Station to O'Neil Pass

LEVEL OF DIFFICULTY: difficult

HISTORICAL HIGHLIGHTS: Nine Stream Camp; O'Neil Pass

Just as the *Seattle Press* published its account of the Press Expedition in July of 1890, Lieutenant Joseph P. O'Neil led a military expedition into the Olympics. He took along a crew of soldiers

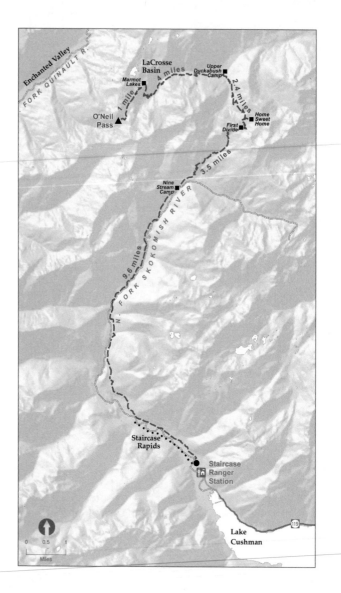

from Fort Vancouver, three scientists sent by the Oregon Alpine Club (later called the Mazamas), and two mineralogists looking for mineral wealth.

The Olympic Exploring Expedition wanted to carve a mule trail through the mountains, an east-west route from Lake Cushman to

Lake Quinault. Along the way, the men planned to climb Mount Olympus and explore as many passes, divides, and ridges as they could. Unlike the well-established Indian trails through passes in the Cascades, there were no known trails across the Olympics, but every river bottom had game trails to follow. O'Neil described the difficulties of penetrating the east side of the Olympics: "The dense forests and denser undergrowth around the base of these mountains . . . render all attempts to enter, but the most systematic trail cutting, abortive." On any day, one crew might be doing the heavy work of cutting trail so mules could constantly resupply the expedition, and two other crews would be following elk trails, looking for the next best route. The biggest challenge was finding a divide suitable for a mule.

Starting from Hood Canal and Lake Cushman, the expedition followed the north fork of the Skokomish River, establishing camps such as Camp 4 at Four Stream and Camp 9 at Nine Stream. After twenty-six days of "chopping and digging," they were still in a valley where a man "could not see twenty yards in any direction except directly upward."

That trail of twenty-six days is now the first long day on the way to the suitable divide O'Neil eventually found. My expedition of two women and a boy began the forty-mile backpack on a rainy day in September. From the Staircase Ranger Station, the North Fork Skokomish Trail follows the east side of the river. O'Neil followed the west side up and over Fisher's Bluff and past Staircase Rapids, but the northern section of that trail has been abandoned because a bridge is out. The North Fork Trail crosses the river just past Seven Stream and joins the old expedition route on the west side. Camp 9, at Nine Stream, was the cache camp from which scouting crews departed in all directions—still a good stop for any traveler.

After nineteen more days of "incessant work," the expedition climbed out of what O'Neil called the canyon of the Skokomish. They reached the high land dividing the watersheds of the Skokomish and Duckabush rivers, which they called the First Divide, and they were right to call it only the first. From Nine Stream, the trail climbs to this divide. Just short of the First Divide, the old O'Neil Trail turns off to the northwest (left) as the North Fork Trail lurches right. O'Neil went through North Pass, slightly to the west of today's crossing of the First Divide.

Ascending the mountains caused the men's hearts to throb "like a stranded locomotive with the violent exertions," but down from First Divide, lovely meadows and fields of blueberries provide rest at Home Sweet Home, the late 1800s base camp for two fur trappers. Then the trail leads over a ridge and down to Upper Duckabush Camp at the Duckabush River—the expedition's Camp 12 and the second night's camp for us.

From this camp, O'Neil's men followed the river upstream, looking for its "rise," its source on the east side of the divide between the Duckabush and Quinault watersheds. They found the rise at a high plateau with several lakes, LaCrosse Basin.[3] Two men climbed Heart's Peak above this basin to sit on the Grand Divide, which separates all east- and west-flowing rivers in the Olympics. They gazed in all directions: to the east as far as Hood Canal; to the west for twenty-five miles to Lake Quinault, which "flashed up like a heliograph in the sunlight." The longer they enjoyed "this marvelous arrangement of nature's work," wrote private Harry Fisher, "the more enchanting it grew."

Enchantment aside, O'Neil's goal of cutting a mule trail depended on finding a pass that heavily packed mules could travel. With proper exertion, the mules could climb the divide from the Duckabush side; descending to the Quinault would be the problem.

O'Neil had already crossed the Grand Divide on a scouting expedition. He and two men had followed an elk trail "as broad as a wagon road, as well beaten as a towpath" where, he reported, "one of the strangest freaks I have ever seen forced its unwelcomed strangeness on us." The trail stopped abruptly at the edge of a precipice.

O'Neil Pass in the Olympic
Mountains.

O'Neil assumed that the elk had either turned around or fallen to
their deaths. Surely no mule could pass here. O'Neil's crews spent
another three weeks mucking about the steep divide, looking for a
way through.

Then another scouting party returned to the precipice where the
trail had disappeared. Private Fisher recorded in his journal that
four men had "prospected the mountain all over and were despair-
ing of success, when they were led by chance" out on a rocky point.
By anchoring logs and stones against trees, the scouts were able to
tack around the point. On the southwest side, they found where the
elk had scrambled down, "though it looked impossible." Thus they
found what became O'Neil Pass. Fisher described it as "the most
absurd-looking point for descent" but probably "the only point by
which the Quinault can be gained with animals." The mules then

zig-zagged down from the pass to the East Fork of the Quinault River and passed through a long "enchanted" valley on their way to Lake Quinault.

Using Upper Duckabush as our own cache camp for backpacks, we headed up the Duckabush River toward the Grand Divide. I clutched a topo map with O'Neil Pass marked as a dot. We contoured Marmot Lake on the south end of LaCrosse Basin. Passing a few marmots and two bears, we entered open subalpine meadows and easily found the pass, which was conveniently marked with a sign. Once through the meadows, the trail drops sharply and enters light woods. Hiking companions quickly disappear from view as they descend the path O'Neil struggled to find. The hiking trail on the west side of the divide now follows a more gradual decline than the zigzagging trail O'Neil's crew cut for the mules.

Once the expedition could see its way to Lake Quinault, O'Neil sent small parties to explore other rivers and peaks, including Mount Olympus. At Lake Quinault, the expedition connected with a crew from Hoquiam who had cut a road thirty miles into the mountains from the coast. Once established, the ninety-three-mile trail from Hood Canal to Gray's Harbor took nine days for a pack train to travel.

Despite O'Neil's persistence in plotting and carving a trail, the route lasted only a few years, then was abandoned and overgrown. Beyond a few homesteads on the edges, the interior was simply too rugged for travel. The mineralogists in the expedition found nothing of value. O'Neil found no military benefit to the Olympics. The peninsula, he said, was "absolutely unfit for any use, except perhaps as a national park where elk and deer can be saved."

In 1897 President Grover Cleveland created the Olympic Forest Reserve to protect the forests from poor logging practices. Twelve years later President Theodore Roosevelt made the Olympic home of Roosevelt elk a national monument. In 1938 President Franklin D. Roosevelt took the next step to make it a national park.

O'Neil closed his report with a prediction: "The scenery, which often made us hungry, weary, and over-packed explorers, the moment our troubles, to pause and admire, would sure people traveling with comfort and for pleasure." Decidedly packed, we legged it back to the comfort of Camp Duckabush the pleasure of hiking down from the hard-earned mountains.

5

Dodger Point Lookout

GETTING THERE: From Port Angeles, take Highway 101 southwest to the Elwha entrance to Olympic National Park. Beyond the entrance, take the turnoff to the Whiskey Bend trailhead, 5 miles.

DISTANCE: 14 miles one way

LEVEL OF DIFFICULTY: difficult; 5,000-foot elevation gain

HISTORICAL HIGHLIGHTS: Dodger Point Lookout

As World War II raged in Europe, the U.S. government feared attacks on the Pacific Coast, a fear realized at Pearl Harbor in December 1941. The next year Japanese submarines approached the Strait of Juan de Fuca and the mouth of the Columbia River. They torpedoed and sank one commercial freighter (with the loss of one crewman) thirteen miles off Cape Flattery. Civilians on the home front started watching the skies, peering out to sea, and listening. Sailors rode on horseback along the beaches; fire-spotters hunkered in beach shacks with radios and guns. In the Olympic Mountains, the army staffed lookouts as part of the U.S. Aircraft Warning Service (AWS).

For a young couple who loved the Olympics and wanted jobs serving the country, lookout duty fit the bill. Leith and Mary Johnson had grown up in Dry Creek, west of Port Angeles, and had

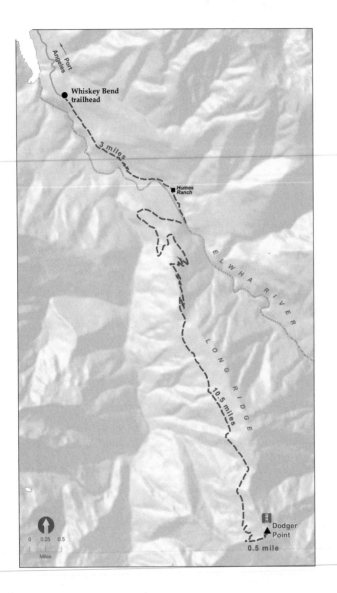

hiked together in their teens. During the war, Leith trained in the Signal Corps, but he developed diabetes and couldn't enlist. "We didn't know what we were going to do," Mary related, "and one Sunday we had taken a drive up this little mountain [in California] and there was a fire lookout up there, a man and his wife." Mary thought she and Leith could do that. The only job openings were back at home—in Olympic National Park.

The Johnsons' first assignment was doing two-week relief stints at seven different lookouts where observers had been alternating six-hour shifts on twenty-four-hour duty. At one lookout they found that the two men had drawn a chalk line down the middle of the tiny lookout and were no longer speaking to each other. On Hurricane Ridge the Johnsons relieved Herb and Lois Crisler, who later became known for their wildlife photography and for building backcountry shelters in Olympic National Park. Mary carried the makings of a home permanent, which she gave Lois in the lookout before her return to the civilized world. After that, the Johnsons settled at the Dodger Point Lookout for the summer of 1943.

Fifty years later, at the age of seventy-nine, Mary Johnson decided to visit all seven lookout stations where she and Leith had served. (Leith died in 1987.) Some of the stations were accessible by car, but she carried a twenty-five-pound backpack to Dodger Point with a friend, Jean Bailey. The climb impressed park rangers, who told me the story.

Dodger Point perches on Long Ridge above the west side of the Elwha River. Long, gradual switchbacks climb the ridge for 13.5 miles and a 5,000-foot elevation gain. My husband and I shared a campfire meal with Mary and Jean the night before we made our own climb to Dodger Point. She brought salt and pepper for a wiener roast and shared her stories.

In late June 1943, the Johnsons started up the Dodger Point Trail with a packer and five horses carrying food, supplies, and a big radio with speakers. The first part of the trail from the Whiskey Bend trailhead follows the Press Expedition route along the east bank of the Elwha River. Beyond Humes Ranch, the Dodger Point/ Long Ridge Trail crosses the river on a suspension bridge as the Elwha comes out of Convulsion Canyon. The trail loops around the northern edge of the ridge, traverses the east side of the ridge for a

Mary Johnson stands in the door of the Dodger Point Lookout cabin in the summer of 1943. Courtesy of Jeanice Johnson.

few miles, then crosses to the western side. As the trail gains altitude, the slopes steepen.

Three miles from the summit, the trail is narrow and steep—as Mary describes it, "straight down on one side and straight up the other." That June the snow had lingered, and one of the horses bumped his pack on the slope. It threw him off balance, and he rolled 200 feet over the side. The packer went down and led the horse back up but declared that that was as far as the pack train would go. The Johnsons continued on foot. During the next month, Leith hiked six miles every day to retrieve all of the supplies.

The lookout cabin is not visible until the last half mile, but the meadows and basin with tarns signal subalpine heights. Northwest poet Gary Snyder camped in the heather meadow with his first wife in the 1950s[4] and met a young man serving as a lonely lookout. He wrote a poem about the quiet meeting of three people in high country: "For the Boy Who Was Dodger Point Lookout Fifteen Years Ago."

A side trail leads steeply up to the cabin, Leith's daily route in 1943. "My husband wore the toes out of his boots just kicking steps in the ice," Mary said. At the top, the point is higher than Hurricane Ridge, which is visible to the east, but at 5,753 feet, it is lower than Mount Olympus, which crowns the southwestern view. Here the Johnsons watched and listened for planes that might fly toward the shipyards and defense industries of Puget Sound. The lookout's job was to radio any identifying characteristics of the planes. Mary took up tatting to stay awake during some of her shifts: "We were on the route to Bremerton, and I was afraid of letting any plane get through." None did.

The name Long Ridge comes from Frank Long, an 1890 settler in the Elwha Valley. Dodger Point was named after Dodger Bender, who did trail and telephone maintenance and construction for the Forest Service. Julian McCabe helped build the fire lookout cabin in 1933, using gables intended to be reminiscent of the popular craftsman style. All of the lumber and windows were packed in by horses. McCabe recalled getting caught in a late September blizzard without much to eat: "We had some rice and . . . I threw rocks and I hit a grouse. That rice and grouse, boy, did it ever taste good!"

After the war, the lookout returned to its primary function as a fire detection station, but it is now boarded up and used only in emergencies. Grouse still patrol the high ground, but by September there are none of the swarms of mosquitoes that plagued the Johnsons after the snow melted. The cabin marks a human presence on the wild, high ground of the Olympic Peninsula. Eyes may scan the mountains that anchor Washington on the west, then wander east toward the dense human history on Puget Sound.

CHAPTER TWO

PUGET SOUND

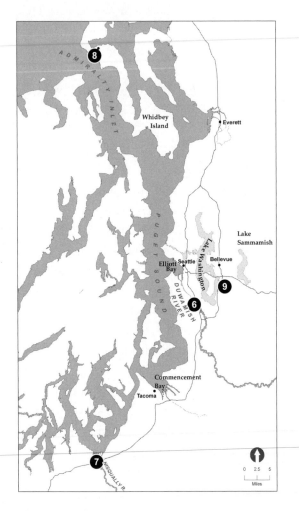

saac Neff Ebey paddled an Indian canoe around Puget Sound in 1850, looking for the best place to homestead. Congress had just passed the Donation Land Law, which allowed a man and his wife to claim 640 acres of land in Oregon Territory if they would live on it before 1855. Starting at the southern tip of the Sound, Ebey passed the mouth of the Puyallup River, now called Commencement Bay, where Tacoma would grow. He scouted Elliott Bay, harbor to the future Seattle. He ascended the Duwamish and Black rivers to Lake Washington and declared that the land between the lake and the Sound "no doubt will be found very valuable." Continuing northward through Admiralty Inlet, he reached Whidbey Island. "What I have seen is no more than a mere outline of a great country," Ebey reported to Michael Simmons, an earlier settler at Tumwater. "The filling up must be done at a future day."

Fill it up the newcomers did. They came off the exhausting Oregon Trail, rafted down the Columbia River, paddled up the Cowlitz River, and trudged the rest of the way to Puget Sound. They claimed the valuable land in the river valleys, in many of the same places the Indians had villages. Treaties signed in the 1850s gave most of the land to the settlers while preserving Native Americans' access to water and fishing.

In subsequent years, population and trade expanded inland from the shores of Puget Sound. The first transcontinental railroad reached Commencement Bay in 1883, linking the hinterland to the ports. Seattle countered with an overly ambitious railroad line that reached only the coal fields of Newcastle, east of Lake Washington. As both Seattle and Tacoma flourished, the Duwamish River and an interurban line connected the farmland communities between them. The river downstream was straightened into an industrial waterway in 1917; from its shores fisheries, ship builders, and heavy cargoes linked the region to Alaska. During the heavy industrialization of Puget Sound in World War II and the following decades, wastewater and stormwater polluted the waterway, which was declared a Superfund site in 2001. Cleanup and restoration has just begun.

Because Puget Sound is the most densely populated and developed region in the state, ancient trails and sites are buried beneath parking lots, apartment buildings, office buildings, pulp mills, and airports. Tribal groups today live a contemporary life yet fight to protect what few village sites, burial grounds, and fishing sites remain. Historical societies, too, preserve photographs and artifacts of rural and small-town life. Rail fans collect photos of stations and favorite streetcars. Trail advocates place interpretive plaques near picnic tables for office workers. Despite constant encroachment, the land itself retains some footprints: a stone fish weir, a fertile prairie, a resource-rich delta, and a coal mine in the suburbs.

We'll begin on the Duwamish River, the "way in" to the country for the Duwamish. Then we'll follow the first settlers into south Puget Sound and into the Nisqually Delta. We'll walk along the border of Ebey's Prairie, high above Admiralty Inlet on Whidbey Island; and hike the railroad grade to the coals of Newcastle. The walks are on land, but they parallel the waters where humans first flourished.

6

Duwamish River

GETTING THERE: The trail is described from north to south, beginning at North Wind's Fish Weir and ending at Fort Dent Park. To begin at North Wind's Fish Weir, take East Marginal Way to 102nd, turn west, stay left, and turn left on 27th, just before the entrance to Highway 99. Park at the end of the road at Cecil Moses Memorial Park and walk to the pedestrian bridge. Parking and access are also available at the Tukwila Community Center and at Fort Dent Park.

DISTANCE: 1.5 miles from North Wind's Fish Weir to Tukwila Community Center; 4 miles from Tukwila Community Center to Fort Dent Park

LEVEL OF DIFFICULTY: easy

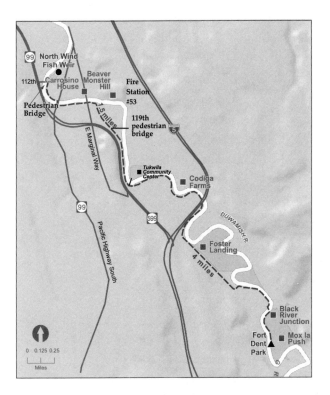

HISTORICAL HIGHLIGHTS: North Wind's Fish Weir; contemporary petroglyphs; Carosino House; Beaver Monster Hill; Foster Landing; Black River Junction; site of Mox la Push

When Isaac Ebey canoed up the Duwamish River looking for a good place to homestead, he was following the "way in" to the Puget Sound lowlands known to the Duwamish people. Their name, duw-ahbsh, meant something like "going inside." For more than 2,000 years, the Duwamish lived in longhouses and camped on the shores of the river. They fished from large tripods and hunted for birds from blinds along the banks.

European-American settlement followed a similar pattern, beginning at the mouth of the Duwamish and working upstream. Homesteads, dairies, and vegetable farms developed in the fertile valley.

Riverboats and then a trolley carried milk and vegetables to market in Seattle. By the late 1900s, this rural, small-town life had been crowded out by industry, transportation routes, and shopping malls.

Now it's hard to even find the river. The first five miles of the Duwamish serve as an industrial waterway; the river here was straightened and dredged in 1917 to facilitate shipping. South of the Turning Basin, where large ships and boats turn around, the river follows its ancient curves, often hidden by warehouses and office complexes. A bicycle and walking trail stays in range of the river from its mouth at Elliott Bay to Fort Dent Park, where the river becomes the Green River and the Duwamish Trail connects with the Interurban Trail. The northern part of the Duwamish Trail passes the sites of a Duwamish village and an immigrant neighborhood that were displaced by the booming Port of Seattle, but the trail is discontinuous along parts of West Marginal Way and through the neighborhood of South Park. So we'll begin at North Wind's Fish Weir, where a formation of rocks reaches back into ancient time.

A Native American oral history, "North Wind and Storm Wind," explains why Puget Sound has rainy weather, how the glaciers retreated, and why a bridge of stones stretches halfway across the Duwamish River. There are several versions of the story, which anthropologist Arthur Ballard collected from Native Americans in the early 1900s. According to a version told by Big John, two peoples lived along the Duwamish River, North Wind's people (the cold wind people) and South Wind's people (the rain wind people). North Wind's people killed South Wind's people, and North Wind stretched a fish weir of ice across the Duwamish so that no fish could swim up the river.

There was one old woman left of South Wind's people. She lived alone on a mountain west of the river and made baskets. Her grandson, Storm Wind, lived among North Wind's people with his mother, Beaver Woman. When Storm Wind grew up, he went to the mountain to find his grandmother, who was cold. Storm

Wind had the power to pull up big fir trees by the roots, and he laid some at her door for fuel. Together they planned to fight North Wind's people.

The grandmother poured water from the baskets she had woven and made rain—big splashes of rain from the coarse baskets and a fine misty rain from the fine ones. The rain caused a flood that melted the fish weir and broke it apart. All of North Wind's people were killed, and North Wind ran away down the valley toward the sea, the land flooding behind him. What was left of the frozen fish weir turned to stone. "It stretches across the river there now. Anybody can see it."

Anybody can see the fish weir—at the right time. As a college instructor eager to share local history, I have taken classes to see the weir, only to find the rocks buried under high tide or a release of water from the Howard Hansen Dam upriver. At low tide, however, the weir is visible. Just north of the pedestrian bridge, rocks from the east bank reach halfway across the river.

North Wind created a fish weir on the Duwamish River to block salmon swimming upstream.

When the Chinook salmon are migrating upstream in the fall, people gather on the bridge to watch and to fish. The Muckleshoot tribe has fishing rights on the river; during fishing season, more than seventy of their boats are on the water. Fly fishermen wade out on the rocks, which force the salmon into a channel. Despite the river's heavily polluted bottom, the Washington Department of Health claims that it is safe to eat Chinook salmon once a week because they move on the surface of the river.

Three granite boulders on both sides of the bridge contain petroglyph images carved by Roger Fernandes recounting the history of the weir. Along the trail south, on the east bank of the river, Susan Point, a Salish artist, has carved and painted petroglyphs in wood depicting the Storm Wind story.

From North Wind's Fish Weir south, the Duwamish River flows in its natural state, as Ebey saw it. The river winds; the banks are lined with brush and trees tall enough to hold eagles; salmon jump in season. The trail crosses the river to the west side on the Tukwila International Boulevard bridge.

In another quarter mile, just before the trail goes under the Sound Transit arch and the East Marginal Way bridge, look across the river at the shingled Carosino House. This farmhouse was part of the community of Italian immigrant farmers who settled here in the late 1800s. The Carosinos, including Rinaldo Carosino and his son Tony, had a truck farm and raised corn, pumpkins, radishes, and other vegetables to sell to the military and at Pike Place Market. A wine cellar on the property once housed 2,000 gallons of wine. An old bocce scoreboard hung from a tree. Sound Transit's light rail now runs right through the front yard.

This corridor has always been the favored route from Seattle to points south. The Seattle-Tacoma Interurban Railway opened along the Duwmamish and White rivers in 1902. South of the East Marginal Way bridge, two thick circular concrete pilings held up a drawbridge used by the interurban. Everything has been crowded into this space: a river, a trail, streets, railroads, an interstate, and a light rail.

To visit more sites mentioned in the North Wind/Storm Wind story, leave the trail and cross the river on the south side of the East Marginal Way bridge. Walk the sidewalk on the east side of the river and pass Beaver Monster Hill (Skaxu), known as Poverty Hill to local residents. This is the site where Mountain Beaver Woman gave birth to her son, Storm Wind. Later it was a defensive position from which the Duwamish could see raiding parties coming from the north. In 2004 the hill was saved from dynamiting by the Cascade Land Conservancy, which gave it to the City of Tukwila with a new name, Duwamish Riverbend Hill. The city plans to create trails and interpretive elements in this preserve.

Two blocks farther, a legend pole at Fire Station Company 53 recounts the tale of North Wind and Storm Wind. The pole was carved by Native American artist Chris Meyers using three different-sized chain saws. The sidewalk and the trail both pass through the community of Allentown, a stop on the interurban. You can cross from side to side on a pedestrian bridge at 119th Street. At the southern end of Allentown, on the east side of the river, the Tukwila Community Center interprets Muckleshoot history.

As Isaac Ebey paddled up the river, he wrote that it "meanders along through rich bottom land, not heavily timbered, with here and there a beautiful plain of unrivaled fertility, peeping out through a fringe of vine-maple, alder or ash, or boldly presenting a full view of their native richness and undying verdure." Although Ebey didn't claim this land, its fertility attracted others, whose names and land claims border the trail south of the community center on the river's west side. Codiga Farms Park, visible at a small bend on the east side, was a dairy run by Swiss immigrant Archie Codiga. The City of Tukwila purchased the land in the late 1990s, and the U.S. Army Corps of Engineers created a back channel for salmon here.

Past a plain of pavement, offices, and industrial buildings, the river rounds Foster Point. Brothers Joseph and Stephen Foster came from Wisconsin in 1853, and Stephen made his claim here; it became a stop on the interurban. A street went through the point and crossed the river on the 56th Avenue South bridge. The trail continues under I-5 to Foster Landing where steamboats stopped to carry farm products from the valley to Seattle. These shallow draft boats could maneuver through the shoals. They stopped at about a dozen established landings, including (from north to south) Meadows, Duwamish, Quarry, Allentown, Riverton, Mortimer, Foster, Tukwila, Black River junction, and Renton Junction. Boats carried their heaviest loads in the winter during high water; traffic stopped during the dry summer months.

At Tukwila's Interurban Avenue Pump Station, a public artwork, *Water Carry*, relates water and the river to local history. The trail parallels Interurban Avenue then comes back to the river north of Fort Dent Park. A marker on a rusty arching pedestrian bridge describes the Black River Junction landing. The steamboat *Traveler* carried passengers and goods on the Black River to and from the Duwamish between 1854 and 1886. The narrow channel coming in from the east is all that remains of the Black River, which disappeared when Lake Washington was lowered in 1916.

A short distance farther is Fort Dent Park, where Joseph Foster made his claim at a strategic confluence. Here the Black and Green rivers formed the Duwamish River. The Duwamish people claimed the land here too, with a village called Mox la Push, which meant "two mouths." In the spring, high waters in the White River coming down from Mount Rainier could reverse the current in the Black River, forcing it back into Lake Washington; hence the Black River had two mouths. At the south end of the park, a young Chief Seal'th once repulsed a raiding party by cutting down a tree so that it blocked the river; the canoes of the raiding Klickitat Indians were swamped when they struck the log in the darkness, and they were killed when they came ashore.

Conflicting claims to the land were addressed in treaties negotiated in 1854 and 1855, but some tribes resisted the transfer of most of the land to homesteaders. Tribes who did not receive sufficient land—particularly those from the south and the east—attacked and killed settlers in the White River Valley, starting the Puget Sound Indian War. Local settlers fled to the new town of Seattle for the winter, and Fort Dent was built at the site of Mox la Push. The fort was never used. The conflicts in western Washington ended when the territorial government tried and hanged Leschi of the Nisqually, blaming him for leadership of the rebellion and the deaths that followed.

Staying out of the war and the "Battle of Seattle" in 1856, Chief Seal'th and the Duwamish cooperated with the founders of the city named after him, as they had from the first landing party at Alki. To address some of the inequities of the treaties, in 1866 the U.S. government proposed to give the Duwamish a reservation along the Black River. This alarmed settlers along the Duwamish Valley, more than 150 of whom successfully petitioned the government not to create the reservation. The Duwamish have been without a reservation or tribal recognition ever since, and thus deprived of land and fishing rights. The Duwamish were gradually crowded away from the river, to other reservations, and to the fringes of the city. One of the last Duwamish children to be born on the river was born in 1902. The village at the confluence remained on maps until 1910. Finally, in 2008, the Duwamish reclaimed their long heritage on the river by constructing a longhouse and a cultural center along the river on West Marginal Way, across from Terminal 107 Park.

Nothing remains of the fort built to protect those who had claimed the land. Instead the park has been leased as a sports complex and recreation area for more recent immigrants, such as the East Indians who played cricket here one September afternoon.

The hill where Storm Wind's grandmother made baskets was quarried away to build I-5. But Duwamish ancestors believed another hill was the center of the world, the hill from which the ancients divided the world into four parts: Sbah-bah-teel still stands high above the Duwamish Valley, west of the intersection of Highway 99 and 116th Way, surveying the constantly changing valley from ancient heights.

7

Medicine Creek Treaty Grounds

GETTING THERE: Take exit 114 from I-5 at Martin Way. Go .25 mile northwest, following signs to the Nisqually Wildlife Refuge.

DISTANCE: 2 miles one way

LEVEL OF DIFFICULTY: easy

HISTORICAL HIGHLIGHTS: Medicine Creek Treaty signing site; Brown farm

The Nisqually River valley and delta are a visual feast for drivers rushing by on I-5, much as they were a veritable feast for the Nisqually people and for homesteaders, a place where game was plentiful and the land was fertile. The Nisqually National Wildlife Refuge encompasses the delta and McAllister Creek, previously known as Medicine Creek or She'nah-nam (from the Indian word meaning "shaman"). This was the site of the Treaty of Medicine Creek, an early instance of both cooperation and conflict in this resource-rich delta.

In 1845 the Bush-Simmons-McAllister party of five families and two single men struck off from the Oregon Trail and headed north to Puget Sound country. The party had crossed the continent from Missouri, rafted down the Columbia River, alighted at Monticello (now Longview), and headed into country controlled by the Hudson's Bay Company (HBC). In doing so they were defying both

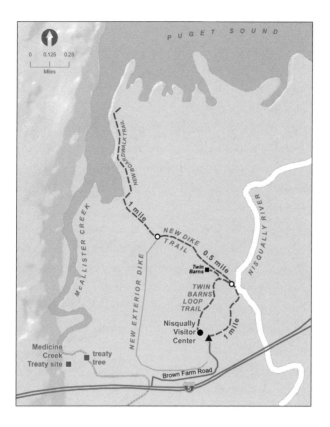

HBC claims and the laws of the new territory of Oregon, but they had good reason; George Washington Bush, a well-to-do business-man and cattle trader in the party, could not make a land claim south of the Columbia because he was of mixed race.

To reach Puget Sound, the party followed the Cowlitz River (its Indian name was the "Cowiliskee"), where Cowlitz rivermen poled scows to transport the families, their wagons, and their goods. At Cowlitz Landing (Toledo), where the river bends east, the party shifted back to wagons or crude sleds for the overland stretch. The men went ahead to widen the trail by clearing brush and downing logs, laboring to turn the trail into a wagon road. When others followed, this route became known as the Cowlitz Trail or the

"Road from Cowlitz Landing to Olympia," a fifteen-day journey through prairies with excellent soil, magnificent forests, and fine streams of water.[1]

In her memoirs, Sarah McAllister Hartmann recalls how her father, James McAllister, chose his land claim. "While waiting at the Cowlitz, they [the party] were met by the Chief of the Nisquallys, Leshi. . . . He met them and welcomed them to this country, making each family a present and inviting them to join his tribe, saying, we might be annoyed by roving Indians, and if we did not belong to his tribe he could not protect us."

Michael Simmons made his land claim on the falls of the Deschutes River, now Tumwater. George Washington Bush made a claim on what became Bush Prairie after the new territorial government acted to approve his petition to own land. James McAllister found the "the soil rather light for farming" on Bush Prairie and accepted Leschi's invitation to move farther north. He selected a farm at the junction of two creeks, the Medicine and the Squa-quid, near the council grounds of the Nisqually, which were formed from a natural opening in the woods, about a mile long and a quarter of a mile wide—just perfect for farming.

The McAllister family lived in two tree stumps while McAllister slowly built a house on the north end of the grounds. Even though the families didn't have bread for a few years, they had plenty to eat. "We had all kinds of game, which was more plentiful than tame stock now, fish and clams, dried and fresh, the Indians showing us how to prepare them."

Today I-5 bends east and west and bisects the council grounds, with McAllister's land claim on the south side of the highway and the wildlife refuge on the north. McAllister Creek wanders through the refuge much as it did in the 1840s and '50s. The council grounds are no longer accessible, but a new trail leads across the bottomland to the creek, whose name changes narrate the history.

The McAllisters were essentially squatters. Not until 1848 did

The Medicine Creek Treaty was signed on these council grounds.

Great Britain give up its claim to land north of the Columbia River, and not until 1850 did Congress grant land claims. When Washington became a territory separate from Oregon in 1853, negotiations for ownership of the land began.

In 1854, during a typically wet December, several hundred Puyallup, Nisqually, and Squaxin gathered along She'nah-nam, or Medicine Creek, to negotiate with the U.S. government in the person of Governor Isaac Stevens. "Rain continues hard at intervals," recorded George Gibbs, a surveyor. The governor's party was camped on the edge of the creek, on a spot "but little elevated above the tidelands"; the Indians were above them, among the timber. Gibbs said the scene presented a curious picture: "Thin temporary huts of mats with the smoke of their numerous campfires, the prows of canoes hauled upon the bank and protruding from among the huts, the ponies grazing on the marsh, the gloom of the firs and cedars with their long depending moss and the scattered and moving groups of Indians in all kinds of odd and fantastic dresses."

After two days of negotiations, many Indians signed the treaty, as did James McAllister and his cousin, John. Leschi did not; he considered the lands reserved for the Nisqually as inadequate and inferior since they did not include the mouth and rich delta of the Nisqually River.[2] In the months that followed, he visited relatives east and west of the mountains and discovered the Yakama were unhappy with white settlement of the land too. Leschi warned McAllister of conflicts to come and urged him not to join the militia, but McAllister joined the Puget Sound Volunteers. According to Sarah Hartmann, her father was on his way to Leschi's stronghold in the mountains to persuade him not to fight when he and others were ambushed and killed. The U.S. government tried and hanged Leschi for leading the hostilities. Medicine Creek was renamed McAllister Creek. The war formally ended in August 1856, and the resulting peace council provided larger reserves for the Puyallup and Nisqually tribes.

From the refuge headquarters building, the trail leads across delta land that was diked and farmed after the conflicts of the 1850s had abated. The land under the trail was shaped by Alson Brown, a Seattle lawyer, who purchased the delta in 1904 and started an experimental farm that became completely self-sufficient. Using horse-drawn scoops, Brown built dikes to hold back the salt water; the enclosed marshlands attracted wild ducks. Brown lost the farm to creditors in 1919; they leased it until the 1970s. An environmental group, the Nisqually Delta Association, successfully urged establishment of the Nisqually National Wildlife Refuge in 1974 to preserve the duck-rich site. Then, in 2004, through comprehensive planning and the advocacy of the Nisqually tribe, the decision was made to let the delta revert to tidelands. The dikes were removed in 2009, allowing salt water to reclaim the delta between the creek and the river.

At the end of the trail, look southeast along McAllister Creek. For more than 150 years, one lone snag survived of the grove of Douglas Fir where the Indians had camped. According to Nisqually member Cecelia Carpenter, in *Remembering Medicine Creek,* it stood just north of the I-5 overpass as a reminder that "the Treaty of Medicine Creek, held beneath its branches, is still in force." The treaty tree blew down in the fierce windstorm of December 2006.

Cultural and land-use conflicts still characterize the valley. Two thirds of the land reserved for the Nisqually became part of the Fort Lewis military reservation in 1917. Fish-ins at Frank's Landing during the 1970s led to a federal court decision by Judge George Boldt reaffirming the tribal fishing rights granted by the Treaty of Medicine Creek. The Nisqually still exercise their treaty rights to place salmon nets in McAllister Creek. The decision to dismantle the dikes and allow the river and creek to return to a natural course aims to restore the health of Puget Sound to the abundance of the 1800s.

8
Ebey's Landing and Prairie

GETTING THERE: Take the ferry from Mukilteo to Whidbey Island. From the ferry, take Highway 525, which becomes Highway 20, to Coupeville. Continue on 20 for .3 miles past a pedestrian overpass; turn left on Ebey Road, and drive 1.7 miles straight ahead (don't follow the curve to the left) to the end of the road at Ebey's Landing. Park in the ten-car lot or on the wide shoulder.

DISTANCE: Ebey's Landing to Sunnyside Cemetery, 1.35 miles.

LEVEL OF DIFFICULTY: moderate

HISTORICAL HIGHLIGHTS: Ebey's Landing; Ferry House; prairies; Sunnyside Cemetery; blockhouses

The prairies above Ebey's Landing on Whidbey Island seem pastoral compared to the rugged bluffs to the north, where surf dashes

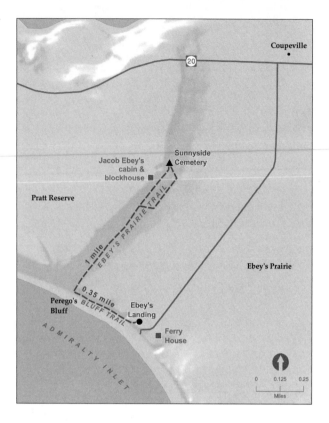

against the rocks. Through the innovative process of creating a historic reserve, the prairies, with awesome views, have been protected from housing development. Isaac Ebey found paradise here, and some of it remains.

Ebey landed on Whidbey Island in 1850 after paddling around much of Puget Sound, looking for the right place to homestead. Once he saw the island, Isaac wrote home to his brother Winfield that he had found "almost a paradise of nature. . . . If Rebecca, the children, and you all were here, I think I could live and die here content." He filed his land claim on the prairie behind the bluff above this landing. His claim commanded the Indian trail that led east to Penn Cove, an inner bay of the island, and three Skagit villages.

Ebey was not the first to claim this fertile land. The Skagit had

Nineteenth-century travelers arrived from the mainland at Ebey's Landing on Admiralty Inlet, Whidbey Island.

burned the prairies seasonally for hundreds of years to preserve them as a source of camas bulbs and bracken fern. In the early 1830s, the Skagit had obtained potatoes from the Hudson's Bay Company and grew them very successfully. Although they had ejected a white settler two years earlier, the Skagit welcomed Ebey and others, perhaps hoping the homesteaders would protect them against Haida raiders from the Queen Charlotte Islands.

Rebecca, Winfield, Ebey's children, and his parents, Jacob and Sarah, soon came. With such support, Ebey became a leading citizen: district attorney, delegate to the territorial legislature, adjutant general for Washington, and collector of customs. From the landing he rowed ten miles across Admiralty Inlet to the Customs House in Port Townsend whenever his services were needed. Ebey raised potatoes too, and his hogs grew fat on the camas bulbs. Life was good. Rebecca wrote in her diary that "the rolling of the surf against the Shore is very loud this evening which sounds romantic and beautiful."

When other visitors came to Whidbey Island, they landed here too. One day in June 1859, James G. Swan, who also held many jobs in territorial Washington, left Port Townsend in a canoe and reached Ebey's Landing about noon on his way to meet with the Skagit chiefs. Swan turned down an offer of horses and chose to walk to Penn Cove. "There is an excellent road to Penn's cove, and the day being very pleasant, I had a most delightful walk," he wrote in his journals. On the way he gathered "a feast of delicious strawberries."

The delightful walks remain, if not the feast of strawberries. From Ebey's Landing, the beach is yours to roam. A few steps north of the parking lot is where Swan, mail, wagons, and passengers pushed through the sixty-foot bank on their way to Coupeville, which was platted on Penn Cove by Thomas Coupe. After 1860, the Ferry House—still visible in the fields just beyond the bank, to the southeast—provided spirits, supper, bed, breakfast, and a mail service. The National Park Service has begun preserving this building and hopes to restore it. Ebey's home was a few yards south of the Ferry House. His land claim extended west of the homesite, and a plaque on a knoll commemorates his life there. William Engle claimed the farm south of Ebey in 1852, after failing to find fortune in the gold fields of California.

By 1853, Whidbey Island was one of the most settled areas of Puget Sound, but paradise was uneasy. Ebey's first wife, Rebecca, died of tuberculosis that year, shortly after the birth of their third child. Two years later, territorial governor Isaac Stevens negotiated treaties with the Indians to legitimize land claims such as the one Ebey and Engle had made, but the treaties did not resolve all of the conflicts. The Skagit complained that the settlers' cattle were destroying their potatoes. Leaders of the Whidbey community joined the Territorial Volunteers and built blockhouses for protection.

The Skagits never attacked, but northern tribes continued to raid Puget Sound. In October 1856, seven canoes filled with warriors threatened Port Gamble, across the Sound, and clashed with a U.S. Navy vessel called out to protect the settlements. One American sailor and twenty-seven Indians (including a chief) were killed in the battle. Seeking revenge, the Kake band of Tlingits from southeast Alaska canoed to Whidbey in August 1857, looking for a white chief to kill. From the landing they climbed the bluff in the middle of the night and called Isaac Ebey out of his cabin by firing a gun. When he came outside, they killed and beheaded him while the others in the cabin fled to the Engle farm.

After Ebey's death, his second wife left the island, but most of his family stayed. Isaac's father, Jacob, surrounded his house with a stockade twelve feet high, a blockhouse at each corner, and in 1860 he built Ferry House. Most of the Skagit Indians left the island, having been crowded off of the prairies and decimated by venereal disease, influenza, and tuberculosis. Chinese workers came to dig and maintain the potatoes already planted, but they were met with hostility and eventually abandoned the island too. Wheat, oats, onions, potatoes, sheep, and dairy cows flourished on the prairies the Skagit had first maintained. Through the efforts of those who kept the land, the prairies have been preserved, making it easy to imagine life on the island in the 1800s and before.

To walk the boundaries of the Ebey claims and find Jacob Ebey's blockhouse, take the bluff trail northwest toward Perego's Bluff, named after George Perego, who lived here as a hermit with his three dogs. Perego had speculated that the army would want this bluff for gun placements. The U.S. Army did build a "triangle of fire" in 1897 to guard the entrance to Puget Sound, including Fort Casey, south of the bluff;[3] however, the army did not choose his bluff, which still commands a sweeping view of both the inlet and the inland prairies.

The highest part of the bluff is in a Nature Conservancy reserve and open to the foot traveler, but before reaching the top, Ebey's Prairie Trail heads inland for one mile along the western boundary of Isaac's land claim. The trail can be overgrown to shoulder height in spring but well defined underfoot. From this trail, much of what we see is what Swan saw. "From the summit of a hill over which the road passes, I had a fine view of Penn's cove . . . and the green fields of the farms rising gently from the water's edge, with a background of forest trees, above which showed the high peaks and snow-covered cliffs of Mount Baker." Mount Rainier is often visible 102 miles in the opposite direction.

The prairie landscape has weathered 6,000 years of human use and still provides crops of beets, corn, alfalfa, cabbage, barley, and wheat. Along its unplowed edges, native camas bloom in early April. The trail goes northeast along a fence line, where perching birds are creating a hedgerow as they drop seeds. Roads and hedgerows in this preserve trace the land claims staked out by early settlers. Much of this prairie is owned by descendants of William Engle.

At the end of the field are Jacob Ebey's former blockhouse and his home, which still oversee the prairies and will become a visitors center. A road from here leads to Sunnyside Cemetery. The prairie trail jogs downhill and turns left along a dirt then a gravel road; follow the trail emblems on posts. The trail then climbs up a gravel path to a prairie overlook (more pastoral views) and ends at Sunnyside Cemetery, where many of the early settlers, including the Ebey family, are buried. The cemetery also shelters the Davis blockhouse, built by James Davis, brother of Rebecca Ebey. The blockhouses reassured the settlers and may have deterred further aggression from the north.

The three large prairies that drew homesteaders—Ebey's Prairie, Crockett Prairie, and Smith Prairie—have been preserved in a National Historical Reserve, the country's first such reserve, created by Congress in 1978. Private landowners have allowed scenic easements and have sold their rights to develop the land so that the visual character of the landscape may remain the same. What preserved this paradise more than the blockhouses was descendants' far-sighted appreciation for the intrinsic value of the prairies.

9

Coal Creek to Redtown

GETTING THERE: Approach the small parking area for the Coal Creek Trail from the east. From I-405, take the Coal Creek exit and proceed southeast through several lights to the intersection with Newcastle Way in Newcastle. Turn around there and return west on Coal Creek Parkway. At 1.2 miles, after S.E. 60th Street the parkway dips where the creek goes under it. Turn right into a small parking area. If you want a one-way hike, leave a car at the Cougar Mountain Regional Wildland Park. From the intersection of Coal Creek Parkway and 136th in Newcastle, turn northeast and follow the Coal Creek-Newcastle Road about one mile to the park entrance on the east side of the road.

DISTANCE: 3 miles one way

LEVEL OF DIFFICULTY: moderate

HISTORICAL HIGHLIGHTS: mining debris; turntable; mine opening

For the first twenty years I lived in Washington, my Bellevue home bordered abandoned coal mines and mining townsites, a dirty history camouflaged by a thick overgrowth of green. Feeling self-conscious in hiking boots, I could walk out the door and follow deer trails to the Coal Creek ravine.

After the sawmills had milled the trees of Puget Sound, the power that drove progress was coal, which was readily available on the eastern shore of Lake Washington. Miners dug nearly eleven million tons of coal from the Newcastle Hills in the mining boom of the 1880s and '90s as Washington became the "Pennsylvania of the West." The rush began when two men brought several loads of coal from Squak Mountain into Seattle during the winter of 1862–63. City entrepreneurs quickly organized a survey of public lands. They hired a school teacher from New York, Edwin Richardson, who had

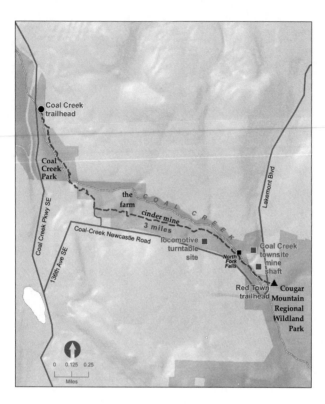

already surveyed some public lands for schools. Richardson marked "Stone Cole Creek" on a map where he had discovered what he thought was anthracite coal, generally called "stone coal."[4] Although his spelling was loose, Richardson was smart enough to file a claim on the land as coal fever began.

Four years later a small development company, including Reverend Daniel Bagley, bought Richardson's claim. Since the company's teachers and preachers lacked the capital for large-scale mining, production began slowly. The first 150 tons of coal were transported on wagons over a road through the present neighborhood of Newport Hills, then barged up Lake Washington and hauled by wagon to Seattle. By 1876, the Newcastle mines produced 400 tons a day and employed 250 men.

Coal Creek Trail follows Richardson's creek through ravines to the mine sites in the Issaquah Alps. Beginning where the creek goes under Coal Creek Parkway, the trail offers simple pleasures at first: birds that seem quite startled by humans, rocks smoothed by centuries of water, two waterfalls from modest heights, fern-covered hillsides, thistle in bloom, and a fragrant meadow. Houses crowd the top of the ridge on the east, and commuter traffic rushes by beyond the ridge on the west, but the narrow ravine obscures most of these intrusions.

The signs of human industry are subtle at first. Watch for unnatural features of the terrain: timber rather than logs in the creek, bricks in the path, coal chunks in the creek, open areas with tall grass, and wide, level paths. For the first .8 mile, the trail follows the east side of the creek, then it crosses to the south bank over a bridge, which has evolved over the years from a simple log footbridge. The creek has water year-round but much less in summer. The trail climbs above the creek. At 1.1 miles, stay on Coal Creek Trail (N1). The Primrose Trail, which goes to the Scalzo mine sites, is now closed. From 1933 to 1939, Tony Scalzo mined the Primrose Seam north of the creek. He had a wood and coal yard at Rainier Avenue and Atlantic Street in Seattle, which he supplied with a relatively poor quality of coal from the mine.

N1 crosses a creek on a log bridge with a handrail then rambles through an old farm overgrown with tall grass and blackberry vines. The trail provides sunny vistas, fragrant smells, and wonderful blackberries in early September. If you follow beaten grass paths, you will spot an old, three-sided shed with a corrugated roof; two apple trees on what is known as the farm still produce fruit.

A new trail was under construction but not yet open in the spring of 2009; the old trail veers left. Up a steep hill from the farm, a yellow iron-gated old trail shows where the abandoned roadbed of the Seattle and Walla Walla Railroad came in from Renton. Seattle and Tacoma competed fiercely to become the leading port in Washington, and both wanted the terminus of the first transcontinental route to the Northwest. In 1873 the Northern Pacific Railway chose Commencement Bay in Tacoma as its terminus, much to Seattle's dismay. Entrepreneurs and land speculators in Seattle decided to build their own railroad to Walla Walla and trade with eastern Washington. Although the Seattle and Walla Walla Railroad and Transportation Company rumbled no farther than these coalfields, it proudly brought President Rutherford B. Hayes out from Seattle on the train in 1880 to celebrate the mines' production.

The trail passes by a fern-covered hill to the south and a valley to the north on a wide, elevated path, the railroad grade. Beyond this panoply of ferns, the trail passes the debris of large-scale mining. In 1880 Henry Villard bought out the mines, and production kicked into higher gear. Operators discovered a coal belt almost 900 feet wide in eleven seams, seven of which they worked. In an open area, an old road curves left and goes downhill to the site of a cinder mine. For decades, mine waste was hauled from Coal Creek and dumped into this handy canyon. The rock waste contained coal, and the pile ignited spontaneously and smoldered for more than half a century, into the 1940s. Thereafter, the cinders were mined and spread on schoolyards and running tracks. A road continues south as the trail veers east.

The last .7 mile of the trail were under reconstruction in the summer of 2009. On earlier forays, there had been unmistakable evidence of industry: a big slab of concrete with rebar sticking out of it, overgrown with ferns. This curious mixture of nature and machine had been a locomotive turntable where the train engines turned around to take cars laden with coal back to Seattle.

Nature dominates again with the sound of water—the North Fork Falls—a gentle waterfall over rocks stained with iron oxide. The planks in the creek were laid to stop the water from leaking into a mine, according to the late Harvey Manning and to Ralph Owen, field historians for this park. Benches near the falls offer a rest.

The remaining trail forks left and leads up to the north side of the ravine and a dark mouth in the earth. This is an air shaft from the Number 4 seam. In 1894, 162 miners climbed through such an airshaft on ropes to escape a burning mine. A display board here includes an Asahel Curtis photograph of the town of Coal Creek in 1909. The photo dispels any misplaced nostalgia for the past; this was an industrial enterprise. Curtis's photograph shows the railroad tracks leading to Seattle, tracks from the mines to the bunkers, the roof of the coal bunkers where the coal was cleaned and separated, a sawmill, a steam plant, the ticket office and depot, the Finnish boarding house, and the Coal Creek Saloon. The creek itself is completely obscured in the photo—it was encased in timbers.

In the fields above the ravine are the site of the Newcastle School, remnants of the Newcastle Hotel, and the foundations of the Generator House. The trail crosses the old Newcastle Road (now Lakemont Boulevard) to Cougar Mountain Regional Wildland Park.

The morning shift poses at the Newcastle mines. Washington State Historical Society.

There trails lead to the company townsites of Redtown and Rainbow Town, to Ballpark Meadow, to China Creek (where Chinese workers mined), and to the entrance to the Ford Slope and the Bagley seam, the center of mining activity.

In the twenty-first century, these wooded paths are frequented by hikers, dog walkers, and cross-country runners. One hundred years ago, Scots, Irish, Finns, Swedes, Belgians, English, Germans, Italians, Croatians, Serbians, Slavs, Greek, Welsh, and Chinese worked the mines. They played baseball and soccer at the ballpark meadow, accompanied by the Ford Mine Band. Groups from Seattle came out to hunt cougar and bear. The Newcastle School built in 1914 offered night classes in reading and writing for the miners. Peddlers passed through the town selling kitchenware, clothes, and sewing machines. There were dances on Saturday night and a Christmas Day ball in 1875 that drew 200 people.

The air is fresh and healthful now, but then the daily grind was dirty and sometimes dangerous. Mules worked underground with the men, hauling out the cars of coal. Aboveground, small boys and men who could no longer work underground sorted rocks from coal at the bunkers. There were occasional fires in the mines, and waste dumps sent smoke, fire, and noxious gases into the air. Seventeen men were killed in one blast caused by a dust explosion.

Villard sold the mines to California investors in 1897, and Pacific Coast Coal ran the mines until 1929. The company pulled out when their bunkers burned and the Coal Creek mine was destroyed by fire. Competition from petroleum and from finer grades of coal was growing. By the 1930s, the towns were abandoned; only small operators continued into the 1960s.

Then began a long struggle by Harvey Manning and the Issaquah Alps Club to establish Cougar Mountain Wildland Park, to preserve this trail and many others from the "filling in" that Isaac Ebey had predicted would happen on Puget Sound. Their efforts were successful enough that by 1989 a million people could take a wildland hike from their suburban front doors.

Centuries have passed since the Duwamish identified the center of the world along the Duwamish River, and more than a century since James McAllister and Leschi lost their lives contesting the Nisqually Delta, Ebey found paradise on Puget Sound, and entrepreneurs found black gold in the Newcastle Hills. Only through persistent effort have the historical features of the land—a winding river, a prairie, a delta, a ravine—been preserved for all to enjoy.

CHAPTER THREE

The North Cascades

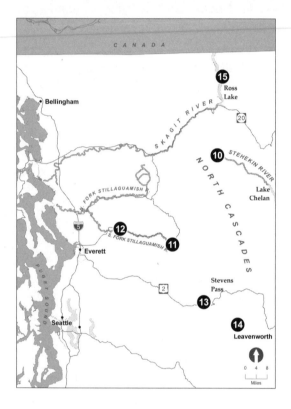

I n her historical novel *The Living*, Annie Dillard describes a
northern Washington beach as "the rough edge of the world,
where the trees came smack down to the stones." As Dillard's
female protagonist steps ashore and the salt water wets her shoes,
she can see "a sharp line of snow-covered mountains." The weather
is coastal Northwest: "It was not quite raining, but everything
was wet."

Spring snow covering Sahale Peak. Photograph © 2007 by Andrew Gorohoff.

From rough beaches to snow-covered mountains, from swift rivers to deep lakes, the North Cascades region has some of the wildest and most remote terrain in the state, stretching from the Canadian border to the Stillaguamish and Skagit rivers, and from the shores of Bellingham over the North Cascades to the Stehekin Valley. The region's remoteness and wetness mean that human intrusions are relatively light or washed away. It is possible to hike for miles in some places and see only scant evidence that someone else has been there. This very remoteness has attracted the most adventuresome travelers.

In 1792 Captain George Vancouver took possession of this region for His Majesty King George III, but no one has ever fully possessed it. Fur traders, soldiers, prospectors, and railroad surveyors crossed the North Cascades looking for wealth and a way through the range, which is eighty miles wide. Few visitors left any permanent tracks until the Great Northern Railway crossed Stevens Pass and Seattle City Light dammed the Skagit River. Even now, the human hold on the land is tenuous. Roads wash out, avalanches cover railroad tracks, and mountain peaks challenge the curious.

In a latter-day act of possession, we'll retrace the steps of a fur trader for the North West Company, an army lieutenant looking for a way through the mountains, a prospector looking for silver, and the railroad engineers who found the right pass. We'll follow a forest ranger who claimed the land by naming 3,000 remote lakes, ridges, and creeks. Finally, we'll climb alongside poets and writers who served as fire lookouts and drew inspiration from the solitude and eternity of the North Cascades.

10

Cascade Pass to Stehekin

GETTING THERE: Drive Highway 20 to Marblemount, then turn east on Cascade River Road, 23.5 miles to the trailhead. The gravel road becomes narrow and steep near the end.

DISTANCE: 3.7 miles to Cascade Pass; 17.5 miles from pass to High Bridge and shuttle service to Stehekin; 1.5-mile side trip to Horseshoe Basin, plus .5 mile to mine opening.

LEVEL OF DIFFICULTY: difficult

HISTORICAL HIGHLIGHTS: Cascade Pass; Horseshoe Basin mine; Cottonwood Camp; Bridge Creek; Rainbow Falls; Boulder Creek

A doggedly persistent U.S. Army lieutenant and his party rode into Marblemount in August 1882 after a gloomy summer journey through the North Cascades. Two Indian families living there refused to believe any white man could have come from the summit. But Henry Hubbard Pierce had persevered for 295 miles from his post on the southern end of Lake Chelan. The next night Pierce and his men found a logging camp in the Skagit Valley, where they ate a "bountiful supper" with "a ravenous appetite."

Pierce had climbed through the Stehekin River Valley and over Cascade Pass, which native people knew for centuries as "the way

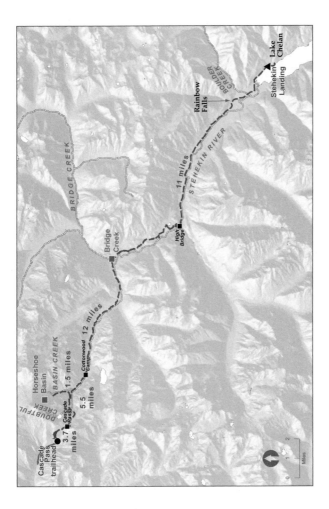

through." Inland tribes crossed the Cascades to barter mountain-goat wool and hemp in return for dried clams, salmon, and ornamental sea shells. Red Fox, chief of the Okanagons, had reached the "Great Salt Lake" (Puget Sound) over this pass several times and told early travelers about the route. The U.S. Army wanted to find out whether inland Indians could join Indians on the coast for military action, at a time when they were protesting white incursions on their land; after his trek, Pierce concluded that the terrain would prevent the Indians from communicating easily with one another.

The forbidding terrain tested many others. Alexander Ross, a fur trader for the North West Company, and Daniel Linsley, a surveyor for the Northern Pacific Railroad, had crossed before Pierce, looking for ways to transport furs and freight over the mountains. Ross reached today's Sedro Woolley before deciding that the route was impractical as an alternative to the Columbia River. Miners built a road halfway from Stehekin to Cascade Pass to transport ore, and citizens hoped this same route would become a highway. Instead, the hike through Cascade Pass has become one of the most popular in the state.

Native Americans and early explorers approached the pass from the east side, converging at the Stehekin River and following the river up to its source at the pass. From there they continued down the Cascade River to the Skagit River, which flowed to the coast. The journey from present-day Twisp to Marblemount took about fifteen days. Today most hikers approach the summit from the west. Continuing on to Stehekin requires Pierce's dogged persistence and his tolerance for the changes in Northwest weather.

A long drive up a difficult dirt road—no highway here—leads to the trailhead. The trail switchbacks thirty-three times in three miles among groves of gigantic cedar trees, which Pierce described as often being forty feet in circumference. Ross saw the cedars bending like saplings during a hurricane-force storm in 1814. Lieutenant George Backus peered through the mist down this side of the mountain and reported that it looked "like the descent to the infernal regions."

Pierce himself reached the summit during a "sleety shower." He had been warned by an old miner that the pass was a "strange, inhospitable place." His party managed to kindle a fire of wet wood and settled for sleep "amidst the gloom of the present and the uncertainties of the future." During the night the sleet became snow (in August); falling masses of ice thundered into the canyons; the torrents roared; the wind howled; and "the situation was rendered dismal beyond description." But—the next morning—"a glorious sun illumined the surrounding peaks" and lifted the group's spirits, robbing the sunlit crest of its "foggy terrors."

On most summer days the ascent can be quite pleasant. After rising 1,800 feet to an elevation of 5,400 feet, the trail opens up into meadows. On glorious mornings the ancient way through has enough foot travelers to warrant a parking attendant at the summit (telling hikers not to "park" on the meadows). On a rainy September day, you'll have "the foggy terrors" and the solitary bench to yourself.

The Mazamas, a mountaineering club, were so inspired by this area that they proposed a national park in the North Cascades in 1906. But various local promoters wanted a road over Cascade Pass; such wishful thinking even appeared on state maps as State Road 1. To gain popular support for the road, a group called the Cascade Pass Highway Pilgrims brought annual foot or horseback pilgrimages to the pass from both sides in the 1920s. The conflict continued when conservationist Bob Marshall walked over Cascade Pass in 1930 and recommended it be designated a "primitive area." In 1932 a tunnel was suggested, but Ivan "Ike" Munson, a location engineer, found cliffs at the pass so steep that his surveyors had to swing on ropes to do their work. Eventually hopes for a North Cascades highway shifted to extending Highway 20 through Washington and Rainy passes. After several more decades of advocacy, national park designation came in 1968. Cascade Pass had eluded road builders in much the same way it had discouraged early explorers—through the ruggedness of the terrain and the unpredictability of the weather.

To tread the entire "way through," descend 2,600 feet from the summit into the Stehekin River Valley. But be forewarned: Ross found this route "steep and abrupt." Spokane chief Quiltanee told railroad surveyor George B. McClellan it was a poor, steep trail, and Daniel Chapman Linsley found it "utterly impracticale" for a railroad in 1870. Pierce went on and on in his journal about the wretched, zigzagging path—it was tiresome, "most imperfect." He described the gray granite canyon walls in this narrowing valley as "exceedingly rugged and forbidding, rising to a height of 4,000 feet above the stream." Thinking more positively, Pierce noted that mountain goats found pasture among the cliffs, lusty trout abounded in the river, and springs flowed from the canyon sides.

Thanks to an old road constructed for mining, most of the trail is easy to follow, if still interminable. There are modern comforts: three campgrounds in the first 5.5 miles down from the pass—Pelton Basin, Basin Creek, and Cottonwood Camp. At first, the trail descends a wooded ridge through Pelton Basin on gentle switchbacks. A waterfall cascades down at the crossing of Doubtful Creek, which can be swollen with heavy snow melt on a hot afternoon. Pelton Creek cascades down the other end of this ridge to join Doubtful Creek and form the Stehekin River. A Pelton wheel,

The Black Warrior Mine operated at Horseshoe Basin into the 1940s.

invented by Lester Allan Pelton in the 1870s, translated power from the waterfalls to a sawmill in the basin.

In the late 1800s, miners joined the search for a way into and out of the mountains, spurred by discoveries of gold, silver, and lead near the pass. Charles von Pressentin, Otto Klement, four other prospectors, and an Indian guide crossed Cascade Pass in 1877, looking for gold, and Klement gave the west side river and the pass their names, after the cascades in the river. A retail store started up at Marblemount, selling coffee transported from Seattle up the Skagit River and providing enough brew to power travelers through gloomy weather.

Once down the steep slope on the east side and past Doubtful Creek, the trail widens. Before the cable bridge at Basin Creek, a 1.5-mile trail climbs into Horseshoe Basin, a horseshoe-shaped cirque with more than fifteen waterfalls falling from the snowfields of the glaciers above. The dark spot in the cliff wall is the Black Warrior Mine, accessible by a half-mile hike. From the first claim in 1889 and on into the 1940s, the Black Warrior was mined for copper, zinc, lead, gold, and silver. During the winter of 1909, miners dug tunnels from their sleeping cabins through thirty-foot snows to reach the mine. A 7,000-foot tramway connected the upper and lower basins. Eventually the ore proved poor in quality, the working season too short, and the way out of the mountains too hard. The U.S. National Park Service has restored part of the mine shafts, so you can explore them if you don't mind darkness, mud, and the scurry of tiny feet. Just inside the shaft is a room that probably served as a warming and cooking area.

From Horseshoe Basin, the trail sometimes follows a mine-to-market road built in the 1930s that transported supplies from Stehekin to the mines. Vehicles used the road as late as 1948, but avalanche debris obliterated it in the 1970s, and the trail detours upward from the road.

At the last campground on the route, a substantial table welcomes heavy backpacks and weary butts. This is Cottonwood Camp, perhaps named for Pierce's "cottonwood swamp" or for the black cottonwoods common along the river. Old Cottonwood Camp is reached by crossing the river, by log or fording. From here the trail descends gradually, with frequent detours around washed-out areas; it is twenty-three miles from Cottonwood Camp to Stehekin Landing at the upper end of Lake Chelan.

A few years ago, a National Park Service shuttle picked up and dropped off hikers three miles east of Cottonwood Camp, cutting twenty miles off the journey to Stehekin. However, a 2003 landslide closed off the upper ten miles of this road, and now a private shuttle service meets hikers twice a day at High Bridge, twelve miles east. To reach High Bridge, hikers can walk the old roadbed, now maintained as a trail, to Bridge Creek. Here Pierce found a "rude bridge of drift-logs, joined with strips of cedar bark, and ballasted with stones, built by the Indians." The road crosses the creek on a better-than-rude bridge, and hikers can join the Pacific Crest Trail on the old wagon road, which was carved higher above the river.[1] This higher road goes through wilderness to High Bridge and cannot be reclaimed for vehicle use without an act of Congress.[2]

The shuttle from High Bridge, covering the last eleven miles to Stehekin, crosses Boulder Creek, which Pierce described as a creek flowing over "a bed of huge granite bowlders." The shuttle stops at Rainbow Falls, "a magnificent cascade . . . with a sheer unbroken fall of 300 feet," and the entire fall is no less than 450 feet. The last stop before the civilized town of Stehekin is the Stehekin Bakery, a sensory paradise to grizzled hikers.

The Golden West Visitors Center offers more insight into this remote town, where history is near. If you take the long, sleepy ride on the *Lady of the Lake* back to Chelan, you will see why no railroad and no highway were ever built along the shores of this deep glacial gorge.

11

Monte Cristo Townsite

GETTING THERE: Take Highway 92 through Granite Falls. Coming out of town, turn left, continuing on the Mountain Loop Highway. Stop at the Verlot Ranger Station for a brochure to the townsite. Some 40 miles east of Everett is Barlow Pass and the trailhead. Park in a lot on the north side of the highway or on the shoulder along the south side.

DISTANCE: 4 miles one way

LEVEL OF DIFFICULTY: easy, except for washed-out portions

HISTORICAL HIGHLIGHTS: markers along the way; Monte Cristo townsite

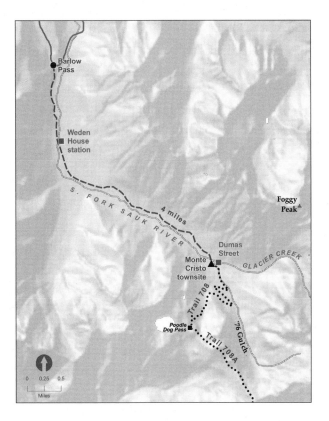

In the 1870s, silver ore was discovered in the watershed of the North Fork Skykomish River, and a rush was on. Silver City rose on the banks of Silver Creek, which originates near Silver Lake and Silvertip Peak. The hopeful names promised more than was delivered, however, so miners such as Joseph Pearsall started looking farther afield for glitter.

From the east bank of Silver Creek, Pearsall climbed to the top of a mountain and looked north through his field glasses. In the watershed of the Sauk River he saw a metallic reflection from a distant mountain, a red-gold glitter that looked like galena, which could contain silver. Crossing over a pass to reach the mountain, Pearsall collected some samples, which turned out to be silver and gold.

He shared the news with a buddy, Frank Peabody, and they found an investor. With a grubstake of $150, Pearsall staked out a claim in a gulch near the headwaters of the South Fork of the Sauk. He named his claim the Independence of 1776, "'76" for short. The two brothers who grubstaked the claim, Fred and John Macdonald Wilmans, were not stay-in-the-office financiers. They made the two-day trek over the pass from Silver Creek and down into '76 Gulch and joined the prospectors around a campfire to consider a suitable name for their investment. Hoping to become as rich as the Count of Monte Cristo, the protagonist of the book by Alexander Dumas, they chose the name Monte Cristo.

Monte Cristo proved up. At its peak in the 1890s, the town had a population of 2,000. Mines on the mountains above the town produced millions of dollars in gold and silver ore. Today, a gentle four-mile walk along the Sauk River leads back into the basin framed by mountain peaks and the best ghost town in Washington.

Within a year of Pearsall's discovery, other prospectors were streaming over Wilmans Pass, looking for a share of the wealth, but soon switched to the lower Poodle Dog Pass, named for a mine and a dog owned by Peabody. The trail was impassable to horses, so the broad backs of mountaineers did the packing for six cents a pound. An average pack of fresh beef and a sack of flour weighed seventy-five pounds.

The scale of mining at Monte Cristo soon surpassed the power of human backs or arms. Lode or "hard rock" mining required drilling and blasting and became more expensive than the Wilmans could sustain. Only railroad or oil millionaires outside the Pacific Northwest had amassed enough capital to build a concentrator, a railroad, and a smelter. Within two years an investment firm backed by John D. Rockefeller—Hoyt, Colby and Company—purchased a controlling interest in the Monte Cristo mines. Rockefeller's firm built the Everett and Monte Cristo Railway along the South Fork Sauk River, to carry ore to a smelter in Everett.

The hike to Monte Cristo follows the railroad grade along the South Fork to its headwaters at the townsite. Extensive flood damage permanently closed the railroad, and the track was taken out in 1936. Just three years later, when the Mine to Market Act required local jurisdictions to build roads across federal land on which potentially productive mines had been located, the road used the abandoned grade of the railroad. The road is gated and accessible only to vehicles of private landowners.

Over the years, the river has meandered, bridges have washed out, and hillsides have slumped. Despite the stern warning signs posted, the detours are relatively easy for a hiker. A bypass trail leads uphill around a slide from the storm of December 2006. Then hikers must choose between crossing logs and wading across the river, which is shallow in late summer.

The road passes trails to the Twin Bridges mine, the Del Campo mines near Weden Lake, and the Weden Creek Trail, an old miners' trail that climbs steeply to Gothic Basin. At 1.7 miles is the site of the Weden House railroad station, marked by a sign on the north side. Peaks come in and out of view: Twin Peaks, Lewis Peak,

'76 Creek and Glacier Creek border the Monte Cristo townsite.

Del Campo Peak, Cadet Peak, and Monte Cristo Peak. At approximately 2.5 miles a stream comes in from Pearsall Gulch, named after the same Joe Pearsall who first saw the glitter.

All of these sites are mere teasers for the townsite itself. The first sign of settlement is the Forest Service campground on the left. Then a bridge crosses over Glacier Creek, one of the two creeks forming the headwaters of the South Fork Sauk. Weary hikers can plop next to a big rock, which historians have used to locate parts of the town in old photographs. The main attraction is just around the bend.

Better than a theme park, Monte Cristo allows the imagination to fill in the people, the smells, the sounds, and the bustle of the era. The townsite lies on a peninsula between Glacier and '76 creeks. Aerial tramways carried minerals down the slopes to the concentrator here. The area of Forest Service cabins, where many people lounge on a sunny day, is the former railroad yard. A large turntable built to head the locomotives back down the valley still turns with a creak.

Most miners lived above the town on Wilmans and Foggy peaks. Workers lived in the lower area across the railroad yards. Managers and businessmen lived in the upper part of town along Dumas Street. The finest residence was built for Charles A. Riddle of the Boston-American Mining Company.

In addition to these homes, the town had a store, five hotels, a school, and a newspaper. Imagine arriving at the train station on the daily train from Everett and lugging your trunk uphill to the fine Royal Hotel. What remains of the three-story structure is an Alpine blue fir planted in the hotel's rock garden in the 1920s. A white picket fence surrounds the tree, and a plaque honors U.S. Navy Commander James Elsworth Kyes. Kyes's family operated a mercantile store here, arriving in 1902 from the Klondike gold rush. As a boy, Kyes had brought the fir tree down from Addison's Peak and planted it. Kyes died after giving his life jacket to a crewman when their ship was sunk by a submarine on Christmas Eve 1943.

Dumas Street, named after the novelist, ran between the creeks and was paved with planks because of the perpetual mud and snow (not a problem in July). In the summer, residents hoisted their alpenstocks for picnics on the slopes. In the winter, life could be very harsh, with temperatures below zero. The town was dependent on the railroad's snow plows to cut through more than seven feet of snow to stave off isolation and even starvation.

A new trailhead at Sunday Creek leads up to Poodle Dog Pass and Silver Lake, then drops to Twin Lakes. This is the route Pearsall and Peabody first took into '76 Gulch. Once the Cascades were no longer a "poor man's" field, mined by men who carried poodle dogs over passes, Joe Pearsall left Monte Cristo in 1897. He headed for the Klondike and was never heard from again. Perhaps he anticipated the usual rags-to-riches-to-rags storyline. At Monte Cristo's peak, several corporations were trying to make a profit from the mines and pay dividends to stockholders. After the financial panic of 1907, the value of the ore couldn't match the costs of prospecting and development. Monte Cristo became a resort for hunters, campers, and sightseers. By 1933 the site was a ghost town with spectacular scenery.

One of the last remaining buildings at Monte Cristo, an old lodge that had been a cookhouse, burned down in 1983 under suspicious circumstances. Since that fire, the Monte Cristo Preservation Association has worked with private landowners and miners to preserve the site for visitors. Where miners and pack teams once wound up the mountainsides, a steady procession of backpackers and leashed dogs rest in the basin, seeking restoration more than wealth.

12

Old Robe Canyon

GETTING THERE: Take Highway 92 through Granite Falls onto the Mountain Loop Highway. Coming out of town, turn left, continuing on the highway about 7 miles. Find the sign for Old Robe Trail on a brick block on the south side of the road after a long, steep hill. The sign is across from Green Mountain Road. Park along the edge of the road, where there is ample space for several cars.

DISTANCE: 1.2 miles to trail closure

LEVEL OF DIFFICULTY: moderate; some rough footing, drop-offs to river

HISTORICAL HIGHLIGHTS: tunnels; troughs cut out of the bedrock for railroad ties

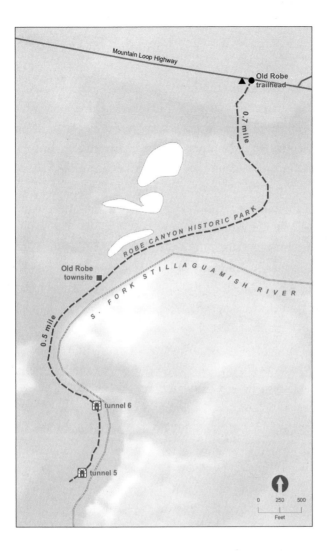

Mining was only half of the adventure in a boomtown like Monte Cristo. Even when silver and gold ore was of high quality, the expense of carting it out could eat up the profits. Undaunted prospectors traipsed all over the mountains, some for the pure thrill of discovery, but only investors like John D. Rockefeller had the deep pockets necessary to take the ore to market. Rockefeller's company acquired the mining claims at Monte Cristo in 1892 and hired J. Q.

Barlow to survey a route for a railroad. Barlow explored the south forks of the Sauk and Stillaguamish rivers, the only level way out of the basin, and warned against running the line through the Stillaguamish's canyon of perpendicular walls. He knew the damage winter snows and spring runoffs could do and suggested trestles instead. Financial backers far from the fury of Northwest rivers described the Stillaguamish as a "trout stream" and disliked the expense of trestles.

Barlow quit, but other engineers forged ahead and carved a railroad line into the canyon walls. "That canyon is one of the most difficult places to build a railroad I ever saw," said T. Tonneson, assistant engineer, as he built a road from Monte Christo to Hartford (near the modern community of Lake Stevens) and then on to the smelter at Everett. The road through the canyon was five miles long, with six tunnels. The crew had to give up on building Tunnel 7 through "a perfect Niagara of mud and water." Instead they constructed a shoofly, a twenty-five-degree curve away from the wall. A November storm flooded all the major Northwest rivers in 1892, and the Stillaguamish flowed through Tunnel 6 instead of below it. Despite these problems, the Everett and Monte Cristo Railway was constructed at a cost of $1.75 million and operated for almost forty years.

Railroad tunnels still cling to the walls above the raging river in a canyon near the old community of Robe. The trail starts at 980 feet, passes a picnic area within a few minutes' walk, then drops to the river level. The first mile winds down the hill on a few switchbacks and continues around a large wetland area, across the river basin, where the wide, gentle river is visible, then leads into a wide bog, the Robe townsite. The Robe family of Granite Falls homesteaded here in the 1890s, and the community grew to 150 people as the railroad and then loggers arrived. A sign at the beginning of the trail shows the approximate location of the former train station, marsh ponds, dry kiln, planing mill, shingle mill, line shed, and freight shed, all now overgrown or eroded by the river.

The trail joins the river at .7 mile, crosses streams, and enters the narrow canyon where the South Fork Stillaguamish flows. This part of the trail comes with warnings that unleashed dogs are unsafe, that children should be close at hand, and that the trail is closed at 1.2 miles due to slides and unstable conditions. Building tracks or even riding on a train through this canyon was not for the faint-hearted. In 1895, when a slide at Tunnel 4 closed the tracks, a second slide killed a member of the crew sent up to clear it.

Moss and ferns deck the steep canyon walls, and several small waterfalls trickle down, testifying to the constant presence of water. Much of the trail is old concrete poured in the bed cut from the rock. Some railroad ties remain; others have left impressions where the rock was chiseled out to hold them. Concrete chunks with embedded river stones have fallen into the river.

The river narrows, gathering speed and noise. The tunnels are numbered from west to east. Tunnel 6 is about 250 feet long, on a slight curve, with enough light to see the end of it; the thick rock wall between the hiker and the river feels especially secure. Tunnel 5 at 1.7 miles is 100 feet long and straight, more a large arch than a tunnel. Just beyond it, one of the many slides that bedeviled the builders has wiped out the old railroad bed.

Venturesome hikers report that the first slide is crossable on a narrow tread, but there is a second slide area farther on. It can be crossed on the remnants of a concrete sidewall, about eighteen inches wide, but the sidewall is suspended in air fifteen to twenty feet above the cascading river. Tunnels 4 and 2 were removed by the railroad in 1911. Tunnel 3 has collapsed. The site of Tunnel 1, known as the Kissing Tunnel because it was long enough to steal a kiss in, is across the river at the end of the Lime Kiln Trail. When I hiked this trail in 2000, Tunnels 5 and 6 were still accessible, but in 2009 the trail was closed before the tunnels.

For a brief time after the demise of mining at Monte Cristo, the railroad continued running, carrying timber to the sawmills of

Lake Stevens. Visitors staying at a large inn at the foot of Big Four Mountain east of Silverton rode self-propelled gas cars with open passenger trailers along the railroad grade, through the tunnels, and into the mountains. In the 1930s the lumber industry collapsed and the river flooded again, closing down the railroad and the fortunes of Robe. The Robe School closed in 1936, and residents moved eastward along the new highway north of the canyon. Sixty years later the Robe Canyon Historic Park was established. In the past decade, Eagle Scouts from troops in Lake Stevens and volunteers from the Stillaguamish Citizens' Alliance and Volunteers for Outdoor Washington have kept the engineering feat open for adventure.

13

Iron Goat Trail

GETTING THERE: For Martin Creek trailhead: Take Highway 2 to milepost 55, 9 miles west of Stevens Pass. Turn north on Forest Service Road 67, the Old Cascade Highway. Go 2.3 miles to the junction with Forest Service Road 6710. Turn left and go 1.4 miles to the trailhead and parking lot.

For Scenic trailhead: At milepost 58.3, turn left at the junction with the Old Cascade Highway, then immediately turn right into the Iron Goat Interpretive Site and trailhead.

For Wellington trailhead: Turn north at milepost 64.3, just west of Stevens Pass on the Old Cascade Highway (this turn is easier coming from the east). This road is not marked on the highway. Go 2.8 miles to the junction with Forest Service Road 50. Turn right into the parking lot.

DISTANCE: Martin Creek to Wellington, 5.5 miles; 1.3-mile loop along the lower and upper grade and crossovers; Scenic to Martin Creek, 2.75 miles; Scenic to Windy Point, 1.25 miles

LEVEL OF DIFFICULTY: moderate

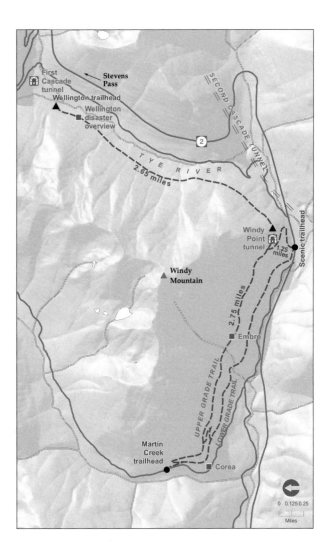

HISTORICAL HIGHLIGHTS: interpretive plaques; shoofly route at Windy Point; remains of snow sheds and back walls; site of the Wellington disaster (brochures are available at the trailheads)

Transcontinental railroads expanding from the Midwest to Puget Sound wanted a low pass through the Cascades, preferably one without avalanches. The Northern Pacific picked Green River Pass (Stampede Pass) and completed the first line through the mountains in 1888 on switchbacked trestles.

Watching this feat with a fierce competitive spirit was James J. Hill. A resident of St. Paul, Minnesota, Hill had already built an empire of steamboats, freight, coal, and a regional railway, but he had a grander vision: a "Great Northern" railroad west across the continent, reaching the coast at Seattle. Hill dispatched a respected engineer, John F. Stevens, to discover passes through both the Rockies and the Cascades. "Find it, and I will name one for you!" Hill promised. From Lake Wenatchee, Stevens followed Nason Creek westward and up, then traced a tributary of the creek (which became Stevens Creek) to its origin at the summit. With some surety this would be a feasible pass, Stevens sent his assistant, Charles Haskell, to survey the route. Haskell found the pass and carved the name "Stevens Pass" in a tree.

Hill himself came out to inspect the route and declared that building the line would require the fortitude of an iron goat—hence the Rocky Mountain goat logo of the Great Northern Railroad. Some called the enterprise "Hill's Folly." Hill's crews carved a route high on the mountainsides above the pass, cutting down trees as they went. Workers had to drill and blast enough rock to create a flat grade on the slope of the mountains. That high route proved an unsustainable folly in winter but a spectacular hike in summer.

The Iron Goat Trail has a mountain goat's view of Stevens Pass. There are three trailheads; the western end at Martin Creek, the eastern end at the Wellington station, and the Iron Goat Interpretive Site at Scenic, the southern point of a loose triangle. The trail also has two elevations: a lower grade trail 2.6 miles long, five feet wide, and barrier-free, with a crushed rock surface, and an upper grade trail 5.5 miles long. The third and newest trail connects the trailhead at Scenic with Windy Mountain, the halfway point on the upper grade.

A Japanese crew straightens the track on the Great Northern Railroad, c. 1928. University of Washington Libraries, Special Collections, Pickett 4176.

The Iron Goat Trail is probably the most thoroughly interpreted historic hike in Washington. Replicas of mileposts measure the distance from St. Paul. Brochures and reader boards at the trailheads describe the possible hikes. There are extensive interpretations at Wellington (the site of a disaster in 1910) and at Scenic, on Highway 2.

For historical drama, begin at the west end, and witness the herculean efforts ordinary men put forth in building a railroad through the Cascades. From the high curving trestle built over Martin Creek, the trail extends east to massive snowshed walls, "shoofly" curves, and horseshoe bends, clinging to the side of Windy Mountain and ending at Wellington and the first Cascade tunnel.

Work began in 1890. The city fathers in Spokane granted the Great Northern a right-of-way through the heart of town. The route was relatively flat across the Columbia Basin until it climbed the switchbacks on the eastern slopes of the Cascades. Stevens planned an intricate set of three switchbacks on the east side of the pass and five on the west.

From the Martin Creek trailhead, the lower grade leads to the interpretive site at Scenic and to crossovers to the upper grade trail. One-half mile down the grade, the trail goes through a wide space called Corea, the site of a tent city. "Give me enough Swedes and whiskey, and I'll build a railroad to Hell," Hill was reported to have said. Like any pithy phrase, the truth was more complicated; workers came from Finland, Japan, Sweden, Canada, and England as well as New York, Illinois, Minnesota, Pennsylvania, and Iowa. Archaeologists have found the remains of ceramic bowls used by Japanese workers and remnants of dome ovens used by Italian workers to bake bread.

Whatever their ethnicity, track layers could spike down more than four miles of track in one strenuous day. After a hard day's work, comforts were few. A photograph shows the tents in the snow, on ascending platforms. Some workers had the added protection of walls. A Japanese worker, Yoshiichi Tanaka, described the living conditions: "Lodging facilities were awfully poor. Two rows of beds made of boards were run along the inside walls of old freight cars. Instead of mattresses, we spread straw on the boards. . . . Innumerable bedbugs marched all over us."

Just after the trail passes Corea, the pattern on the moss, called corrugation, reveals the path of the old railroad ties, which were left to rot. Further on, you may take the Corea crossover, constructed by volunteers, to the upper grade. The mileposts on this lower grade show an increasing distance from St. Paul as you walk east. That's because trains had already followed the upper grade, crossed Martin Creek on a trestle 165 feet high, and made a 170-foot turn in the Horseshoe Tunnel headed east again to Scenic before winding around to the west of Scenic—all in the interest of not having to climb or descend too steeply.

The lower grade trail passes milepost 1718 and a rock cut blasted out of the mountains with dynamite. After the harsh winter of 1915–16, the Twin Tunnels were built along this stretch. In 1990 a debris flow of earth, water, trees, rocks, and mud washed out sections of these grades and left a jumble of rocks where the trail is today. The lower-grade tail ends at Scenic, an apt name for this station.

The upper grade also leaves from the Martin Creek trailhead, departing from the lower-grade trail via the Martin Creek crossover. This trail passes many concrete snowshed walls, the railroad's valiant efforts to hold up the mountainside and deflect sliding snow from the tracks. Small waterfalls cascade over the walls. Iron spikes, concrete chunks, and rusted metal line the path.

At milepost 1714.93 is the site of Embro, a camp for workers, and a station first known as Alvin. A side trail leads to a small dam that provided water to protect the wooden snowsheds from fire. Discards such as rope, wash basins, and a coffee pot remain down the slope where they were thrown, long before the days of packing it out (these are protected artifacts).

After two years of backbreaking work, track layers from west and east met at Scenic, thirteen miles west of the summit, in January 1893. Two superintendents drove the final spike at 8 p.m., illuminated by lanterns and locomotive headlights. They celebrated with shouts and gunshots. The first regularly scheduled passenger train reached Seattle on July 4. Glassware graced the dining car tables even through the switchbacks. Resort hotels flourished at Scenic, beginning with the Great Northern Hot Springs Hotel built in the 1890s.

Scenic lies below Windy Mountain, where trains used to "shoofly" around a rock outcropping. Trains could go no more than five miles per hour there, to avoid tipping over. Walking around the curve eliminates all doubt about why a tunnel was built in 1913. The Windy Point Tunnel is unsafe to go through, but you can shelter at either end for lunch or sit in the sun outside on rocks overlooking the Tye Valley and the west portal of the second Cascade Tunnel, now used by the Burlington Northern Santa Fe and Amtrak's Empire Builder. Like a ghost of trains past, the sound of a train wafts up the mountain before it emerges from the woods, and smoke lingers above the portal after the train has disappeared.

Ghosts abound in the three-mile stretch from Windy Mountain to the station of Wellington, where disaster struck in 1910. The same wet weather that annually drifted down each winter on most of northwestern Washington dropped about thirty-five feet of snow in this stretch. Snow and ice from the mountain walls regularly slid over the tracks. The mountainsides of Stevens Pass had once been covered with forest but were denuded by loggers cutting railroad ties, which made the slopes even more avalanche-prone. For the first few years, snow plows and hundreds of men shoveled the tracks clear each winter, creating piles as high as twenty-five feet on either side of the tracks. Rotary snow plows went ahead of trains inching down the steep western slopes. The slanting roofs of the wooden snowsheds carried some of the snow over the tracks.

When Hill could afford it, in 1897, the railroad built the first Cascade Tunnel, which bypassed the highest slopes and brought trains to the Wellington station. In late February 1910, a passenger train and a mail train bound for Seattle emerged from the west end of the tunnel and parked at the Wellington station, blocked by late winter snowstorms that covered the tracks ahead. For five days and nights, rotary snow plows and human snow shovelers worked to free the tracks, but as soon as one slide was cleared, another came down.

After five days spent confined in the cars, a few of the passengers decided to hike the three miles to Windy Mountain, through snow that covered the tops of telephone poles. From there they slid down the steep slope to Scenic. The less able-bodied passengers remained on board, waiting for rescue. Then, in the middle of the night on March 1, an avalanche of snow broke loose from Windy Mountain and swept both trains down the mountainside and into the creek below. Only eight passengers and fourteen railway and postal employees survived. More than ninety-six were killed, making this the deadliest accident in American rail history. Rescuers spent a week retrieving bodies from the wreckage and sledding them and the injured survivors down by rope to Scenic. The hike from Scenic to Windy Gap switchbacks up and down the avalanche chute they used.

The Great Northern reacted to the disaster in three ways. First it built more and longer snowsheds on the ten miles of track between Scenic and Wellington. One of those massive wooden snowsheds east of Windy Point has collapsed and now forms wooden waves on the mountainside. Concrete backwalls, built in 1914, 1915, and 1917, still retain the wet slopes. In the final half mile of the upper grade, going east, the remains of one long, concrete snowshed shelters the trail. An interpretive site just west of Wellington helps the visitor visualize the path of the avalanche and the trains' plunge into the valley.

The railroad's second response was to change the Wellington station's name to Tye, after the Tye River, so that trains no longer went through "Wellington." Then a slide at Corea engulfed another stopped train in January 1916, killing seven people. So in its third response, the railroad constructed a new 7.8-mile tunnel under Stevens Pass and below Windy Mountain. When completed in 1929, it was the longest railroad tunnel in North America. That's the tunnel visible from Windy Point. The first tunnel was abandoned, and trains no longer took the dangerous high route through Stevens Pass.

Over the decades, railroads have merged and disbanded. The Northern Pacific and Great Northern became the freight-carrying Burlington Northern Santa Fe. Amtrak's Empire Builder still runs through the second Cascade Tunnel under Stevens Pass on its way from Seattle to Chicago. The abandoned route above it reverted to the Mt. Baker-Snoqualmie National Forest. Volunteers for Outdoor Washington approached the Forest Service about transforming this route into a trail, and work began in the early 1990s. Countless volunteer hours, led by tireless advocate Ruth Ittner, have made the once-disastrous route a recreation trail. Trees all along the trail have reclaimed much of the mountainside and seem to grow out of the tops of the walls, but the constant flows of water and deadly snow still bedevil the best of human engineering and hard labor.

14

Ladies Pass

GETTING THERE: Take Icicle Creek Road south from the west end of Leavenworth. At 13 miles, it becomes dirt road 7600. At 17 miles, go left at a Y-junction. Branch left toward the Rock Island Campground, over a bridge that crosses Icicle Creek. At the end of this road is the Black Pine Campground (for horses) and the trailhead for the Icicle Creek Trail.

DISTANCE: 24-mile loop from Icicle Creek trailhead; 20.5-mile loop to Chatter Creek Campground on Road 7600

LEVEL OF DIFFICULTY: difficult

HISTORICAL HIGHLIGHTS: lakes and pass named by Sylvester

Lakes named after women, such as Mary, Alice, and Margaret, dot the Cascade range. Who were all of these women? Many were related to Albert H. ("Hal") Sylvester, who roamed the Wenatchee National Forest as a surveyor and forester for more than thirty years, from 1897 to 1931. As part of his job, Sylvester named every uncharted ridge, creek, and lake he found in the forest, which stretches east from Snoqualmie Pass across the Wenatchee Mountains and north to Stehekin at the northern end of Lake Chelan.

"I seldom went on a field trip without coming back with some new names to add to the map," Sylvester related in an article he wrote

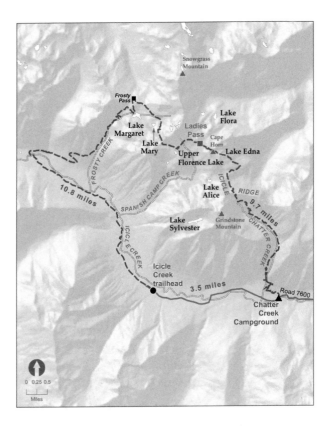

about his work. By 1931, he had named more than 3,000 places. On two days of a trip along Icicle Ridge, which cuts across the midsection of the forest, he named nine lakes, all of them for women he knew. This hike shadows Sylvester along the ridge, through aptly named Ladies Pass, gradually revealing four of the lakes looking just as they did when Sylvester discovered them.

Sylvester came to the Northwest as part of the U.S. Geological Survey, which was conducting an official mapping of every wilderness mile. When President Theodore Roosevelt created national forests in 1907, including the Wenatchee and Snoqualmie national forests, Sylvester switched to working for the Forest Service. To help fire-fighting crews locate fires, he continued adding names to the USGS quadrangle maps, which were updated every two or three years.

Most of the time Sylvester took a systematic approach to naming. Main waterways already had names given by Native Americans, so Sylvester gave the same name to ridges, ranges, and divides on the left of the waterway, looking upstream. Icicle Ridge, for example, he adapted from the Indian name for the creek, *na-sik-elt,* meaning "narrow canyon." The word "icicle" sounds like the Indian name if you put an "n" at the beginning and a "t" at the end, Sylvester explained. In addition to Indian names, Sylvester often used Chinook names (from the trade jargon developed by coastal tribes) or the names of settlers, miners, prospectors, or sheepmen. Tumac Mountain, for example, is named after two Macs—McDuff and McAdam, Scottish sheepherders who raced their herds to get to the pasture first in the summer. Lakes he tended to name after women.

When Sylvester ran out of names of friends and family, he picked whatever name was at hand. Index Creek was named because it forms the index finger of the Chiwaukum drainage system. Kodak Peak (near the headwaters of the Little Wenatchee River) he named when an assistant left his camera there. Overcoat Peak, northeast of Snoqualmie Pass, was named after a coat that became more of a burden than a help on Sylvester's climb; thirty years after he left his coat on the mountain, a party of Seattle Mountaineers found its remnants and sent him the shreds as a souvenir.

Some of the names were slight mistakes. A ranger submitted the name Pomas Creek for a waterway in the Entiat Mountains, and Sylvester tried to figure out what the location had to do with the French word for "apples." He realized that the ranger meant "pumice," after the pumice blown out by Glacier Peak, which fills the creek. Less imagination is required to guess the origin of Dishpan Gap, Saucer Lake, Cup Lake, Lake Camp Fire Girls, and Dirtyface Mountain, but Whistling Pig Meadow?

The nine-lake naming spree happened in the fall of 1909 when

Sylvester entered the high country of the Icicle Creek watershed with ranger Burne Canby. They approached Icicle Ridge from the east, and the naming began. "Rather late one evening, we camped in a little meadow well up toward the top of Icicle Ridge. It was cold. We didn't realize how cold until next morning, when we found our meadow heavily covered with white frost. I hadn't been giving any names thus far on this trip but called the meadow Frosty and the little creek that ran through it Frosty Creek." The next morning, they packed up and rode to the summit of Icicle Ridge to a fairly low pass, which he called Frosty Pass.

Some ninety years later, on foot with my husband Al and his hiking buddy Bill, we intersected Sylvester's route at Frosty Pass. The Icicle Creek Trail approaches Icicle Ridge and Frosty Pass from the west, from the Black Pine Campground, and winds among cedar trees for 4.5 miles along this far-reaching creek. The trail crosses several creeks, including French Creek, before reaching the Upper Crossing, a new route created after a 1990 flood took out the old bridge. The "new" bridge is two large logs, one falling into the creek, with no wires or handrails. Bill coaxed me across.

On the other side, a new section of trail connects with the old Frosty Pass Trail. It crosses Frosty Creek on two skinny logs; then switchbacks begin as the trail becomes overgrown and almost obscured by weeds and wildflowers. The first lake Sylvester named— Lake Margaret—comes into view before Frosty Pass and makes a good campsite at 10.8 miles.

Sylvester and Canby first saw and named Lake Margaret after camping at Frosty Pass and then hiking east along the ridge. "[We] hadn't gone far, when we saw below us, in a glacial pocket, a beautiful lake of perhaps sixty acres." Sylvester consulted his 1900–1901 Chiwaukum quadrangle map for the name of the lake "—but lo and behold, it was not shown! The topographers had missed it." Sylvester sketched it in and turned to Canby for a name. Canby's two sisters were named Margaret and Mary, so this lake became Margaret.

From the campsite on Lake Margaret, the trail continues to Frosty Pass and turns east, as the namers did, on Icicle Ridge Trail 1570. A side trail leads to Sylvester's higher-elevation view of Lake Margaret. Continuing along the ridge and into alpine meadow country, Sylvester and Canby came upon another lake that they named Mary (the second sister), now a popular backcountry campsite. Next came a lake they called Florence, after a friend of Margaret's and Mary's. This was getting interesting, and Sylvester remarked to Canby: "If we find another, we will name it for Mrs. Sylvester."

The three lakes lay in the shadow of Snowgrass Mountain, which was named between 1908 and 1912 by sheepherders, probably because the peak is almost entirely covered with grass, which would be revealed in the summer as the snow gradually retreated. Ladies Pass is a junction of trails; marmots claim the upper trail. The faint "main" trail leads downward and continues around the mountain. An even lower trail leads to Upper Lake Florence, in view below.[3] Sylvester brought friends back to this ridge between Lakes Mary and Florence in 1944, pausing at Ladies Pass to point out Snowgrass Mountain.

Past Florence, rounding the shoulder of a small ridge, the pair saw another lake glittering through the alpine fir and mountain hemlock to the south—Lake Alice, naturally, named after Alice Peirce Sylvester. The trail continues along a narrow ridge, then switchbacks down a slope to a branch of Spanish Camp Creek. In the meadows near the creek we paused to chat for a few minutes with a man out for a day hike with two large, friendly dogs. At the head of Spanish Camp Creek, Sylvester and Burne spotted a deep emerald green lake to the north—called Flora, after another ranger's wife. (Lakes Alice and Flora do not come into view from Trail 1570.)

The trail then climbs and rounds the windy lee of a high, sharp peak that Sylvester named Cape Horn. "Somewhat scared" by the peak's appearance, the two took the trail and found their sixth lake of the day, Lake Edna, "Burne's best girl." It was "nestled in a hollow in a barren field of rock"; the nest is still barren rock.

Here Sylvester and Canby camped the second night and then continued east along Icicle Ridge the next day, naming Augusta (for Sylvester's mother), Ida (his wife's sister), and Victoria (the Queen of England). That ended the lake finding and naming on that trip, but it marked the beginning of a practice. "The numbers of ladies' lakes grew, until practically all rangers' and other Forest Service men's wives, sisters, sweethearts, mothers, and daughters had lakes named after them," Sylvester recounted.

We departed from Sylvester's route at Lake Edna and headed south toward the Chatter Creek Trail to complete the loop begun at the Black Pine Campground. There are two southbound options at Lake Edna. One is marked by a large cairn, cuts over a knoll, and descends to basins forming the headwaters of Chatter Creek. The second is a more defined trail that leads part of the way around Lake Edna, over a knoll, and down to a junction with the Chatter Creek Trail. This trail, 1580A, almost disappears as it crosses several meadows. Follow the cairns and the lowest path of least resistance. The trail becomes more distinct as it crosses the rocky slopes of Grindstone Mountain, whose inspiration will be obvious.

After a steep ascent over Icicle Ridge, the trail switchbacks down to follow Chatter Creek. The rocky Chatter Creek Trail is a steady descent of 5.75 miles from Lake Edna to the Chatter Creek Campground, which is 3.5 miles by road from the Black Pine Campground.

During his years in the Forest Service, Sylvester made efforts to rehabilitate soil damaged by erosion caused by the overgrazing of sheep and wildlife. He was an avid outdoorsman; in the summer of 1916 he led a pack trip to the summit of Mount Stuart, the highest peak in Chelan County. He also named the Enchantment lakes.

After his retirement in 1931, Sylvester continued to roam remote

Lake Mary was named by Albert H. "Hal" Sylvester.

terrain. In September 1944, he invited three friends on a trip back
to Ladies Pass and the lakes. With four saddle horses and two pack
horses, they approached the pass from the northeast, following
a trail up Chiwuakum Creek. They spent the first night at Lake
Chiwaukum, then proceeded up through the valley to Larch Lake,
switchbacking steeply on a granite talus slope and following a very
rough trail. At Deadhorse Pass one of the packhorses slipped and
fell end over end to its death. When the group started out again,
they side-hilled below Lake Grace and camped under Snowgrass
Mountain at Lake Mary.

The next day the five-horse caravan set out, with Sylvester guiding the pack horse, its lead rope thrown around the horn of his
saddle. They traversed the sawtooth ridge between Lakes Mary and

Florence on a steep switchback trail. Just after crossing the ridge, with Lake Florence in view below, Sylvester paused to point out Snowgrass Mountain. The horses bunched up as the group gathered so they could talk more easily, but as they did, the lead rope caught under the tail of Sylvester's horse. His horse stepped off the trail, bucked, and lost its footing. Sylvester was trapped in the saddle, with his leg pinned down by the rope. Both his horse and the pack horse fell over the side into a jagged rockslide area. Sylvester was pinned under his horse. Through sleet and snow, he was carried out on a stretcher by relays organized by the Forest Service. Despite these efforts, Sylvester died a week later. Lake Sylvester, one of the highest lakes in the Cascades, was named after him. Located straight south of Ladies Pass, it overlooks Lake Alice.

Despite its glittering lakes with their feminine names, Ladies Pass is still rugged territory. On our way down, we were overtaken by the day hiker and his dogs, but he was carrying the older dog in a makeshift pack on his back. The dog had slipped and fallen down a rocky slope, suffering a fatal injury. Choosing not to leave the dog in the mountains, the man carried a heavy load, with the younger dog following sadly behind.

15

Desolation Peak

GETTING THERE: There are several ways to reach the Desolation Peak trailhead; all require advance planning. Park at milepost 3.4 on Highway 20 at the Ross Lake trailhead. Hike 1 mile and 450 feet down to a gravel road; go right (north) to the dock and telephone for the Ross Lake Resort water taxi (make a reservation ahead of time at 206-386-4437). The taxi will take you to campgrounds along the lake or to Desolation Landing. Arrange for pickup too. Or hike the East Bank Trail 16 miles to

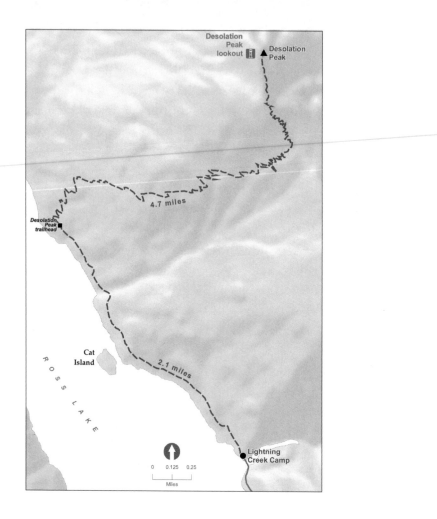

Desolation
Peak
lookout

Desolation
Peak

4.7 miles

Desolation
Peak
trailhead

Cat
Island

2.1 miles

R O S S   L A K E

0   0.125   0.25

Miles

Lightning
Creek Camp

the Desolation Peak Trail. Or boat to Desolation Landing from Hozomeen
Campground, south of Hope, British Columbia.

DISTANCE: 4.7 miles from landing; 6.8 miles from East Bank Trail

LEVEL OF DIFFICULTY: difficult; 4,400-foot elevation gain

HISTORICAL HIGHLIGHTS: lookout station

Jack Kerouac, Beat novelist of the 1950s, spent a lonely summer on
Desolation Peak in 1956. "On Desolation, I was the alonest man in

the world," he wrote in his journals. In sixty-three days he had no visitors and returned to base only once, when he ran out of tobacco. Yet he stayed, searching for a Zen-like solitude and inspiration. Kerouac predicted in *Desolation Angels* that countless pilgrims and sages would form a "rucksack revolution, with all over America millions of Dharma Bums going up to the hills to meditate and ignore society." Kerouac made Desolation Peak famous when he wrote about his experience in two autobiographical novels, *Dharma Bums* and *Desolation Angels*. On any sunny summer day, a few pilgrims may climb Desolation Peak, seeking the same muse.

Fire-watch cabins on high North Cascades peaks lured several Beat writers. Northwest native Gary Snyder, the "Thoreau of the Beat generation," manned Crater Mountain above Ross Lake in 1952 and Sourdough Mountain in 1953, spotting fires and writing poetry. A few summers later, Snyder met Kerouac at a famous poetry reading in San Francisco. Kerouac had already written but not yet published *On the Road*, his account of crossing the country in search of meaning through adventures. Looking for more, Kerouac went hiking in the Sierras with Snyder and loved the experience. Snyder persuaded him to go to the Skagit country, "the greatest place in America."

The next summer Kerouac hitchhiked north. Washington State had more than 600 fire-watch cabins, and Kerouac had requested Desolation. After fire training and crew work, he and one ranger, one packer, two mules, and three horses were rafted up Ross Lake with the summer's provisions on board. At Desolation Landing, they disembarked in rain, sleet, and snow in July.

Reaching the trail today is equally complicated, even without a summer's provisions. Hikers approach either by boat to Desolation Landing, or from a nearby campsite such as Lightning Creek, or by long trail from Highway 20. Kerouac, an urban guy from Lowell, Massachusetts, climbed this trail only twice—his first trip on horseback, the second on foot after replenishing his tobacco. The trail ascends relentlessly, more than half in light woods, then gradually opens to subalpine meadows, high rocks, berries, and bear country. The only water source is a small creek halfway up, which is often dry by August. Kerouac melted snow for much of his water.

The lookout first shows itself—still a long mile away—around the curve of a false summit, then disappears from view in the steep foreground. Kerouac described it in *Dharma Bums* as "a funny little peaked almost Chinese cabin among little pointy firs and boulders standing on a bald rock top surrounded by snowbanks and patches of wet grass with tiny flowers." It perches 6,000 feet high on chert, toolstone mined by Native Americans and used for blades 8,000 years ago.

At the top, the peaks of the North Cascades surround the cabin. To the north looms Hozomeen, which Kerouac mythologized as "the Void." His first view of the peak came in the middle of the night when it appeared like a huge black monster standing in the window, a witch's tower shape: "What a mountain! . . . Hozomeen, Hozomeen, the most mournful mountain I ever seen," he wrote, then later, "the most beautiful mountain I ever seen." Jack Mountain and its glacier, Nohomeen, loom to the south, but Kerouac was obsessed with Hozomeen.

Kerouac spent the long daylight hours meditating, studying the Diamond Sutra, and writing madly. He stayed close to the lookout, enjoying the solitude of the meadows and the spartan comforts of the cabin. Visible through the windows are seventy-year-old furnishings: a bed suspended on ropes rather than a metal frame because of frequent lightning strikes; the round Osborne fire-finder secured to a pedestal in the center of the room; a stove; an old ice chest; a wooden table with a bench. Outside, tanks hold the summer's propane, the heavy wooden weather door is stashed under the cabin, and shutters are propped open to the mountain air on all four sides. The 2007 occupant pasted the "alonest" quote on the inside of a window for fans to read.

Jack Kerouac spent the summer of 1956 at this lookout cabin atop Desolation Peak.

Bear, grouse, deer, osprey, and pika keep company in the meadows. Although a cool wind often flows from the southwest, "There were days that were hot and miserable," Keroauc wrote, "with locusts of plagues of insects, winged ants, heat, no air, no clouds, I couldn't understand how the top of a mountain in the North could be so hot."

In contrast, he described Ross Lake as "a beautiful cerulean pool far below with tiny toy boats of vacationists, the boats themselves too far to see, just the pitiful little tracks they left rilling in the mirror lake. You could see pines reflected upsidedown in the lake pointing to infinity." The view hasn't changed in fifty years, since the lake's creation by the final dam on the Skagit River in 1953.

Most poet lookouts had few fires to spot, but dramatic weather punctuated the summers; lookouts stood on lightning stools grounded in glass feet during thunderstorms and felt the hair on their necks rise. The name Desolation comes from an Upper Skagit forest fire in 1926 that jumped the undammed Skagit River from the west and desolated these slopes, which explains the preponderance of young trees. Fire returns to Desolation about every fourteen years, and the Forest Service still hires would-be hermits to scan the skies at Desolation and Sourdough mountains, where poets Gary Snyder and Phil Whalen spent summers. Both cabins were placed on the National Register of Historic Places in 1989.

Alone on this peak, Kerouac felt the eternity, majesty, and cruel fatalism of nature. Although Snyder came down from the Northwest peaks reluctantly, Kerouac was happy to leave in September when fire danger had passed. He headed to Mexico for chocolate, women, and drink, but he, too, knew what he was leaving: "Now comes the sadness of coming back to cities."

The descent is easier—at least for young knees. Kerouac humped seventy pounds down to Desolation Landing in two hours with aching feet and quivering thighs. Because his boots were worn out, he filled them with cardboard slip-ins for soles; he kept hitching his thumbs through the packstrap to hunch it high on his back, a motion any burdened backpacker would recognize. His good-bye verse described the end of a pilgrimage:

Desolation, Desolation
   so hard
   To come down off of.

CHAPTER FOUR

The Central Cascades

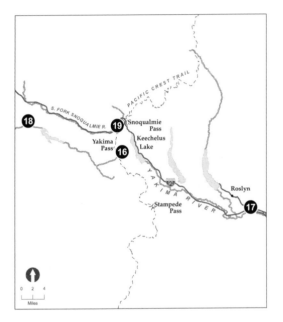

Fifteen million travelers drive through Snoqualmie Pass each year on eight lanes of I-90, an interstate that traverses North America from Seattle to Boston. Of the many passes through the Cascades, this one has become the major east-west route across the state.

One hundred and fifty years ago, it was hardly known. The Snoqualmie Indians knew where the pass was, but the first American explorers saw only snow and forbidding peaks—"no possibility of effecting a passage in that direction," George McClellan wrote. Washington Territory's citizens were convinced, however, that Puget Sound cities would never prosper until the right pass could be found through the Cascades. The search began.

Ancient travelers found mountain passes by following water to its source. Four rivers led to three major passes through the Central Cascades. From the central Sound, the South Fork Snoqualmie River leads to Snoqualmie Pass, and the North Fork Cedar River leads to Yakima Pass (which has also been known as Cedar River Pass). From the east, the Yakima River leads to tributaries flowing from the same Yakima Pass. From south Puget Sound, the Green River leads to Green River Pass, later named Stampede Pass.

At 3,022 feet, Snoqualmie Pass is the lowest of these three but the hardest to find because it is not visible from the west or east. Instead, the pass is topographically hidden, shaped like the eye of a needle in a north-south loop. The Snoqualmie Indians, traveling on foot and by canoe, approached Snoqualmie Pass along the south fork of the Snoqualmie River. Descending from the summit south to Lake Keechelus, they crossed on canoes or kept to Keechelus Ridge on the east side of the lake.

Approaching the Central Cascades on horseback, the Yakama Indians followed the Yakima River up to Lake Keechelus, which was only half as long as the reservoir along I-90 today, and rode on a ridge around the southern end of the lake. Continuing west to Lost Lake, they climbed to Yakima Pass, just a few miles south of Snoqualmie Pass. Descending, they followed the north fork of the Cedar River down the west side of the mountains. This route was better for horses because it was higher and less blocked by brush and fallen timber.

Both tribes roamed the mountains in summer to hunt mountain goat and deer, fish for crayfish and freshwater mussels, and gather grasses for basket weaving. They picked huckleberries and dug roots and bulbs, such as wild onion, camas, kouse, and sweet potato. They also crossed the mountains to trade, gathering every few years at a large camp called Che-lo-han in the Kittitas Valley (see chapter 6).

To protect this trade, Native Americans were sometimes reluctant to share their knowledge of the trails. The Hudson's Bay Company learned little of the Central Cascades and relied on the Columbia River for trade and transportation. The first railroad survey in 1853 found Yakima Pass but overlooked Snoqualmie Pass. Decades passed before Snoqualmie Pass became the route of choice. This chapter will trail the Snoqualmie and Yakama people over the passes and track George B. McClellan and Abiel Tinkham in the 1850s as they explored for a transcontinental railroad route. We'll walk a coal-mine railroad built from Cle Elum to Roslyn in 1886, then trek parts of the old Milwaukee Road, where rails crossed Snoqualmie Pass in 1909. Finally, we'll shadow wagons and tourists in Model Ts on corduroy roads and the Sunset Highway, which parallel I-90 at the pass. Most of the old routes have faded, but a few have survived the heavy treads of wagons, railroads, and cars.

16

Yakima Pass

GETTING THERE: The Pacific Crest Trail goes through Yakima Pass. Access it from Mirror Lake Trail 1302. Take exit 62 from I-90 (Stampede Pass-Lake Kachess). Turn south on Road 54, which is paved for one mile. At the fork under the power lines, turn right on Forest Service Road 5480, a dirt road, and stay right. At a five-way intersection at Lost Lake, take the road on the north side for a rougher 2 miles. It's best to park at 7.4 miles, before the road becomes steep. Walk the last .5 mile to the Mirror Lake trailhead.

DISTANCE: 2.6 miles one way

LEVEL OF DIFFICULTY: moderate; climbs to two lakes, then down to the pass

HISTORICAL HIGHLIGHTS: Yakima Pass; Twilight Lake; Lost Lake

Just south of heavily traveled Snoqualmie Pass is little-known Yakima Pass, a pass once identified for the first transcontinental

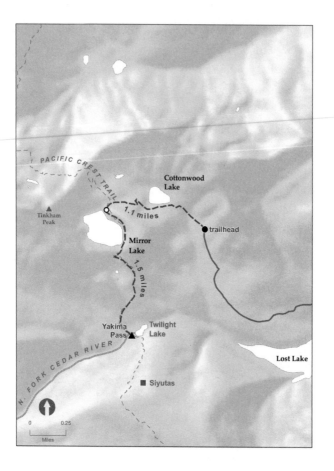

railroad in Washington. Army engineer George B. McClellan found the pass on horseback while following the old Yakama Trail in 1853. Today, the Pacific Crest Trail goes through it, with hardly a pause for what might have been. Only berry pickers and hikers find this low spot between the ridges, marked by a small wooden sign.

Before the Civil War, the U.S. Congress tried to bind the union by building railroads across the continent. The key question was which part of the West—north, central, or south—would lay the first tracks. Avoiding tough political decisions, Congress decided to explore all of the proposed routes and let nature decide. Surveys for the northern route began in 1853, the same year Washington Territory separated from Oregon Territory.

The main obstacle for the northern route was crossing the Cascade Mountains. Settlers coming off the Oregon Trail would float down the Columbia River and portage its rapids, then head south to the Willamette Valley or north to Puget Sound, shifting their loads from wagons to boats and back to wagons (see chapter 2). A suitable pass through the Central Cascades would eliminate these shifts and cut miles off the journey.

McClellan's job was to find that pass, survey the grades, estimate the snow depths, and make a recommendation for a route. Leaving Fort Vancouver on the Columbia River in July 1853, McClellan traveled northeast at a leisurely pace, with a military expedition of 60 men and 160 animals. His plan was to approach the Cascades from the east, following rivers such as the Yakima up into the mountains. He had quickly discounted the first pass he explored, Naches Pass, as unsuitable. Instead he accepted the suggestion of Catholic priest Charles Pandosy, who had established a mission at Ahtanum, southwest of today's Yakima, that he take a look at Snoqualmie Pass. Indians warned, however, that snow was twenty-five feet deep at the summit.

Taking a party of nine, McClellan left camp near Ellensburg and rode along the Yakama Trail. He passed the first two lakes that nest in glacial grooves—Lake Cle Elum and Lake Kachess—and stopped at the foot of Lake Keechelus, where the Yakima River begins. There he made the choice of what became the less traveled path, toward Yakima rather than Snoqualmie Pass.

Continuing on a high ridge overlooking a lake, he followed a steep trail and camped on the ridge on the evening of September 6. McClellan started out on horseback the next morning. After about a mile and a half, he wrote in his journal, he "found that we had crossed the divide."

Logging has obscured McClellan's route above Lost Lake. The

better approach to Yakima Pass is on the Pacific Crest Trail, via Cottonwood and Mirror lakes. From the trailhead for these lakes, climb gently a half mile to Cottonwood Lake, a tranquil spot, and then continue a half mile to the larger Mirror Lake. Here, in 1929–30, a laborer who had worked on building the highway through Snoqualmie Pass, Morris Jenkins, decided to spend his winter trapping. Jenkins lived in a cabin that was completely covered with snow, with only the top of the stovepipe visible. He dug a tunnel to check his trap lines and to get to a spring for water. The snow reached more than twelve feet in depth that winter, and temperatures reached minus thirty-two degrees. The possibility of such deep snow had worried McClellan seventy years before Jenkins.

A sign at Mirror Lake proclaims Snoqualmie Pass eight miles to the north and Stampede Pass ten miles to the south; unheralded Yakima Pass is only a mile away. From Mirror Lake, descend the Pacific Crest Trail, hiking through logged-over country open to sweeping views of the land. Yakima Pass is the low point to the south, between this ridge and the next. The Pacific Crest Trail crosses two gravel and dirt logging roads, then descends through a narrow, brushy, sometimes wet trail to Twilight Lake. Here is a small wooden sign for Yakima Pass.

For two days McClellan explored this pass, setting up camp on a prairie. Ethnologist George Gibbs recorded its Indian name, Si-yu-tas. McClellan ventured three miles on foot, following a creek into today's Cedar River watershed (now marked by "No Trespassing" signs to protect Seattle's water supply). He came to the fork of two streams that run toward the Sound (the origins of the Cedar River), but the way was narrow and rocky. An Indian guide told him that the river emptied into a lake, with a "cascade about as high as a pine tree" at the other end (Cedar Falls). From his day's explorations, McClellan concluded that it would be "extremely difficult to put a road over the pass."

It was nearly twilight of his first day of exploring when he came upon "a pretty little lake with good grass around it." The next day he observed that streams flowed out of it to both the west and the east, placing it "directly upon the summit of the divide." McClellan thought a road could be carved along the banks of the lake, but today the area is only a wet bushwhack.

Beyond Twilight Lake, the Pacific Crest Trail continues up an even brushier path and over the end of a ridge. This is the ridge McClellan approached from and followed between Meadow and Roaring creeks from Lake Keechelus. Somewhere on the ridge he made his base camp. From the top he described "a fine view of the Mtns. Mt. Rainier was in full sight—more imposing and majestic than ever. At our feet—some 1000' below us, lay a pretty lake—scattered around us the most jagged mountains of the range."

A small bench lies south of Yakima Pass on the Pacific Crest Trail, with a view of Twilight Lake, the pass, and two curving roads that nearly converge. Forest Service environmental coordinator Susan Carter believes that McClellan's camp lay between the two roads. Carter was working as an archaeologist in the Wenatchee National Forest in the late 1970s when Morris Jenkins showed her segments of the old trail used by the Yakama and a meadow whose stripped trees indicated Indian use. At that time, the deeply embedded horse trail was still visible, but it has since been obscured by clear-cutting practices that destroy the top six inches of soil.

The larger lake visible to the east is Lost Lake, which McClellan called by its Indian name, Wilailootzas, "a long narrow lake—about 2/3 or 3/4 mile long, by 400 or 500 yards wide." He thought that the lake's steep banks would be a "considerable tho by no means insuperable" difficulty for a railroad. Instead, those steep banks have preserved the lake's relatively "lost" status. Declaring himself "pretty well tired after our 2 days divide walking, slipping, and climbing," McClellan retraced his route east along the Yakima River. He stopped at Lake Kachess to try fishing, "but the wretches would not rise to the fly."

McClellan never found Snoqualmie Pass, noting in his report that the mountains in that direction "are very lofty, generally bare at the top, often of solid rock, with sharp outlines, most of them with considerable snow upon them." He traveled farther north, along the Cascades, the Stuart Range, and Lake Chelan, but found no way through. In December he tried once again to find Snoqualmie Pass by approaching it from the west but turned back at today's North Bend.

McClellan was skeptical that a train could travel through any of the passes in the winter snows, and he ended up recommending a route along the Columbia River. Territorial Governor Isaac Stevens was unhappy with McClellan's report, so he called on Abiel Tinkham, who had already crossed the difficult Bitterroot Mountains of Idaho in December. Traveling on snowshoes, without even a tent, Tinkham and his Yakama guides crossed Yakima Pass in January 1854, and arrived in Seattle seven days later. Tinkham found the snow only six feet deep at the summit and abandoned his snowshoes at Nook-Noo Lake (Cedar Lake).

Despite Tinkham's efforts, Congress listened to McClellan. The first transcontinental railroad to the Pacific Northwest—the Northern Pacific—followed the Columbia River in 1869, turning north at Kalama. A branch was later built through Stampede Pass to Tacoma, but no rails, steam, or soot would ever mar Yakima Pass. The area northeast of Yakima Pass has been logged, but the contours of the land, the course of the streams, and the shapes of the lakes have remained much the same.

Retrace your steps to Mirror and Cottonwood lakes and back to the trailhead, or go downhill on either of the logging roads that cross the trail. If, like McClellan, you've been exploring, perhaps you've found Siyutas or remnants of the old Indian trail or even some of the fish that would not "rise to the fly."

17

Coal Mines Trail

GETTING THERE: To begin in Cle Elum, take exit 84 off I- 90 into Cle Elum along First Street. At First Street and Stafford Avenue, park at the small city park on the north side of First Street or at the Coal Mines trailhead, one block north of First Street. To begin in Roslyn, come into town on Highway 903, turn right on Pennsylvania Avenue, the main cross-street, and go .1 mile to Visitor Parking and the Coal Mines Trail. To begin in Ronald, continue through Roslyn on Highway 903.

DISTANCE: 4.7 miles one way

LEVEL OF DIFFICULTY: easy

HISTORICAL HIGHLIGHTS: coal mine sites; Roslyn Cemetery; Northwest Improvement Company Store

Although the first railroad surveys found no suitable pass through the Central Cascades, Northern Pacific Railway magnates never gave up on the idea of a direct route to Puget Sound. In the 1870s, railroad engineers discounted Snoqualmie Pass and chose a pass to the south, Stampede Pass. Workers built elaborate switchbacks up the mountains on trestles, then a tunnel through which the Burlington Northern still runs, practically unseen and unheard.

Powering a train through mountains consumes huge stores of energy, so while engineers looked for routes, they also kept an eye out for resources. In 1886 engineers located large seams of coal near lakes Cle Elum and Kachess, just east of Snoqualmie Pass. Wasting no time, the Northern Pacific Railway formed the Northern Pacific Coal Company, set up a company town on part of the railroad's land grant, opened a company store, and imported 400 miners from Italy. They named their town Roslyn.

For the next thirty-five years, coal dominated Roslyn's life.

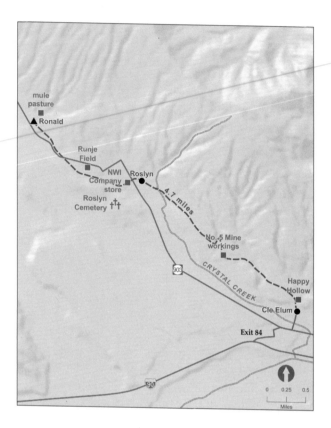

A mixture of immigrants soon followed the Italians: experienced miners from Wales and England, then Germans, Czechs, Serbians, Croatians, Poles, and Lithuanians. By 1900, 40 percent of the population was foreign-born, all crammed together in a bowl of houses ringed by the hills. At its peak, the town's population was 4,200; two-thirds of the males fourteen and older worked in or around the coal mines. The children in the elementary school were of twenty-four different nationalities or ethnic groups.

Roslyn was a company town, but Cle Elum developed as a result of land speculation and enticements to the railroad to locate a depot in the area. In December 1886, Roslyn miners carted the first coal out of the mines and shipped it on a branch line to the depot in

Children from many backgrounds attend a Roslyn school, c. 1905. Roslyn Museum Collection.

South Cle Elum. The coal kept flowing from the mines and the depot until 1963.

Thirty years after the last mine closed, the towns purchased the broad, flat roadbed of the spur line for a trail. Twenty numbered sites, from Cle Elum to Roslyn to Ronald, trace a coal mining history fraught with both conflict and prosperity. (You can pick up a copy of a tour guide to the Coal Mines Trail at various sites, including the Cle Elum Chamber of Commerce.) The sites are sparsely strung out over the first four miles, but the walking is pleasant, with a few benches and shaded spots, and Crystal Creek on one side. The mine sites are generally numbered in reverse, from Mine No. 7 just outside of Cle Elum to Mine No. 1 in Roslyn.

Indications of mining come gradually: slabs of concrete, coal, rusted cable, and heaps of slag and cinder covered with slight vegetation. As coal was dug out of the mines, the rubble that came with it was dumped in piles nearby. The first site past the backyards of Cle Elum is the dump of the No. 7 Mine, which extended from the top of the ridge to 400 feet below Cle Elum. The second site is Happy Hollow, a hamlet on land that settlers leased from the Northwest Improvement Company. Next was a settlement of Eastern European immigrants, who worked in No. 5 and lived in thirty-two company houses. A spur rail line led one mile west, to No. 9; Slavic miners nearby lived in "Ducktown," named for the poultry they raised for food. The No. 4 Mine was closer to the tracks. An explosion in that mine killed ten miners in October 1909, leaving twenty-one children without fathers.

Mining activity and historic sites pick up as one gets closer to Roslyn, including the Shaft Street Power House, the Roslyn Foundry, the Northwest Improvement Company horse barn, the warehouse, the wash house, the machine shop, and the No. 1 Mine, which exploded in May 1892. Forty-five men died in the explosion, which was caused by faulty ventilation and an accumulation of gas. Rescuers had to wait three days while repairs were made to the ventilating equipment before entering the lower levels. In addition to the bodies of the miners, rescuers found a cat and seven mules still alive, quartered in a stable on a lower level.

From the No. 1 Mine site, the trail leads into town, and the numbered sites continue: the coal office, engineers' office, official residences, doctor's office, the Roslyn Depot on East Washington Avenue, and the block-long Northwest Improvement Company Store, which opened in 1896, closed in 1957, and now houses a variety of stores. Maps of downtown and a tour guide for the trail are available during business hours at the Roslyn Administration Building at Pennsylvania and First.

The same year the No. 1 Mine exploded, Roslyn Bank was the site of a different calamity. Owned by cattle baron Ben Snipes, the bank held large shipments of cash used to meet the mine payrolls. In September, five armed men on horseback robbed the bank of $5,000 (the $40,000 mine payroll had already been transferred to the mining offices). A $1,000 reward was offered for their capture, and the governor added another $500, but the robbers were never brought to justice.

The Coal Mines Trail leads through town on Washington Avenue, crossing Highway 903 (North First Street), then continuing two blocks to Third Street. The road curves to Runje ("Run-gee") Field, formerly a Yakama gathering place, where many Roslyn heritage celebrations now occur. The trail continues straight ahead, out of town, past houses and horse pastures. Markers note the powder house, the No. 3 Mine structures and dump, and a mule pasture, where mules who had spent much of their lives underground were put out to graze, having been blindfolded to protect them from the bright light. The fired red color of the slag piles comes from years of intense heat from burning. A thirty-minute walk from Roslyn is the hamlet of Ronald, where the trail ends.

Ronald was the site of the No. 3 Mine, which employed black miners during labor strife in the late 1800s. Two years after Mine No. 1 opened, the first labor unions in America tried to organize miners in Roslyn. In 1888 the Knights of Labor led a strike for higher wages and an eight-hour workday. In response, the company brought fifty African Americans from Illinois on trains guarded by federal marshals. After a chilly welcome, the new workers descended into the No. 3 Mine, where they worked eleven-hour days for lower wages than the striking white miners. The railroad line to Cle Elum was closed temporarily, to prevent guns and outsiders from entering the community. Hundreds more African Americans were soon added to the workforce, significantly increasing the black population of the state.

After a second strike by white miners, the company closed the Roslyn mines and kept operations going with black workers at the mine in Ronald. This tactic succeeded, and the strike failed, resulting in lower wages for all. Only about half of the striking miners ever got their jobs back, and within a few months, more than 200 left Roslyn. Despite the hard feelings aroused by the strike, many of the strikebreakers stayed on in Roslyn. In 1976 Roslyn elected the state's first black mayor, William Craven.

Coal production slumped during the financial depressions of the 1890s, and the Snipes bank failed. Although production recovered and peaked in 1920 at 1.8 million tons, Roslyn faced competition from other regions and other sources of energy, such as oil. For years, the Northern Pacific ran on Roslyn coal, but the railroad that finally barreled through Snoqualmie Pass—the Chicago, Milwaukee, St. Paul, and Pacific —switched to electricity. In 1963 the last large commercial mine (No. 9) closed, although four-fifths of the coal deposits in the area remain unmined.

Make your next-to-last stop the Historical Museum, where a map shows all of the mines underfoot. Then visit the cemetery just out of town; it has thirty-two different ethnic and cultural sections. The Mount Olivet section was deeded by the railroad to African Americans after the mine explosion of 1892. Gravestones tell of epidemics of smallpox, cholera, whooping cough, and diphtheria.

Roslyn now combines its mining heritage with tourism. Visitors frequent cafes, taverns, the historical museum, and filming sites for the television show Northern Exposure, which was ostensibly set in Alaska. Annual summer celebrations draw many mining families back even as a large resort community outside of town, Suncadia, challenges Roslyn's historic identification with coal.

18

Iron Horse Trail

GETTING THERE: There are many entrances and exits from this trail in the Central Cascades. From the west, access the trail at Rattlesnake Lake. From exit 32 on I-90, turn south on 436th Avenue/Cedar Falls Road

S.E. and proceed 3.5 miles to the Iron Horse State Park parking lot and trailhead on the left. From the summit, take exit 54, Hyak, turn south, then immediately turn left on the frontage road, following signs to Snoqualmie tunnel (in winter, a Sno-Park permit is needed). Other access points are at exit 34, Twin Falls Natural Area; exit 38, the eastern end of Twin Falls; exit 42, a mile up the McClellan Butte Trail; and exit 47, 1.4 miles up the Annette Lake Trail.

DISTANCE: 21 miles from Cedar Falls to Hyak

LEVEL OF DIFFICULTY: easy on trail; moderate via McClellan Butte or Annette Lake trails

HISTORICAL HIGHLIGHTS: exhibits at Cedar Falls; site of Change Creek accident; Hull Creek trestle; Hansen Creek trestle; Snoqualmie tunnel; Milwaukee Bowl

By 1893 two transcontinental railroads crossed the Cascades, the Northern Pacific through Stampede Pass and the Great Northern through Stevens Pass. Watching these Herculean efforts, the Chicago, Milwaukee, St. Paul, and Pacific Railroad gambled that a third railroad could run at a profit through the Cascades. The Milwaukee Road, as it became known, claimed Snoqualmie, the last and lowest of the railroad passes. Operating between 1908 and 1980, the Milwaukee Road crossed the backbone of the state from Spokane to three Puget Sound ports—Tacoma, Seattle, and Everett.

The costs of construction were huge; the road from Montana to the coast totaled $234 million. Unlike the Northern Pacific, which it paralleled in some places, the Milwaukee Road received no government subsidies or land grants to help finance construction. Instead, the railroad negotiated with local land speculators, who offered concessions for the prosperity they were sure the rails would bring. Today the gentle grade of the wide railroad bed has become the I-90 of cyclists, skiers, and hikers. The grade spans some 300 miles, and all but 40 of these can be hiked. West of the Columbia River,

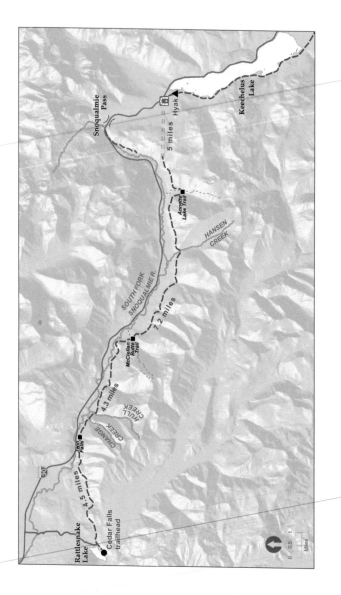

the Iron Horse Trail leads through towns the railroad built—Cedar Falls, Hyak, Easton, South Cle Elum, Horlock, and Thorp. From Ellensburg, the line crosses army land to the Columbia River. The trail begins again at Beverly, on the east side of the river, steams through Othello, takes a branch line to Spokane, and then crosses the Idaho border on its way to Chicago. (See chapter 6 for the Milwaukee Road Corridor Trail from Beverly to Smyrna.) The 113 miles of the western third are best hiked, skied, or biked in parts.

The main trunk line over the Cascades starts climbing at Iron Horse State Park, near Cedar Falls. This station was a key terminus from which branch lines went to Puget Sound ports. One of the lines, to Everett, has become the Middle Fork Snoqualmie Trail. The railroad station itself has been dismantled and moved to Kent, but the Cedar River Watershed Education Center recounts the history of the watershed, of homesteading in the area, and of the brick plant town of Taylor, the logging town of Barneston, and the railroad town of Moncton—all of them now gone. From Cedar Falls (a newer name for Moncton), the grade leads upward toward Snoqualmie Pass, skirting the Cedar River watershed, to reach Twin Falls at 4.5 miles.

As the third kid on the block, trying to compete with the Northern Pacific and the Great Northern, the Milwaukee Road became known as "America's most resourceful railroad." Often building its own equipment rather than buying it, the railroad came up with bay-window cabooses and skytop-dome observation cars. Diesels were painted a distinctive orange and black.

The biggest distinction, however, was the railroad's decision to electrify much of its line. From 1916 to 1920, quiet electrical power replaced diesel on every part of the 654-mile line, except for the section between Othello, Washington, and Avery, Idaho. Overhead wires known as catenary carried electricity from twenty-two substations to run the trains like trolleys. The company staged tug-of-wars between steam locomotives and electrified engines to prove that electric engines were more efficient as well as being less expensive, quieter, and cleaner. In several places on the trail, overhead supports that held the electric lines still stand above trestles. When the spring rains came, the enormous weight of melting snow could break the lines. Line men tied ropes around their bodies and were let down over the mountainsides to reach and repair the wires.

Past Twin Falls, the road rounds a curve 600 feet above Change Creek, near the old Garcia station and Deception Crags, a popular climbing area. In 1922 a freight train with four motors encountered a rock slide on this curve that had carried away the track but not the electrical lines. When the train was unable to stop in time, all four motors rolled down the mountainside, one after the other. A work crew used two big hooks to retrieve the engines, and section gangs rebuilt the track. Towering trestles still rise from the depths of ravines to hold the trail above Change Creek, Hull Creek, and Hansen Creek, at 12.1 miles.

From the intersection of the McClellan Butte Trail (at 8.8 miles) and the Annette Lake Trail (16 miles) to the west portal of the tunnel, this snowbelt portion of the trail is especially popular with cross-country skiers. Miles of often virgin snow are broken only by rabbit tracks, with views of the pass and the sweep of the mountains far above I-90.

For all three railroads through the Cascades, the biggest obstacle was snow. When railroad surveyor Abiel Tinkham snowshoed through nearby Yakima Pass in January 1855, he reported snow depths of only a few feet, but that turned out to be a mild Snoqualmie winter. During the first winter of the railroad's operation, in 1909–10, snow was more than eight feet deep at Snoqualmie Pass. Six feet of snow fell in a single storm, closing the railroad line for ten days. Snowsheds more than a mile long were added at the summit the next year between Rockdale and Laconia. They were said to be the longest snowsheds ever made on an American railroad.

In the winter of 1912–13, snow drifted more than forty feet high, and the railroad decided to build a tunnel to bypass the deepest snow at the summit. The tunnel formed the base of a triangle from Rockdale to Hyak, with the summit at its peak, thus eliminating the Laconia station. "Tunnel stiffs" used 340 tons of dynamite to

The Columbian sits at the Rockdale Station, just west of the crest, in the early 1920s. Washington State Historical Society.

blast a straight line through the mountain, with a daily goal of ten feet blasted. For every foot blasted past that goal, workers received a bonus of an hour's wages. Even with that incentive, the 2.25-mile-long tunnel took five years and 700 workers to complete. It opened in January 1915, shortening the route by four miles, eliminating a steep grade, and protecting the tracks from snow.

As the trail approaches Snoqualmie Pass, the valley of the South Fork Snoqualmie narrows, crowding a river, a railroad, and an interstate highway together. Once the tunnel was completed and the railroad was electrified (eliminating the dangers of fumes and gases), the Milwaukee Road became for many years the one reliable form of transportation in winter. Early car tourists often put their cars and themselves on the train to go over the pass. The tunnel from Rockdale to Hyak is usually open to cyclists and hikers (closed in June 2009), but it is dark, cold, and drippy. The end of the tunnel opens to the high sunlight of Hyak.

Maintenance facilities for the railroad were at Hyak, where a one-room school educated employees' children. Seventeen children attended, at least one in each grade in the 1920s. The children shoveled snow from the roof and windows of the school to let the light in during the winter. When school was out, they skied, without the help of tows.

In the summer, these same children made rafts and poled around the beaver ponds along Gold Creek and Hyak Creek (today's Cold Creek), according to Hamilton Howard, Jr., whose mother was the schoolteacher. The children were strictly forbidden to play in the railroad tunnel. Hamilton tells of a time when he and a friend disobeyed and were caught in the tunnel when a train came through. They were able to squeeze into a depression in the wall as the train roared by. "We never did that again," he told journalist Yvonne Prater.

The natural bowl at Hyak (which means "big hole") became a playground. During the summer months, thousands of people would ride into the mountains and picnic on Lake Keechelus. In the winters of the 1930s, skiers came from Ellensburg, Seattle, and Tacoma on weekend ski trains. The Milwaukee Ski Bowl's five runs were named after trains: Olympian, Hiawatha, Chippewa, Arrow, and Pioneer. An interpretive sign at the Hyak Trailhead (and Milwaukee Bowl) shows the 1920s version of ski school for teens.

From the summit, some of the most scenic parts of the trail lead along the west side of Lake Keechelus and then follow the Yakima River's descent into the Kittitas Valley. Remnants of old snowsheds were present along avalanche stretches of Lake Keechelus when I first skied the trail in the 1980s. At Lake Easton, tracks for the Burlington Northern on the south side of the river parallel the trail on the north side. South Cle Elum grew from land speculation around the railroad's plans. Since the Northern Pacific already had a lock on Roslyn's coal and the station in Cle Elum, an entrepreneur named Samuel T. Packwood organized the "Cle Elum Land and Development Company" and platted land south of the town. When Milwaukee's locating engineers came through in 1906, they surveyed the right-of-way through Packwood's plats. Eventually South Cle Elum became a major stop on the Milwaukee Road, a place for changing crews. The solid brick electrical substation in South Cle Elum and the depot and railyard have been restored by volunteers. The Iron Horse Inn was a dormitory for crews; the rooms were named after engineers.

The Milwaukee Road was never highly profitable, but at one point it had 75 percent of the container load business that ran out of the Port of Seattle. At its peak of efficiency in 1947, the train sped from Chicago to Seattle in forty-five hours. The Milwaukee's resources ran out in 1970 when the Great Northern, Northern Pacific, and others merged into the Burlington Northern, forming a Goliath that the Milwaukee Road could not match.

The railroad continued running until 1980, when service was abandoned west of Montana. Hustling to prevent the Union Pacific from purchasing the route, the Burlington Northern acquired the Snoqualmie Pass route and pulled the rails. The right-of-way was bought in subsequent years by the Washington State Parks Department and developed as a trail.

The trail seems to go on forever. It has the same endless feel in the dry, hot stretches of eastern Washington during the summer as it does on the long, gentle climb to Snoqualmie Pass in the winter. To relieve the long miles, imagine the headlight of an orange and black locomotive of the Olympian Hiawatha, carrying revelers high over the creek ravines, through the long dark tunnel, along the river canyons, and into the bright sunlight at the peak of the Cascades.

19
Snoqualmie Wagon Road

GETTING THERE: Take exit 47 from I-90 (Denny Creek/Asahel Curtis). On the north side of the highway, follow the signs to the Denny Creek Campground. Beyond the campground, turn left at the Franklin Falls

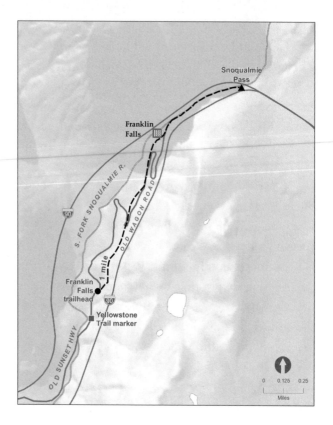

Trailhead, and park just before the bridge over the river. Look for
the wagon wheel display on the east side of the road; it identifies
the beginning of the old wagon road.

DISTANCE: 1 mile one way, plus walking on the shoulder of Sunset
Highway

LEVEL OF DIFFICULTY: easy, but wet during times of high water

HISTORICAL HIGHLIGHTS: numbered posts marking sites along the
old wagon road; the rockslide of the early 1960s; old highway bridges;
Yellowstone Trail marker

When the middle class could afford Model-T Fords, the family
vacation began. Auto tourists enjoyed the scenery at Snoqualmie

Pass and a slow ride over rough roads, then camped overnight in the mountains—along the old road between Cabin Creek and Lake Keechelus or at the Midway Resort, midway between Yakima and Seattle, near Lake Easton. The oldest remaining auto campground is at Denny Creek, near an intersection of historic routes. Converging at the pass, usually right on top of one another, were the Snoqualmie Indian path, a cattle drive, a footpath for miners, the Pioneer Wagon Road, the Yellowstone Trail, the Serpentine Trail, and the Sunset Highway, all predating I-90. A stretch of the old wagon road and the little-used blacktop of the Sunset Highway reveal these iterations.

Along the road to the campground, note an artifact of vacationing: the yellow and black circle on a rock right before the one-lane bridge. With the proliferation of cars, a nationwide Good Roads Movement advocated for better scenic roads. A group of businessmen in Roscoe, South Dakota, formed the Yellowstone Trail Association in 1912 to mark "a good road from Plymouth Rock to Puget Sound." The association hired W. Warwick to put up markers: a yellow and black circle with an arrow pointed in the direction of scenery such as Yellowstone National Park, the Rockies, Glacier National Park, Mount Rainier, and the Cascades. Working his way across the country, Warwick brought his can of paint to Snoqualmie Pass and to this road to the Denny Creek campground.

The old wagon road begins at the Franklin Falls trailhead, where a wagon wheel next to a post announces "Wagon Road Trail." David Denny, son of the family that landed at Alki in 1851, was a dogged believer in the link between roads and progress, as was his father Arthur. Not coincidentally, the family owned iron mines at Snoqualmie Pass. When territorial legislators first asked Congress for money to build a military road through Snoqualmie Pass in 1861, the other Washington was busy fighting a civil war. Soon gold was discovered in the Colville region east of the mountains, and Seattle citizens decided to act locally. In 1865 an exploring party that

The Snoqualmie Wagon Road
climbs to the summit.

included Arthur Denny came back from Yakima, Naches, and Snoqualmie passes, recommending Snoqualmie Pass for a road. Over
the next few years, with money from the legislature and local match-
ing funds, a pioneer wagon road was built along the old Indian trail
on the South Fork of the Snoqualmie River.

Fall rains and spring snowmelts soon washed out these efforts,
however. "What is called a wagon-road is nothing but a rough
uneven trail, full of obstructions, with the trees cut down on either
side, very often barely wide enough for a wagon to be urged along,"
commented English mountaineer Edmund T. Coleman.

On the east side of the pass, Kittitas Valley bustled with mining
and ranching, and founders there also wanted the road. In 1883 a
private company, the Seattle and Walla Walla Trail and Wagon
Road Company, built a toll road on top of the foot-trail-turned-
wagon-road, from Taneum Creek on the east side to Ranger's
Prairie (North Bend) on the west. Then, in the 1890s, argonauts
returning from gold strikes in the Yukon found gold on Gold
Creek, just north of Lake Keechelus—more reason for a road. At

the age of sixty-seven, impoverished by the financial panic of 1893, David Denny spent the last summer of the century rebuilding the "Famous Lost Wagon Road." He put down 412 feet of bridges and 1,200 feet of corduroy planking, and set off 200 blasts of dynamite to remove rock.

In 1970 the Chief Seattle Council of Boy Scouts took on the restoration of this road. Along the trail, a few numbers still on posts correspond to an old brochure no longer in print. Not all numbers mark specific sites. Number 1, at a new bridge over soggy land, points out that rot-resistant Western red cedar made good puncheon—split planks—to keep wagons from sinking into the bog. Number 2 marks decayed stumps and logs, indicating the kinds of obstacles that road builders such as Denny faced. Number 7 is an old pole, a remnant of the postal telegraph system that followed the wagon road. Number 9 marks a remaining section of the cedar puncheon. Number 10 marks the remains of narrow-gauge railroad iron used to cart ore from nearby mines to the surface.

When he was clearing the road, David Denny found that water was just as much a problem as rock and trees; the south fork of the Snoqualmie River was cutting away at the road as he worked. One hundred years later, after a day of heavy rain, Forest Service personnel were out, trying to keep the wagon road trail from again becoming a creek.

As you emerge from the woods, the trail at the top shifts to blacktop and continues to the pass. The first car went through Snoqualmie Pass in 1905. Just ten years after Denny's road-building, four cars in a transcontinental auto race slogged over the dirt road, arriving in Seattle for the 1909 Alaska-Yukon-Pacific Exposition. As car tourism spread, Washington created the office of State Highway Commissioner and a State Highway Department, both funded by gas taxes. One of the department's first tasks was numbering what already existed. The one-lane gravel and dirt road Warwick had marked became State Road 7. Dedicated as the Sunset Highway in

1915, it stretched westward from Idaho through Spokane, Wenatchee, and Ellensburg, then across the pass and into the sunset.

The blacktopped section at the top of the wagon road trail follows the Yellowstone Trail and Sunset Highway. It switchbacks from Denny Creek to Snoqualmie Summit, where State Road 7 connected with U.S. Highway 10, which approached the summit under the lanes of today's I-90. Highway 10 was not open during the winter until the 1930s, when the highest seventeen miles were paved with concrete. Concrete snowsheds were added in 1950, and the highway was widened to four lanes west of the pass.

The old road switchbacks through a huge rockslide that closed the main highway for a summer in the early 1960s. Once Highway 10 reopened, this one-mile section of the old highway was preserved. If you walk the narrow shoulders, watch and listen for cars, which have limited visibility coming around the switchbacks. Sections of the Sunset Highway also appear at Lake Easton and Olallie state parks. The bridge at Lake Easton, from which someone is always fishing, was built in 1927 to carry the highway.

The Interstate Highway Act of the 1950s spurred more road building, at which time I-90 superseded U.S. Highway 10. In 1970 a new five-mile section divided I-90 into westbound and eastbound lanes with the river between them. A viaduct carries the westbound lanes over Franklin Falls and Denny Creek. White concrete stanchions lift the pavement to the sky, creating new space high above the earlier paths.

Near the summit is an old concrete wall separating the road from the South Fork Snoqualmie River. Snoqualmie Pass is crowded by multiple lanes of I-90, power lines overhead, fiber optic lines underground, paved sections of the Old Sunset Highway, the roadbed of the Milwaukee Road, the old wagon road, and the Indian trail. All of these share the narrow corridor with the South Fork Snoqualmie River, which has not changed; at the beginning of its long tumble to Puget Sound, the river still defines the once-hidden pass.

CHAPTER FIVE

The South Cascades

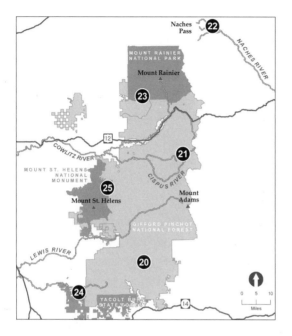

When the air cleared on a summer day 150 years ago, a botanist on a railroad survey saw five snowy peaks from one spot. Doctor J. G. Cooper was stopped with George McClellan's expedition near a Klickitat encampment southeast of Mount Adams. Rain had extinguished the smoke from forest fires and "revealed to us a scene probably unsurpassed in magnificence by any in America. Five snowy peaks surrounded us, rising many thousand feet above our camp."

On a short climb up Windy Ridge at Mount St. Helens, four of these peaks can be seen today. St. Helens is the gray, grizzled survivor on the western edge of this diamond; Mount Rainier looms in bright whiteness to the north; Mount Adams stands off on the eastern horizon; and Mount Hood thrusts a rocky peak from the south in Oregon.¹ These mountains startle the horizon, as they have for centuries.

According to Indian oral tradition, these mountains fought among themselves often, knocking off one another's heads and leaving a slew of debris. In one myth, two jealous brothers, Wy'east (Mount Hood) and Klickitat or Pah-toe (Mount Adams) were fighting over beautiful Loo-wit (Mount St. Helens). They "fought as great mountains do, shedding their beautiful white coats and belching forth lava, steam and ash. They threw great white-hot stones at each other, setting fire to the forests, killing game and driving people into hiding or causing them to flee the country." The large rocks they threw shook the earth so hard that a natural stone bridge spanning the Columbia River broke and fell into the river.

This tradition interprets the many earthquakes and eruptions in the South Cascades within human memory. A Spokane chief called Cornelius told a scientific expedition that in the late 1700s, when he was about ten years old, he was "suddenly awakened by his mother, who called out to him that the world was falling to pieces. He then heard a great noise of thunder overhead, and all the people crying out in great terror." Something was falling very thickly. They first thought it was snow, but it turned out to be volcanic ash, which fell to a depth of six inches. Both Mount Hood and Mount St. Helens are known to have erupted in the late 1700s. It was probably ash from Mount St. Helens that reached the Spokane Indians, whether they were at home in northeastern Washington or traveling to trade and fish.

Despite this unsettling history, these peaks have provided both sustenance and adventure to humans: berries, pasture, timber, horse racing, hiking, and mountain climbing. The trails in this chapter lead through places of benign splendor, such as Indian Heaven near Mount Adams, Indian Henry's Hunting Ground on Mount Rainier, and Snowgrass Flats near the Klickitat Trail. The hikes cross high passes that lead from one watershed to another, such as Cispus Pass and Naches Pass. They also tread areas of sudden mass destruction: the Yacolt Burn of 1902 and the 1980 eruption of Mount St. Helens.

We'll hear the complaints of travelers such as McClellan, who groused, "I've just returned from the mountains, and a glorious old range it is—to look at; but awful to travel in." We'll catch the admiration of others, such as the botanist Cooper. We'll hear the last words of volcanologist David Johnston when Mount St. Helens erupted. Hiking these historic routes reveals a delicate balance between sustenance, beauty, and destruction.

20

Kalama't:
Indian Heaven and Racetrack

GETTING THERE: To the southern trailhead, take Forest Service Road 23 south from Randle. At Highway 141, turn west to Trout Lake. Beyond the Mount Adams Ranger Station, take Road 60 to Goose Lake Campground, 12.5 miles. Stay on 60 for 5.2 miles to 6048, which may be closed by a gate (check beforehand at the Ranger Station). The last three miles are on "primitive road." Drive as far as you are comfortable and park in a turnout.

DISTANCE: 1.5 miles one way

LEVEL OF DIFFICULTY: moderate

HISTORICAL HIGHLIGHTS: deeply worn grooves of the Indian racetrack; lookout on Red Mountain

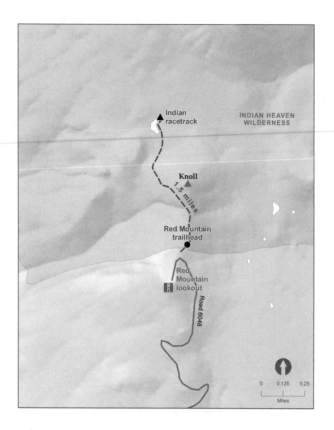

Mount Adams, named by an Oregon promoter for President John Adams, was first called Pahto. After Pahto lost her head in the fight with Wy'east (Mount Hood), she turned mean. "When she was angry, she would send a big thunderstorm and much rain. In the winter, she would send big snows, and in the spring there would be floods." So, according to Yakama legend, the Great Spirit sent eagles to Pahto so she would not act so mean, and she calmed down.

Under this calmer mien, Indian people claimed the high country around Pahto, creating an "Indian Heaven" in a meadow full of huckleberries. For several thousand years many groups—Umatilla, Yakama, Wishram, and Klickitat—came to the wilderness west of Mount Adams. Women gathered and dried bulbs and berries. In later centuries, men grazed horses, raced them, made bets, and pounded a rut 2,000 feet long in the wilderness.

"The racing season is the grand annual occasion of these tribes," wrote George Gibbs, a naturalist on the McClellan expedition. "A horse of proved reputation is a source of wealth or of ruin to his owner. On his steed he stakes his whole stud, his household goods, clothes, and finally his wives. They ride with skill, reckless of all obstacles, and with little mercy to their beasts, the right hand swinging the whip at every bound." In 1878 a traveler saw more than 1,000 ponies at a camp on the slopes of the mountain.

The ponies are sparse today, but some of the meadow and the racetrack remain. The Indian Heaven Wilderness is about ten miles long, lying southwest of Mount Adams. Trail 171 leads to Kalama't, the racetrack meadow near the southern boundary of the wilderness from both a western and southern trailhead. We'll approach from the southern Red Mountain end, and Forest Service Road 60, which follows an old Indian trail.

Many Indian trails crossed this wilderness in the early 1800s, but they were hard to follow. Traveling south toward Hudson's Bay Company headquarters at Fort Vancouver in 1830, John Work passed through woods that were "thicketty" and country that was "dreadfully bad, a considerable portion of it burnt woods, immense trees fallen in every direction, and several deep ravines to cross, very steep for the horses to ascend and descend." Despite having Indian guides, he nearly gave up, concluding in his journal, "There is no way through this space."

The approach from Randle today is seldom blocked with "immense trees fallen," but Forest Service Road 23 does wind through dense and "thicketty" woods that block views of Mount Adams. The mountain suddenly looms into view as the road comes out on the plain. Stop at the Trout Lake Saturday market for handmade quilts and homemade jam and fudge, and then at the ranger station to check whether the gate is open on Red Mountain. From the station, head southwest on Forest Service Road 60, which was probably paved over the Indian trail that Work tried to follow.

At Goose Lake, interpretive boards show the progression of railroad surveyor George B. McClellan. In 1853 McClellan followed the same Indian trails as Work with an expedition of sixty-six men and 173 horses and pack mules. His slow-moving caravan averaged only five miles a day as they looked for a way through the Cascades for a transcontinental railroad. Going from west to east, from Red Mountain to Trout Lake, along what are today's Forest Service roads 60 and 24, they encountered Indians who were suffering terribly from the smallpox brought into this heaven by whites. The caravan passed by the Klickitat encampment of Chequoss, where Cooper saw the five peaks. After traveling through an extensive bed of lava, they reached this "very pretty lake surrounded by lava."

Gibbs, the naturalist on the team, described the water in Goose Lake as shallow, clear, and cold. "It was somewhat remarkable that this pond was surrounded by gigantic cottonwood trees though the elevation was no less than 3300 feet," he wrote in his journal. Most of those trees are dead today.

Past Goose Lake, the last three miles of primitive Road 6048 lead to the Red Mountain lookout and its views of Mount Adams. The trailhead to the racetrack comes before the road's final climb to the lookout. The trail descends through light woods, but you may leave the trail and drop down to a saddle between Red Mountain and a pumice knoll. Just over the other side of this knoll, we sat on the red pumice and peered down at a meadow, searching for the ancient rut, which I had pictured as an oval. In fact, the visible track is a straight line, only a few hundred feet long but deeply worn.

When we reached the meadow, an old wooden sign heralded its history: "Kalam't (Indian Racetrack)." According to elders interviewed by Forest Service archaeologist Rick McClure, riders raced in a straight line from one post to another post. Rounding the post, they rushed back to the starting point.

Horse racing continued at Indian Heaven until the 1920s. During the Prohibition era, according to Ernie Childs, a recreation technician, several local horsemen trained horses especially for this event, "betting moonshine whiskey against money, horses, or whatever the Indians had."

Where hundreds once camped, people now trickle into this meadow from all directions; on a recent summer day, we saw four horses with riders, three dogs, and three other hikers in less than an hour. Trees have invaded much of the meadow that the Indians regularly burned to encourage the growth of bulbs and berries. There are shallow lakes here early in the summer, but they were gone in early August. Huckleberries have grown here in sunlit fields for thousands of years.

Berry picking remains popular. During the first week of August, 1853, the botanist Cooper noticed that the hills had "a profusion of berries of several kinds, which the Indians were engaged in collecting. . . . The whole region looked more like a garden than a wild mountain summit." So many people discovered the huckleberries during the hard years of the Great Depression that an agreement was made in 1932 between the Forest Service and Native Americans: with a handshake, Yakama chief William Yallup and Forest supervisor K. P. Cecil reserved specific areas of the Sawtooth huckleberry fields for local tribal members. These areas are still reserved and marked with signs.

On the way back we ate blueberries, thankful we had timed our hike before late August or September, when Indian Heaven becomes a mosquito haven. Climbing to the Red Mountain lookout at the end of the hike provided a full view of the splendor of Mount Adams. As Supreme Court Justice William O. Douglas wrote in *My Wilderness: The Pacific West,* "There is enough glory in one of these hikes to tide a man [and a woman] over the dark days."

21

Klickitat Trail

GETTING THERE: For Trail 7, take Forest Service Road 22 to the east trailhead and Forest Service roads 23, 55, 5508, and 5508.024 to the west trailhead. The last quarter mile segment to the west trailhead is quite rutted, requiring high clearance. For Trail 96 to Snowgrass Flats and Cispus Pass, take Forest Service roads 21, 2150, and 2150.014.

DISTANCE: Trail 7, 17 miles one way; Trail 96, 7.3 miles one way

LEVEL OF DIFFICULTY: difficult

HISTORICAL HIGHLIGHTS: the trail itself; peeled cedar trees; Snowgrass Flats; Cispus Pass

The Klickitat Trail over Cispus Pass is ancient by Washington history standards. People first lived in the Cispus River Valley 7,000 years ago. We know this from archaeological evidence found at Layser Cave, rediscovered by Timothy Layser in 1982. The cave preserved the bones of more than 108 deer that had been hunted not with the more recent bows and arrows but with the atatl, a throwing board that launched stone-tipped darts. Acting together, hunters drove deer and elk into a steep-walled box canyon and killed them with atatls and short thrusting spears. Family members gathered at the cave to butcher the animals, feast, and make tools and clothing. When Mount St. Helens erupted between 3,500 and 3,900 years ago, spewing ash and pumice for hundreds of miles and destroying food sources, ancient people abandoned the cave.

A thousand years later, an Upper Cowlitz group called the Taidnapam migrated from east of the mountain to the Big Bottom of the Cispus River Valley. They avoided the volcanoes of Mount Adams and Mount St. Helens but traveled the mountain ridges every summer, on foot and on horseback, to hunt mountain goats and gather

Trail 7

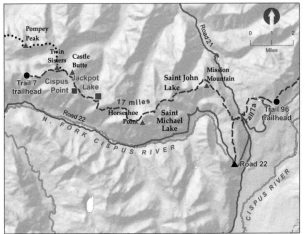

Trail 96

huckleberries. On occasion, they crossed Cispus Pass, which separated the Cispus River drainage on the west from the Klickitat River drainage on the east, and traded with the Yakama and Klickitat peoples, who lived in the Ahtanum Valley. Over the years, these travels etched a ridgetop trail that has lasted for 2,000 years—the Klickitat Trail, named after the river.

Archaeologists Rick McClure and Bill R. Roulette have tracked thirty-eight miles of the Klickitat Trail by identifying seven sites where Native Americans harvested cedar bark, concluding that these sites must have been close to the trail. About twenty-one miles of this trail have been maintained or restored by the Forest Service. The longest accessible stretches are seventeen miles on Trail 7 and seven miles on a combination of trails 96, 97, and 2000.

Unlike the centuries when people moved together, a trip along Trail 7 can be a relatively lonesome experience today. On a rainy two-day hike, my husband and I heard only the sound of our own squishy boots and the unmistakable whoop of someone jumping into a cold lake. Near the end of the second day, we encountered two elk hunters with high-powered bows, who helped us decipher an out-of-date map.

The trail follows much of the old Klickitat Trail east and west along the ridgetop between the north fork of the Cispus River and Johnson Creek. After planting a car at the eastern trailhead, we drove dirt and gravel roads back to the western trailhead and began the trek late in the afternoon. To the west of Trail 7 is an abandoned and unmaintained segment of the old trail, too difficult to follow. Trail 7 heads eastward, gaining elevation and views to the south. It winds first around the Twin Sisters, then is joined by a northern branch of the ancient trail that went around Pompey Peak, now Trail 128.

Past Castle Butte, the trail reaches Cispus Point, the site of a look-out constructed in 1926 and burned down in the 1960s. The views from the spur trail (Trail 127) are said to be spectacular, befitting a lookout site, but our day was shrouded in fog. Past a grass-covered pond and down through wet brush we hiked to a campground at Jackpot Lake. Sheepherder camps once dotted this path from Sisters Camp, near the lookout, to Camp Willson, east of Jackpot Lake.

The next morning, we dried our boots on a log in the sunlight that slanted through the trees, then contoured around Horseshoe

Point, admiring the occasional volcano view. The trail crosses a small pass and a dry creek, climbs a hill, and cuts through a clearcut. Downed logs provided seats for our lunch and platforms for drying our socks.

When Americans came into the Cispus Valley in the 1850s, the Upper Cowlitz and Lower Cowlitz held on to the land, refusing to sign treaties with the territorial governor. The U.S. Congress extinguished their claims in 1864, and thirty years later President Benjamin Harrison declared the area a Pacific Forest Reserve. In 1896 commissioner Gifford Pinchot came west to see the reserved land firsthand. Despite a storm of protest from lumber, stock, and mining interests, Pinchot recommended that even more land be set aside as public timberland. His recommendation resulted in the Mount Rainier Forest Reserve, which eventually became the national park, and the Gifford Pinchot National Forest, where today logging coexists with ancient trade routes.

The Klickitat Trail continues over Cispus Pass into Klickitat River headwaters.

Under Pinchot's jurisdiction as the first chief of the U.S. Forest Service, rangers used the ancient trail to cross the large reserve. They established lookouts and telephone lines and eventually roads. Sheep were allowed to graze in some of the mountain meadows, and part of the trail became a sheep driveway and was trampled by hundreds of hooves. In the mid- and late-1900s, more roads were built so that large areas could be logged, and some of the trail was destroyed by clear-cutting and road construction before Roulette's archaeological study identified its historical significance.

Frequent views of Mount Rainier, Mount Adams, and Mount St. Helens lift even a wet spirit. Trail 7 passes St. Michael's Lake, which is south of the trail, and Cold Spring Camp, where sheepherders camped near good water along the southern edge of Stonewall Ridge, then veers northward past St. John's Lake, a beautiful aquamarine lake with fish in the water and signs of human camping around it. East of the lake, the trail grows faint, but it keeps leading on, and there are no other trails to follow. Indians preferred these high, sparsely timbered ridges for their ponies rather than the more heavily wooded valleys.

After a hard climb toward the thin edge of Mission Mountain, Adams is visible in one direction and Rainier in the other. At foot level, an orange piece of tape beckoned from a tree across a very exposed saddle. The trail zigzags along a great view of Goat Rocks, goes up and down, then sidehills the mountain, with Mount Adams visible again. More orange tape on bushes marks the way through a wet meadow. Trail 7 eventually reaches Road 22 and the eastern trailhead.

The ancient path doesn't end with Trail 7. Another historical segment is Trail 7A, a horse trail, which cuts off from Trail 7 and goes east across Road 21, past Hugo Lake and Chambers Lake to the site of the Berry Patch Guard Station. Then, a short distance from Berry Patch, Trail 96 continues the climb along historic routes to

Snowgrass Flats and Cispus Pass, where the Taidnapam, Yakama, and Klickitat peoples crossed over.

Here solitude ends; day hikers, weekend warriors, and long-trekkers on the Pacific Crest Trail cross the meadows, moving less as a people than as individual adventurers following their own strands. In 1911 the Mountaineers, a Seattle-based climbing club, came this way on their trek from Longmire to the Columbia River. Later, such large parties were banned from camping on the fragile meadows. In 1980 the eruption of Mount St. Helens dropped more ash here than on any other alpine area, and ash still coats many of the trails.

Trail 97, which bypasses Snowgrass Flats, is the original Indian route. After crossing a creek through meadows, Trail 97 joins the Pacific Crest Trail at an impressive arrangement of cairns. In its climb to Cispus Pass, the trail winds along the side of the mountain and crosses numerous creeks starting their downward glide into the Cispus River watershed. An aerial photograph by archaeologist McClure shows that the ancient tread diverges from the Pacific Crest Trail, which in this area was constructed by the Civilian Conservation Corps. The older route heads across the high lands of the basin, just south of the Pacific Crest Trail. The basin below was used as a sheep allotment from 1903 to 1941.

At Cispus Pass the Pacific Crest Trail continues south, briefly crossing the Yakama Indian Reservation. The ancient trail goes north, across a steep slope called the Cispus Wall, then drops into the Klickitat River watershed and the Yakama reservation. It once reached to the Cariboo Trail, a major north-south cattle route to Canada (see chapter 6). Although the old trail east of the pass is seldom used, a remnant is still visible in this steep, bare landscape.

On a later hike toward Cispus Pass in the record heat of late July 2009, a friend and I lingered along Trail 97 in a diligent search for basket trees. Native American women peeled the bark from cedar trees to make rectangular folded baskets for collecting huckleberries. After examining the back of every cedar tree we saw, above and below the trail, we roamed away through a boggy meadow to a hunters' campsite looking out to Mount Adams. Nearby were cedar trees with stripped bark and cut marks. Could they be the fabled trees?

With sore heels and depleted energy, we gave up on reaching the pass and headed back down the trail, looking for cedar trees we might have missed as well as a camera I left at a rest log. Just east of Goat Creek, we saw in plain view what we thought had been hidden—a small grove of three cedar trees with unmistakable basket patches. With more good fortune, we found a note duct-taped to the trailhead signboard that gave a phone number to call for my camera. We may no longer move as a people, but we still know the trail code.

22

Naches Pass

GETTING THERE: To approach Naches Pass from the east, turn north on Little Naches Road (east of Chinook Pass and east of milepost 92 on Highway 410). In half a mile, an obvious old road crosses this new dirt road. Park beyond it.

To approach Naches Pass from the west trailhead, take Forest Service Road 70 north (ten miles east of Enumclaw on Highway 410 and almost two miles east of Greenwater, just east of milepost 44). At about 9 miles, turn right on a road for Greenwater Trail 1176. The Naches Trail (not the same as 1176) begins right before the parking lot, marked by a large old wooden sign.

DISTANCE: 6.7 miles from the east side, 5.25 miles from the west side to Government Meadows

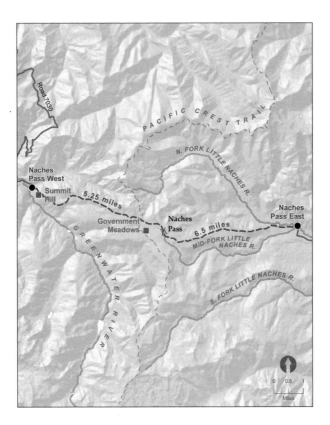

LEVEL OF DIFFICULTY: difficult

HISTORICAL HIGHLIGHTS: Government Meadows at Naches Pass; Summit Hill; notches in trees

In early August 1853, a wagon train of 155 men, women, and children rested in Grande Ronde, Oregon, before crossing the Blue Mountains. As wagon trains did, the party had come together at various points on the Oregon Trail. The Longmire family left Shawnee Prairie, Indiana, in March. At Council Bluffs they joined a party with Asher Sargent and, after crossing South Pass, they joined the Himes family from Lafayette, Illinois. All were headed toward the new territory of Washington, but they faced the expense and hazards of a raft trip down the Columbia River and a river/overland journey north to the Puget Sound lowlands.

"At Grande Ronde a happy surprise awaited us," recalled George Himes, who was nine years old at the time. Nelson Sargent, son of Asher Sargent, already lived in Olympia, the capitol of the ambitious territory. Nelson met an advance member of the train with the welcome news that a party of workmen had started out from Olympia and Steilacoom to make a road over the Cascades through Naches Pass, a shortcut from Walla Walla to Puget Sound that would bypass the Columbia River trip. This news was "so alluring that most of the company decided to go thither," Himes said. They struck off from the Oregon Trail at the Umatilla River, crossed the Columbia River at Wallula, then followed the Yakima River and the Naches River toward Naches Pass.

An Indian trail had long climbed through Naches Pass, just northeast of Mount Rainier. In the early 1800s, the Indians had grazed cattle east of the mountains for the Hudson's Bay Company (HBC) and had driven them through Naches Pass to the company's fort at Nisqually. A French Canadian trader for the HBC, Pierre Pambrun, and Cornelius Rogers of the Whitman Mission traveled through the pass from the east in September 1839. In 1841 the U.S. Navy's Wilkes Expedition sent a party over the pass from the west to explore the interior; they encountered snow ten feet deep in May.

None of these crossings created a route suitable for wagons, so Washington's territorial delegate persuaded Congress to appropriate some money for a road, and Puget Sound entrepreneurs raised $1,200 on their own. Because of the short season in the mountains, two citizen crews started work early in the summer of 1853 from both sides of the pass, cutting down trees and marking others with blazes. Nelson Sargent, eager to help his family get through before the fall snow in the mountains, worked on the east-side crew. Unknown to Sargent, the government's surveyor, George B. McClellan, crossed

Naches Pass in July of that year and dismissed it as unsuitable for a railroad. Federal money dried up.

The Longmire Party set out with the expectation of a road suitable for wagons, but the road they found was hardly worthy of the name, little more than a few blazes on trees. Theodore Winthrop, a recent graduate of Yale College, was "going home across the continent" in August that same year. Riding horseback from Nisqually, east of Tacoma, over an old Indian trail, he came upon the rude beginnings of a road in the midst of thick trees. In his book *Canoe and Saddle*, he described the road building as more destruction than construction: "Woodchoppers had passed through the forest, like a tornado, making a broad belt of confusion. . . . Stumps were in it, fresh cut and upstanding with sharp or splintered edges; felled trunks were in it, with wedge-shaped cuts and untrimmed branches." Calling the road "a failure, a miserable muddle," he went back to the Indian trail.

The road was also a great disappointment to the lumbering wagons and families on foot. "At the first night's camp in the pine timber at the edge of the Cascade Range," said Himes, "we began to realize that all previous experiences in crossing mountain ranges were insignificant as compared with those which we were about to encounter. . . . but there we were, and the idea of retracing our steps could not be thought of for a moment."

Pushing on, the party crossed the Naches River sixty-eight times as hills and mountains crowded right down to the river and blocked their way on one side or the other. Encountering sagebrush "as high as the top of a covered wagon," they had to cut it out of the way. Three days after leaving the river, the wagon train came to the summit of Naches Pass and stopped to rest in the meadows.

The main trail to these high meadows, now called Government Meadows, leaves from the west side of a trailhead on the Greenwater River. But it is also possible to hike from the east, as the Longmire Party did. We took a jeep drive from the east, which begins at the foot of a 2,000-foot climb and goes mainly up, with no switchbacks. After a few miles, the phrase "strong as an ox" takes on new meaning. The first view of Mount Rainier, through a clearcut, comes after more than an hour of hiking. At 5.7 miles, the sign for Naches Pass gives a brief history. Shortly thereafter, amid the smell of mint, we crossed the Pacific Crest Trail and arrived at Government Meadows. Here Winthrop had found cold springs, wild strawberries, and enough head-high grass to feed his horses for days.

A Boy Scout troop has put up signs showing where the Longmire party camped. As we explored the boggy area, tired from our climb, three jeeps full of adults and kids merrily chugged into view, arriving up the same trail we had hiked.

West of Government Meadows, the trail is on high, fairly level ground, going through meadows the settlers called "burns," now enlarged by clearcuts. As it descends, the trail becomes very steep, dry, and rutted in places. After two days' rest, the wagon train headed down from the pass, not realizing that the west-side crew had stopped work. False information had reached them that no wagon train was coming through in 1853. In the lower wooded areas, the road is "corduroyed" with heavy planks, nails, rebar, and edging—signs that it was once a road but constructed much later than 1853.

Three miles west of the pass, the emigrant train came to a halt. "My mother, the younger children and I were somewhat in the rear at this time," wrote Himes, "and as we came close enough to discover the cause of the delay, she exclaimed, 'Well, I guess we have come to the jumping-off place at last!'" Himes describes a bluff thirty feet high and almost perpendicular, followed by a longer stretch so steep "an animal could scarcely stand up."

The group concluded that there was no choice but to unhitch the ox teams and lower the wagons with rope. They sent the oxen single file down a more circuitous trail. When no rope proved long enough to stretch down the 800-foot hill, they killed the weakest three steers and spliced a rope out of the hides.

"One end of the rope was fastened to the axles of the wagons, the other thrown around a tree and held by our men and thus, one by one, the wagons were lowered gradually," said James Longmire, who was also in the party. When the rope broke, two unoccupied wagons were crushed to pieces, with a loss of badly needed provisions.

Several spots on the west side of the pass could earn the title of "jumping-off place." Erastus Light, who was also in the party, describes safely descending two steep slopes before reaching a third, "to look down which was enough to take the starch out of any living being except a pioneer." George Himes described the cliff as a drop of 1,000 feet at a thirty-five- to forty-foot angle with a square, rocky surface, a quarter-mile wide. When his party crossed, the cliff was overgrown with trees, bushes, and ferns. Beside the cliff was a narrower trail, three to four feet wide, a switchback that the wagons couldn't go down. This description best matches the very end of the trail, just above the Greenwater River. An old wooden sign there marks the place as Summit Hill.

The trail just above and below Summit Hill is a true foot trail, off-limits to vehicles, and hard to imagine as a wagon road, although a tree here has what look like rope burns. An old wagon wheel with a large oak hub, loosened spokes, and a rusty hand-welded iron rim was found along this trail in the 1930s and probably belonged to one of the wagons that broke.

It took almost two days for the Longmire Party to descend the western slope. After the loss of provisions, some families ate little but salal berries as they trudged along. Nearing starvation and anxious about beating the fall snow, two women and their children hurried ahead of the wagon train. They finally encountered a road builder, Andy Burge, who was bringing supplies from Fort Steilacoom, not

A pack crew pauses on the Naches Pass Trail. University of Washington Libraries, Special Collections, UW28579.

knowing that the road crew had gone home. Burge handed over his surplus food and returned to Fort Steilacoom, blazing the way on trees as he went. He also left semi-encouraging signs, such as "This stretch is a shade better"; "This stretch worse"; "This is the worst."

The wagon train crossed the Greenwater River sixteen times and the White River seven times and finally reached Connell Prairie, eighty miles from the top of Naches Pass. They camped together for the last time near the present site of Buckley, then left to find their own homesteads.

A second party of immigrants followed the same route in November 1853, but they left their wagons on the east side, at Ahtanum Mission. They were caught in the fall snow but were saved from starvation when help was sent from Fort Steilacoom. A few more parties crossed in 1854, including that of Winfield Scott Ebey, who joined his brother on Whidbey Island (see chapter 2). After these travails, dreams of a road over Naches Pass were abandoned.

Although the Naches Trail never caught on as a quick route to Puget Sound, it has caught on as a trail for outdoor recreation. The original Naches Pass Trail was marked by the Washington and Oregon state historical societies in 1910. After a Yakima jeep club drove the trail in 1951, others soon followed. The muddled trail of 1853 is now gouged by vehicle tracks. One July day I encountered three motorbikes, four off-road vehicles, twelve sport-utility vehicles, and two trucks between Greenwater River and Government Meadows— twelve of these on the trail itself. Some of the meadows where the emigrant parties rested have become playgrounds for "mudding," a sport played with trucks. Off-road vehicles glory in the higher "jumping-off places," charging up them and looping back down again. Once again the trail has become a muddle that requires an active imagination to restore it to history.

23

Indian Henry's Hunting Ground

GETTING THERE: The Wonderland Trail leaves from Longmire in Mount Rainier National Park.

DISTANCE: 6.2 miles from Longmire on the Wonderland Trail

LEVEL OF DIFFICULTY: difficult; 2,300-foot elevation gain

HISTORICAL HIGHLIGHTS: Longmire Springs; Indian Henry's Hunting Ground; the patrol cabin

Of the five volcanoes J. G. Cooper saw in 1860, Mount Rainier, or Tachoma, was the king, the mountain that has inspired poets and climbers alike. The traveler Theodore Winthrop had been crossing

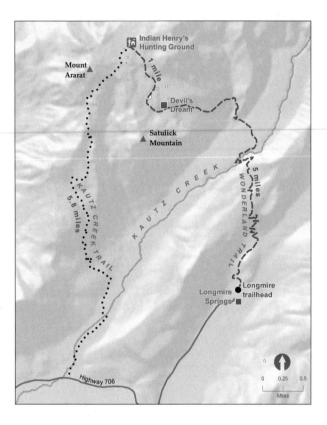

a dark and lonesome ridge for hours as he approached the crest of the Cascades in 1853. At last he "stormed a ragged crest, gaining a height that overtopped the firs," and halted to catch his breath. "As I looked somewhat wearily and drearily across the solemn surges of forest," he wrote in his book *Canoe and Saddle*, "suddenly above their sombre green appeared Tacoma. Large and neighbor it stood, so near that every jewel of its snow-fields seemed to send me a separate ray; yet not so near but that I could with one look take in its whole image, from clear-cut edge to edge." He observed, "No foot of man had ever trampled those pure snows."

It's true that Native Americans left the awe-inspiring Tachoma well enough alone, but the emigrants who followed Winthrop felt compelled to challenge the mountain. Beginning in the 1850s, a succession of climbers reached the summit and left behind their names, poles, and cans of beans they didn't want to carry back down. Now a million visitors come to the park around Mount Rainier every summer, and 10,000 of those try to climb the mountain. Another 500 hikers circumnavigate the peak on the Wonderland Trail. For those less ambitious, a hike on just one part of that trail, through a favorite subalpine hunting ground, yields a slice of the mountain's rich history.

In the 1860s, the hunting ground for elk and mountain goats was the province of a Klickitat man named Sotulick. Five different tribal groups hunted game and gathered berries in the high meadows beneath the glaciers of Mount Rainier. An arrowhead used for hunting mountain goats was found at 7,500 feet, more than halfway up the mountain's 14,000-foot height. Sotulick was hunting on the southwest slopes in 1862 when he encountered three white men. One of them was James Longmire, who had come across Naches Pass in the first wagon train. Longmire was homesteading at Yelm on the Nisqually River, and the men were searching for a mountain pass through which they could drive cattle. They promptly gave Sotulick a "Boston" name—Henry—and thereby began a long friendship and business relationship.

As encounters between Indians and whites became more frequent, Henry settled along the Nisqually River at Mashell Prairie, west of the mountain. He fenced the fields, planted wheat and vegetables, built a log cabin, and supported three wives on his prosperous farm. Indian Henry's Trail led up the mountain slopes toward the Nisqually Glacier, and the meadow in which he hunted became known as Indian Henry's Hunting Ground.

Three trails in the national park lead to this mountain meadow, which has become a crossroads on the way to higher ground. The Tahoma Creek Trail is the shortest and probably follows the original Indian Henry's Trail, but West Side Road has been closed for

In 1908 mountain tourists could rest at Camp Wigwam on the flanks of Mount Rainier. Washington State Historical Society.

several years, making the trailhead hard to reach. The Kautz Creek Trail is the longest and winds around Mount Ararat, named by Ben Longmire, who thought he had found the remains of Noah's Ark there. Kautz Creek was named after August V. Kautz, who made the first known summit attempt on Rainier in 1857.

The third trail begins at Longmire, a resort developed late in the life of James Longmire. In 1883 P. B. Van Trump, George Bayley, and William C. Ewing hired Longmire, who was sixty-three years old, to be their guide on a summit attempt. Longmire enlisted Henry, who agreed, for two dollars a day, to guide the group to the highest point that could be reached by horses above the snowline. They camped the fourth night on the bank of the Nisqually River near "soda and iron springs of great variety." From there Henry cut a zigzag trail for the horses up a timbered ridge to the snowline.

Henry refused to go farther, but the four white men continued past the base camp, and three of them, including Longmire, reached the summit, where they spent a cold night in the crater.

For Longmire, the discovery of the soda and iron springs proved more important than reaching the summit. He filed a claim on the land at the springs and built a camp for mountain climbers, which featured restorative baths. James's son Elcaine turned the springs into a resort, which remained in the family until 1916. Soon there was a well-worn trail from Yelm, with stops at Indian Henry's, Karnahan's Ranch, and Longmire's Springs before reaching Paradise and the ascent to the top through Camp Muir. John Muir stayed in Henry's barn on his way to the top in 1888. Yelm schoolteacher Fay Fuller, the first woman to climb Rainier, also stopped at Henry's two years later.

Although Fuller's feat is inspiring, my hiking cohort of four women, ranging in age from fifty to seventy, aimed for the hunting grounds instead of the summit. Starting at Longmire, now a national park lodge, restaurant, and museum, we embarked on the Wonderland Trail, past mineral springs, dipping and climbing between Ramparts Ridge and Evergreen Ridge. The trail crosses Kautz Creek on a long bridge with a wire to hang on to. (Satulick Point, the promontory overlooking Kautz Creek, derives from Sotulick's name, which has various spellings.) After five and a half miles, we camped at Devil's Dream, among the mosquitoes.

The trail from Longmire is part of the Wonderland Trail, which evolved as word of the mountain's beauty spread. Mount Rainier National Park was created in 1907 and a corps of rangers had the job of protecting its forests from fire. The rangers traveled around the mountain on an encircling trail and stayed in patrol cabins, including one at Indian Henry's.

The year the trail was completed in 1915, about ninety members of the Mountaineers Club of Seattle hiked around the mountain in three weeks. About half of the group went on the Skyline Route on the glaciers, and half on the lower encircling trail. The two groups met at the end of the last day, with men and women camping on different sides of the ridges. The Mountaineers were known for their military-type discipline. Hiking proceeded at a regulated pace, with everyone staying in position and starting and stopping when a whistle blew. The Wonderland Trail today is ninety-three miles long and skirts the toes of the glaciers, with constructed bridges and trailside campgrounds.

Unencumbered by skirts or backpacks or discipline, we four spent the next day hiking one mile more to Indian Henry's Hunting Ground and back, with a stop to cool off at Mirror Lake. Here, in 1892, Van Trump and Bayley camped while climbing Mount Rainier. They pitched their tent on the "extreme edge of the meadow nearest the snow line," probably at the foot of Pyramid Peak, and summited Rainier the next day. George B. Hall ran a tent camp on this meadow in the late 1800s for climbers coming on foot or horseback from Longmire Hot Springs. He charged seventy-five cents for a bed and meals. When he died, his wife, Susan Longmire Hall, invited Van Trump to operate a guide service there in the late 1890s and early 1900s.

No camping is allowed on the meadow today; the meadow is thus preserved as a sensory delight, abuzz with both insects and wildflowers in early August. The usual trio of volcanoes, and a distant fourth, Mount Hood, are visible from the porch of the ranger's cabin. Flies, bees, and mosquitoes whined over our heads as we napped in the shade on a weathered bench. (Even John Muir complained about the yellow jackets in the park.) The images of lupine, paintbrush, bear grass, white rhododendron, pearly everlasting, valencia, and aster dancing under our eyelids compensated for the pests.

The rangers' cabins provided summer residences, bases for poaching patrols in the fall, emergency shelter in the winter, and places to cache supplies and fire-fighting equipment. During the winter, rangers on wooden skis made the rounds to check the cabins' phone lines and shovel snow off the roofs. This cabin is now the oldest in the park, and the register on the porch is a treasure trove of hikers' reports. In 1996 hikers had started coming early in July, although the unmelted snow made the trail hard to find. In 1999 the first visitors didn't log in until August.

In 2002 my family of four tromped through early in the morning of a twelve-mile day. As I pointed out the cabin and our voices carried across the meadow, a seasonal volunteer called a distant "Good Morning!" from the porch, a polite way of saying "occupied." We trudged on, a bit disappointed at not adding our names to the history of a crossroads.

24

Yacolt Burn

GETTING THERE: For Tarbell Trail: Take Railroad Avenue south out of Yacolt and continue on County Road 12 about three miles to NE Sunset Falls Road. At 2.5 miles take the Dole Valley Road south. After 2.5 miles watch for a small brown sign for the Tarbell Picnic Area and Road 1100. Follow Road 1100 to the intersection with Road 1210 and the Tarbell Picnic Area.

For Silver Star Mountain Trail: Take Road 41 from the Sunset Falls Campground 3.5 miles to Road 4109 (a sharp turn back to the right). At a junction, 4109 continues to the left. The trail begins at the parking area at the end of the road.

DISTANCE: 7.3 miles to Silver Star Mountain from Tarbell Picnic Area; 2.6 miles to Silver Star Mountain from end of Road 4109

LEVEL OF DIFFICULTY: moderate; elevation gain

HISTORICAL HIGHLIGHTS: George Tarbell's path; burned-over areas; Silver Star lookout site

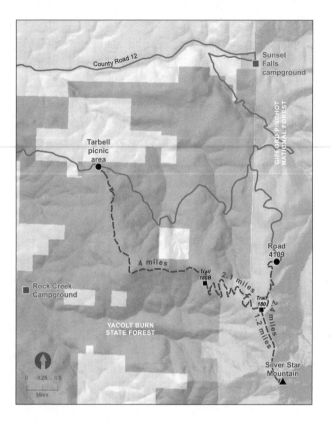

The peaks of the Cascades offered splendid challenges for the adventuresome, but the slopes had timber, and the valleys had fertile bottomlands. By the 1880s, small towns and homesteads lined the banks of the Lewis, Cowlitz, Cispus, Nisqually, and White rivers under the mantles of the mountains. One such town was Yacolt, near Yacolt Creek, which flows into the Lewis River.

Yacolt means "haunted spirits." Indians told an anthropologist of a time when they went huckleberrying, and some of their children were mysteriously lost. When they could not find the children, the Indians concluded that they had been stolen by the wild spirits of the forest, so they called the prairie Yacolt. With its acres of once-dense forests, this area has a tradition of spirits, from child stealers to hermits to reported sightings of Sasquatch.

Settlers claimed Yacolt prairie for farming in the 1870s, and, like the Native Americans, they used fire to clear the land. The first Yacolt post office was granted in 1895, and the town had fifteen buildings and fifty residents by 1902. That was the year of the most lethal forest fire in Washington history, the Yacolt Burn, which burned more than 238,000 acres and twelve billion board feet of timber, and claimed thirty-eight lives.

Fires reach this forest between Mount St. Helens and the Columbia Gorge because of an unfortunate combination of moisture and wind. Fed by moist air and rains from the coast, the forest grows profusely. From east of the Gorge, a dry wind blows, sucking moisture from the dead wood and underbrush and turning it into tinder; settlers called it the Devil Wind because it often started wildfires.

The Yacolt fire began north of Carson on the Columbia River during the night of September 12, 1902, probably in several places at once, from wildfires or from land clearing fires. Fires set by loggers and settlers had been lingering throughout the dry summer. By midmorning, wind had whipped the flames into a front twelve miles wide that was moving northwest toward Yacolt. Orange columns of flame, suffocating heat, and choking smoke roared and raced from ridge to ridge. A farmer, Edgar Rotschy, recalled that by three o'clock in the afternoon the sky was darkening, and at four o'clock he lit the lamps. By five o'clock the next morning he heard the low rumbling of the approaching fire.

Before the years of rapid communication, people relied on their experience of the weather and land to sense danger. Since smoldering fires were common in the area, settlers thought little of smoke in the air. A wagon bearing two families toward a lakeside picnic on the western slope of Mount St. Helens was overtaken by the fire before they could reach Speelyai Creek. Others died in their homes. One woman delayed leaving her house, trying to save a Singer sewing machine and 200 jars of fruit. A mother and her four children were smothered in the cellar beneath their house. Many who survived

The forest fires of 1902 left a forest of snags at Silver Star Mountain. Gifford Pinchot National Forest.

fled to Chelatchie Prairie, where more than forty people crowded into one house and a barn. Some shared a field with six bears, eight deer, and a lynx. A larger group built rafts from fallen trees and paddled onto a lake for two days and two nights to avoid the burning shores. "What a week ago was the beautiful valley of the Lewis River," wrote a stringer for the *Columbian* of Vancouver, "is now a hot and silent valley of death."

Today, the valley of the Lewis River and the town of Yacolt bear no evidence of the fire that came close enough to blister paint but stopped within a half mile of town when the wind shifted. The near disaster became a boom. One year later, the Weyerhaeuser Company came to salvage timber from the ashes and established its first camp of 100 men on a prairie at the edge of town. Soon a railroad passed through Yacolt, carrying lumber from the hills to Vancouver and Portland.

Evidence from the fire remains instead in the forests, which have seen fire, replanting, and more fire. Hiking trails wind through scarred land in the Yacolt Burn State Forest and the "hind foot" of the Gifford Pinchot National Forest. Two main trails, the Tarbell Trail and Trail 180 to Silver Star Mountain, cross burned-over areas where only wildflowers will grow, interspersed with forests only fifty to seventy years old. Trees once 500 years old, 200 feet high, and six feet wide were lost in the 1902 fire. Then eight more major fires swept the region in the fifty years after the burn. Despite decades of replanting and attention to the forest, weather conditions haven't changed, and signs still warn of "Extreme fire hazard year round in the Yacolt Burn area."

Soon after the fire, George Lee Tarbell moved into "the burn" and stayed until his death in 1932. He became a hermit whose only connection to the world was a trail from his cabin to the end of a road leading back to Yacolt. The trail now named after him meanders through much of the state forest, going in and out of the boundaries of the burn. It's a twenty-six-mile loop, used more by horseback riders and mountainbikers than hikers, but a spur trail leads to Silver Star Mountain, site of a lookout tower built to watch for fire. The Tarbell Picnic Area defines the top of the loop; a large wooden sign describes Tarbell and marks his trail.

Follow the Tarbell Trail southeast through areas of reburns. "The place looked lonely and desolate under the dark, rainy skies," wrote Edwin Hill when he arrived in the 1930s as part of the Civilian Conservation Corps. In his book *In the Shadow of the Mountain,* Hill described "widow-makers," fire-blackened snags left tottering on the hillsides, a menace to woodsmen working near them.

Seventy-five years after Hill's visit, the oft-burnt and logged forests are thin but much less desolate and lonely. Although most of the snags are gone, charcoal shows on some large, tall stumps. The remnants of a water system—pipes and boards—lie close to a creek bed. Two sides of a large downed log have been carved into armchairs that face each other across the trail, inviting a rest. The woods allow enough sunlight for some plants to thrive—Indian paintbrush, columbine, Oregon grape, penstemon, tough-leafed iris, devil's club, and bear grass, which the Indians used to make baskets.

The woods are still dense enough to stir the imagination and inspire claims that the ape-like creature known as Sasquatch could be living in Washington's wildernesses. Locals reported Sasquatch sightings in 1963, 1966, and 1969, and Skamania County subsequently declared itself the only Sasquatch refuge in the world. The county council passed an ordinance against killing the animal, a policy largely designed to keep sasquatch-hunters from shooting each other in the woods.

Four miles along this section of the Tarbell Trail, a spur trail cuts off east and crosses over the boundary into the Gifford Pinchot National Forest. The Chinook Trail (180B) climbs through meadows and wildflowers toward Silver Star Mountain, providing wider views of the Yacolt Burn and ribbons of the Columbia River far to the south. From this trail on the first Fourth of July after September 11, 2001, we could see dark clouds over Mount St. Helens and Mount Adams. On the long, sloping ridge of the mountain, however, a group of nine children and adults strolled along the trail, carrying a full-sized American flag, unfurling in the wind.

Trail 180B reaches the Silver Star Trail (180) in a little more than two miles, and an old road leads another two miles to the summit. (Ed's Trail, which is narrower, parallels the old road and rejoins it before the summit.) A more direct route to the summit of Silver Star Mountain starts at the end of a road from Camp Sunset, just below Sunset Falls on the East Fork Lewis River. The Civilian Conservation Corps (CCC) camp where Hill and his comrades lived is now a forest service campground. Instead of barracks, small tents in primary colors dot the banks of the river. A paved path leads to the falls and deep pool below it, where "the boys" took swim breaks. From Camp Sunset, the young flame-tamers could see a trail winding through the burned-over forest, up Silver Star Mountain. They carried building materials by packhorse up the trail and constructed a fire lookout on top. By 1938, crews from the Vancouver Barracks district of the CCC had built ninety-three lookout houses and forty-five towers, and had felled snags on nearly 30,000 acres in southwest Washington.

What is left of their work? The Yacolt Burn spurred the Washington legislature to pass fire protection laws and create a board of forest commissioners, who appointed a fire warden. The destruction caused by the fire inspired the creation of the School of Forestry at the University of Washington. The federal government created forest preserves like the Gifford Pinchot and sent in the CCC. The last big Yacolt reburn was in 1952. After that, the state used prison labor to fell snags, build an extensive network of roads and fire trails, construct water holes, and fight fires when they occurred.

In the last fifty years, fires whipped up by the Devil wind in the old burn have been much less frequent. Trees planted in the 1930s have since been logged. Firefighters today rely on the technologies of satellite imaging, cell phones, and aerial surveillance. The cabin built by the CCC was replaced by a new cabin in 1955 but was later abandoned. On the summit of Silver Star Mountain on a rainy, misty day, a friend and I could see little except for the bright rain gear of a hiking group from Vancouver. Only a concrete slab remained where the lookout once stood.

25

Mount St. Helens

GETTING THERE: From Randle, take Forest Service Road 25 for 20 miles, then Road 99 toward Windy Ridge for a little more than 9 miles. For the

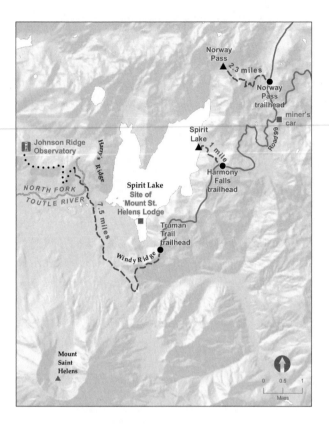

Norway Pass trailhead, turn right on Road 26 to Ryan Lake, marked Norway Pass. The Harmony trailhead is 4 miles farther on Road 99. The Truman Trail departs from Windy Ridge at the end of the road.

DISTANCE: Harmony Trail, 1 mile one way; Norway Pass, 2.3 miles one way; Truman Trail, 7.5 miles one way

LEVEL OF DIFFICULTY: moderate; elevation gain, no shade

HISTORICAL HIGHLIGHTS: views of Spirit Lake, mining operations, and volcanic destruction

Every Washington resident of more than thirty years has a Mount St. Helens story to tell: where they were, what they heard, what they saw, and what they breathed when the volcano blew. Friends of mine told of hearing the explosion, streets darkened with ash, and their children being evacuated from camps in the Cispus River Valley.

The most dramatic stories came from those closest to the volcano—a volcanologist who lost his life reporting the blast; two photographers who were circling the mountain in a small plane when it erupted; miners, campers, and a resort owner who did not heed warnings to leave. Their stories are told in fine detail at the Coldwater Visitor Center and Johnston Ridge Observatory, but the history of the first moments of the eruption can also be found on foot, on several trails through the devastation that killed fifty-seven people.

Mount St. Helens, named by George Vancouver for a British diplomat, is the youngest and most explosive peak in the South Cascades. Native Americans called it Fire Mountain, and their legends suggest it has been smoking continuously. Debris evidence confirms multiple eruptions. Large mudflows from the mountain's slopes have flooded the Lewis, Toutle, and Kalama river valleys within the last three thousand years.

Spokane leader Cornelius told missionaries Elkanah and Mary Walker about an eruption in the late 1700s. "They say some forty or fifty years ago there was a great fall of ashes, the truth of which is very plain now to be seen in turning up the ground," wrote Walker in his 1839 report to the mission board. "They say that it was a very long night with heavy thunder. They feared the world would fall to pieces and their hearts were very small."

Occupants of Fort Vancouver observed a similar ashfall in 1835. "I believe this is the first well ascertained proof of the existence of a volcano on the west coast of America, to the north of California on the mainland," wrote Dr. Meredith Gairdner, the Hudson's Bay Company's official physician.

A longer eruptive phase that began in 1842 and lasted for fourteen years was captured in both paint and sketches by Canadian artist Paul Kane. A Jesuit priest also noted the activity. "The volcano which I spoke of at the end of my journal erupted last night with a frightful noise," wrote Father J. B. Z. Bolduc at the Cowlitz Mission on March 6, 1843. "The flames rose to a considerable height, and this morning it is still smoking very much."

Most of these explosions took people by surprise; there were no volcanologists to predict them. Indians regarded the mountain with respect, from a distance. When the artist Kane tried to hire guides to climb the mountain with him, he was told stories of "Skoocooms," evil spirits who had eaten a man visiting Mount St. Helens. The fish in the lake at the bottom of the mountain were said to have heads "like those of bears." The lake's name, Spirit Lake, derived from the same kind of spirits that haunted Yacolt Prairie.

By 1980, accounts of the eruptions were buried in history books. After 123 years without a peep from the mountain, Washingtonians were quite comfortable in its shadow. When frequent earthquakes rumbled the mountain in March, however, volcanologists, timber companies, the state government, and the national press corps began to pay attention. In early April, governor Dixy Lee Ray declared a state of emergency. By the end of the month, as a bulge on the north flank grew as much as six feet a day, a red zone was drawn around the mountain. Only scientists and law enforcement officers were allowed in the zone.

Despite the warnings, the force and direction of the eruption at 8:32 a.m. on Sunday, May 18, took many by surprise. After a 5.1-magnitude earthquake shook the mountain, the bulge on the north flank began to slide, followed by an explosion of debris, a pyrotechnic blast, and a huge cloud of ash. The mountain had lost 1,000 feet.

When the air cleared, the 1980 eruption had also imposed distances between the volcano and would-be hikers. The former state highway leading to Spirit Lake from the west is now buried under 600 feet of debris. The viewpoints and trailheads that come closest to the mountain on both the west and east sides are a four-hour drive from each other. The trails up and around the mountain are hot and dry in the summer, but the views are spectacular on a clear day because there is no forest to block them. The lure of the volcano is even stronger.

From the east side, each of three trails reveals a different part of the disaster. The trail to Norway Pass goes through the heart of the timbered land most affected by the blast, once the site of mining. Prospectors were some of the first to ignore the dangers of eruptions and the warnings about evil spirits. Beginning in 1892, miners filed more than 100 claims on gold, copper, and silver deposits. The Mount St. Helens Consolidated Mining Company, in which Teddy Roosevelt owned stock, operated the Sweden and Norway mines near Spirit Lake. The camp employed forty men, who in 1905 tunneled into the side of the mountain and produced thirteen tons of ore. The transportation costs were high, however, and mining subsided.

Although the company's mines had long been closed, a few independents were still operating in 1980. Miners who had been in their cabin at a nearby mine were killed in the eruption. Their car, grossly distorted from the force of the blast, lies just beyond the turnoff for the trail.

From the parking lot, the trail to Norway Pass climbs through low bushes, wildflowers, and small evergreen trees. It switchbacks along ridges, through pumice and large white and gray logs and through trees downed in the explosive phase of the eruption. Other trails intersect before the hiker comes around a corner to the first view of the mountain.

At Norway Pass, late on a July afternoon, a small cloud hung over Mount St. Helens. Spirit Lake lay beneath it in full splendor, sparkling blue, with logs around the edges and some in the middle, the remnants of trees swept into the lake. A few trees are still standing behind a knoll that sheltered them from the blast, but their tops are gone. The views are vast: cars winding down the road from Windy Ridge, a small stream that feeds into the lake, Mount Adams to the west, and Mount St. Helen's looming over Spirit Lake. A 1975 photograph from the same spot, taken by Harvey Manning and Ira Spring, shows a symmetrical mountain and a much smaller lake with tree-covered shores.

Soon after prospectors arrived, the beautiful views attracted vacationers too. The federal government made Mount St. Helens a forest reserve after the Yacolt Burn of 1902, protecting both the commercial crop and the scenery. The director of the mining company, Dr. Henry Coe, built two cabins on Spirit Lake. The YMCA sponsored a camp, the Forest Service established a public campground, and several lodges were constructed.

The best-known resort was Mount St. Helens Lodge, owned since 1926 by Harry Truman, who had developed the fifty-acre resort on land leased from Burlington Northern at the headwaters of the north fork of the Toutle River. He constructed a restaurant, a lodge, a boat house, and fifteen to twenty cabins, all covered with hand-split cedar shakes.

A practical joker, Truman created his own Sasquatch sighting. He carved a pair of big wooden feet, fastened them to an old pair of shoes, and tromped around the mountain after the first fresh snowfall of the ski season. "When those skiers saw those giant footprints, they were sure Big Foot was around. Some of them ran off the mountain so fast you could have shot marbles on their coattails," he recounted to his niece, Shirley Rosen.

An early partner of Truman's, Jack Nelson, split off to build his own Harmony Falls Lodge across the lake. The only access to the shores of Spirit Lake is via the Harmony Trail to the site of the lodge. The trail is a one-mile hike down from the road to Windy Ridge and 600 feet of elevation gain coming back up. Having learned about the climate from the Norway Pass hike, I started early in the morning for this one. There is very little shade but a few moist, brushy spots as the trail goes past a spring, the remnants of Harmony Falls. Harmony Falls itself disappeared in the explosion. "All that was left was a little slope colored an ugly brown," wrote Shirley Rosen, who saw the spot from a helicopter soon after the eruption.

Coming around a bend on the level of the lake, I suddenly saw Spirit Lake again: bright blue water with the gray mountain reflected against an equally blue sky. A lake that was covered with logs and too hot for life after the blast now has fish and amphibians—probably from the ponds up-valley that were still frozen over in May 1980. Many of the logs ended up in a thirteen-mile debris dam where the lake used to drain into the Toutle River. The U.S. Corps of Engineers tunneled through the debris to provide an outlet for the lake and prevent a disastrous break.

The shoreline of the lake is restricted because of ongoing research, but sitting on a log nearby, I'm close enough. At this peaceful spot on a sunny, summer day, it's hard to imagine the terror of May 18. It is not hard to imagine why Harry Truman refused to leave when the red zone was drawn. "Spirit Lake and Mount St. Helens are part of me—they're mine," he told journalists. "You couldn't pull me out with a mule team." Truman claimed that he knew the mountain well and that a lava flow would not reach him three miles down from the bulge, on the southern shore of Spirit Lake.

Truman and his resort were buried in the first phase of the eruption. The landslide roared into Spirit Lake, creating a tidal wave that climbed 800 feet up Harry's Ridge (named after geologist Harry Glicken). When the wave came down, it swept hundreds of trees that had been downed in the blast back into the lake. When the ashes cooled, devastation surrounded the mountain; no sign of life was visible for miles.

The Truman Trail, named after Harry, comes closest to the gray crater of the mountain. Truman and his lodge are probably about 200 feet under the new bottom of Spirit Lake. Of the piles of logs still in the lake a few years ago, the third pile of logs east of the overlook may mark the spot. The Truman Trail leads south from the parking lot at Windy Ridge, along an old logging road, for two and a half miles, then heads down through the pumice plain. It crosses three creeks responsible for bringing low shrubs and wildflowers to life among the pumice.

The only sounds are of wind and water. On a gray day, when clouds and mist cover the mountain until noon, a walk through this lonely plain is humbling. Three researchers move soundlessly over the landscape, leaving plenty of space for skoocooms and for the explosive potential of the gray hulk looming above. Mount St. Helens speaks most eloquently of the beautiful yet destructive history of the South Cascades.

CHAPTER SIX

Central Washington

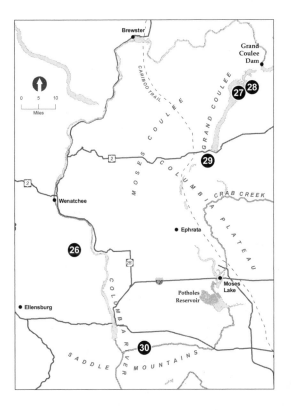

The Columbia River bisects central Washington like a wriggling snake, bending south at Brewster and then west at Wallula Gap. The land on both sides of the river is high and dry. Mountains, hills, ridges, and canyons crowd the river's western shores, defining the Kittitas, Wenas, Naches, Yakima, and Klickitat valleys. The Columbia Plateau and two long coulees, Moses Coulee and the Grand Coulee, stretch north and south on its eastern side.

A century ago, the Columbia River was still wild. "This river exceeds in grandeur any other perhaps in the world," wrote the artist Paul Kane in 1847, "not so much from its volume of water, although that is immense, as from the romantic wilderness of its stupendous and ever-varying surrounding scenery."

That scenery discouraged many foot travelers. Passage was faster on the river, but dangerous rapids forced portages and hauls over the mountains. Kane himself crossed the deep gully of the Grand Coulee on foot, but described days of traveling through sandy country with "weather intensely hot, and no water procurable all day." Since foot trails here can be sparse and harsh, we'll follow the early adapters—the riders, wagons, and stagecoaches.

For much of this region's history, cattle outnumbered people. Megaranchers such as Ben Snipes saw golden opportunities in selling beef to miners, particularly in the new gold fields in British Columbia. Snipes came to this western country as a teenager, driving an ox team in a wagon train from Iowa. After a short time prospecting in California, Snipes acquired his first herd of cattle with an I.O.U. He fed them on bunchgrass and ryegrass in the Klickitat and Yakima valleys, with permission from the Yakama chief, Kamiakin. By the late 1800s, Snipes had amassed a herd of 125,000 cattle that ranged over 800 miles, from the Columbia Hills in the south to the Cariboo mining district in Canada in the north, from the Kittitas Valley in the west to Moses Coulee in the east.

Thus, Central Washington became ranch country. Trails in this chapter follow a fur trader in search of horses, an artist wandering up the Grand Coulee, railroad and military explorers, stagecoaches going over the mountain passes, homesteaders who tried to live on the land, and, always, cowboys.

26

Colockum Pass Road

GETTING THERE: From Wenatchee, drive 14 miles south on the road signed to "Malaga," which begins as Wenatchee Avenue then becomes South Wenatchee Avenue then veers left as Malaga-Alcoa Road, and finally turns into Colockum Road. At a junction with Tarpiscan Road, stay right on Colockum. At 4.7 miles from this junction, enter the Colockum Wildlife Recreation Area. At a sharp turn, curve left, staying on the paved road. At the end of the county road, the road becomes rutted and rocky. Park in any wide spot.

DISTANCE: 5 miles to the halfway station

LEVEL OF DIFFICULTY: moderate; uphill; exposed to the elements

HISTORICAL HIGHLIGHTS: site of halfway station on the stagecoach road

Colockum Pass through the Wenatchee Mountains marked a halfway spot for cattle and people—halfway between The Dalles, Oregon, and British Columbia gold mining camps, and halfway between the developing towns of Ellensburg and Wenatchee. Colockum Pass Road was the preferred route through the high country for more than fifty years. Hardy pioneers could cross these mountains in thirteen hours on foot or five hours on horseback. A few brave souls drove cars over the pass in the early 1900s, but the rocky, rutted road never quite caught on for anything but cattle.

Today, Colockum Pass Road traces the historic route of stagecoaches, wagons, and cattle drives. From the north end, a seven-hour hike leads to the halfway site over high country with wide vistas. The road is marked on maps and posts with a green dot, which means it is open to vehicles, but on a sunny Sunday in August only six trucks, two motorcycles, three off-road vehicles, and one Subaru disturbed the silence.

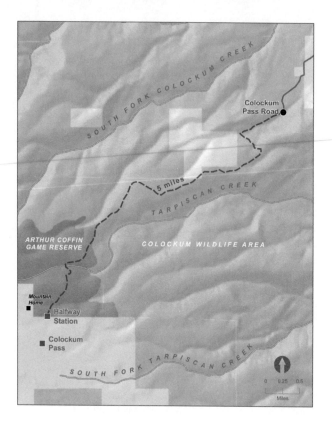

The fur trader Alexander Ross rode this way on horseback in the summer of 1814, headed for Colockum Pass. He was hoping to buy horses from the Yakama at a glorious summer gathering in the Kittitas Valley called Che-lo-han, which settlers transcribed as "Colockum." Ross had left his post in Okanagon country, accompanied by an American clerk, two French Canadian boatmen, a baby, and two Native American wives, who came along to help in driving the horses, for Ross had discovered that "women in these parts" were as expert as men on horseback. After losing bedding and provisions in the rapids of the Columbia River, they camped at the mouth of the Wenatchee River.

If the party had continued canoeing on the Columbia, they would have found more rapids. If they had walked along the west side of the river, sharp canyons and deep gorges would have blocked their way. Also jutting out into the river was Cape Horn, a precipitous 2,000-foot basalt cliff. So the group headed overland toward Colockum Pass, climbing the ridges between creek canyons.

Begin your hike, as Ross did, at the foot of the mountains on the Wenatchee side, at the end of the paved road. An early settler here made a dessert wine like the Spanish Malaga, giving the area its name. The old road ascends a ridge between Colockum and Tarpiscan creeks, the first miles through Ponderosa pine.

Seventy years after Ross, cattle grazed on every hill and down every canyon. Ranches and homesteads spread out along this route: Haley and Reed ranches on the north end of the road, Stone and King just north of the pass, and Smythe, Cooke, Stewart, and Peterson on the Ellensburg side. Spring and fall roundups, when the cattle were collected, sorted, and branded, became community events. Ellensburg and Wenatchee prospered from this ranching, and Kittitas Valley settlers constructed this road in 1880 to connect the towns.

From the beginning it was a crude affair, and travelers had to cut trees, grade the hillsides with plows, lower wagons with rope, and tie trees on behind the wagons to act as a drag. "For miles the ruddy rocky wagon road twisted up the side of the mountain," recalled one family that used the road in 1887. Their two young children, ages six months and two years, were carried or walked a great part of the way. Gradually, rocks were thrown out of the roadway or piled along the side to form banks that still define the road in places.

The territorial government made the road official in 1888, signing an agreement with E. A. Haley to repair and improve the road and put it "in condition of a good mountain wagon road." "No part of said road was to be less than ten feet in width, with suitable and convenient meeting places," which explains the wide roadway. Haley built with grades as easy as practical, which makes the climb gradual but steady.

After the first hour, the road finds open country, with nearly 360-degree views and sportsmen's camps along the side. After a junction with North Fork Tarpiscan Creek Road, Colockum Road continues past a location marker. Sun glints off the Columbia River; Crescent Bar lies on its east flank, across the river from West Bar and, above it, Cape Horn, neither of which is visible.

The road climbs toward a game reserve on a large cattle ranch run by the Coffin family. Three brothers—Arthur, Lester, and Stanley Coffin—first bought a ranch at West Bar, then expanded to 100,000 acres along this road, where they amassed herds of 3,000 cattle, 160 horses, and 60,000 ewes and lambs. During the summer grazing season, the brothers stayed in a log cabin built with a shake roof and square nails. In the fall, the Coffins moved the cattle down to West Bar, negotiating the cliffs of Cape Horn one cow at a time. From the bar the cattle were ferried across the Columbia River to range on the east side.

The boundary of the Arthur Coffin Game Reserve signals the top of the ridge. Beyond two intermittent streams that form Tarpiscan Creek is a plaque on a rock honoring Arthur Coffin. The old cabin here was burned down by vandals. A larger log cabin built in 1913 had four spring beds, which folded up against opposite walls in the daytime. The mountain home of Lester Coffin is in the game reserve, which is fenced and marked "No trespassing." The largest herds roaming the high country now are not horses or cattle or sheep but elk, which we watched, at a respectful distance.

On the steepest part of the road, just north of the headwaters of Tarpiscan Creek, was Dead Man's Hill. Miners carried heavy freight over this route. One wagon was carrying a load of dynamite, which blew up, sending the wagon into a canyon and the driver into a tree. The road has been rerouted in this area, and Dead Man's Hill does not appear on today's topographical maps.

Beyond the Coffin plaque is the halfway station that provided a change of horses for the stagecoaches carrying passengers and mail. The only stagecoach robbery in central Washington occurred on this route in 1891. A man wearing a gray cutaway coat, pinstripe pants, and a white cowboy hat and carrying a shotgun stepped out from behind a tree as the stagecoach headed down toward Ellensburg from the pass. He demanded the mail sacks and the lone passenger's wallet. Although a posse was formed, the bandit was never caught. The men who robbed Ben Snipes's bank in Roslyn also escaped to this area (see chapter 4).

Colockum Pass itself is unmarked—it lies a bit south of the halfway station. Alexander Ross headed south from this pass, down canyons, toward the Kittitas Valley (the Valley of White Chalk). As the valley came into view, spread out before Ross was a sight he would never forget: a huge Indian camp, "of which we could see its beginning but not the end. This mammoth camp," he said, "could not have contained less than 3,000 men (exclusive of women and children) and treble that number of horses." This was Che-lo-han, the annual gathering of Northwest Indians. The camp stretched from the present small town of Kittitas, at the eastern end of the valley, north and northwest to the creeks and canyons that lead over the mountains the way Ross had come. "It was a grand and imposing sight in the wilderness, covering more than 6 miles in every direction," Ross wrote in his journal.

An inscription at the Yakama Nation Museum describes the same grand gathering of many tribes:

Down from the West came the Coastal People,
In their packs, dried salt sea clams, and colored shells.
Out of the East came the High Plateau people,
Driving before them horses for the trade.
From the North came the Mountain People,
Dressed in skins of beaver and of bear.

From the south, up the winding river canyon,
Came the Yakama People, with woven blankets and
   baskets for exchange.
From all directions into Kittitas they came,
And camped together on the fertile plain.

"Councils, root-gathering, hunting, horseracing, foot-racing, gambling, singing, dancing, drumming, yelling, and a thousand other things which I cannot mention were going on," wrote Ross. "All was motion and commotion. The din of men, the noise of women, the screaming of children, the trampling of horses, and howling of dogs was more than could be described."

Ross and his party were met with hostility. The two wives feared being enslaved and found it prudent to leave in the middle of the night, with the baby. Avoiding the main trail, they set out "without food, guide, or protection" due north across the mountains and waited for the men at the mouth of the Wenatchee River. To make their escape, the women had stolen two horses, ridden them all night, and turned them loose at daylight, continuing on foot. Over four days they rode eighteen miles, walked fifty-four, and paddled sixty-six. After several days, Ross secured horses but not before giving up his knife and the belt around his waist in trade. His party reunited with the women, who had a canoe ready to ferry them across the Columbia River.

It is also possible to reach Colockum Pass from the Ellensburg side, either in a hardy vehicle with high clearance or as a long hike (thirteen miles one way), with opportunities for wandering ridges, following streams, and finding springs and meadows. At 6.3 miles the traces of an old road can be found to the left, which makes a good hike to a view of Cooke Canyon, Mount Rainier, and the Kittitas Valley. Spread out below is the terrain Ross saw, but there will be no Che-lo-han at the foot of the mountains. The land now is a quiet network of country roads, ranches, and farms stretching out from the hub of Ellensburg.

Colockum Pass Road remained the favored route over the mountains until the early 1900s. In 1910 John A. Gellatly of Wenatchee and his wife, four children, and a nanny drove a Thomas Flyer over the pass on a trip to southern Oregon. Gellatly described the road as very steep and rugged. Because of his car's simple clutch system, "at the first steep grade, we were in for trouble." On steep grades, fifteen-year-old Lester stood on the running board and scooped dirt between the two discs of the clutch to keep them from slipping. The rest of the family walked. Because of such trouble, the road never became a highway. Instead the state built a road over Blewett Pass, which was later replaced by Highway 97, and Colockum Pass Road faded into the travel standards of "a good mountain road."

27

The Grand Coulee and Steamboat Rock

GETTING THERE: Take Highway 155 about 11 miles south of the Grand Coulee Dam or 15 miles north of Coulee City to the main entrance of Steamboat Rock State Park. The trail heads off in three places from the main road, but day parking is in a lot near the end of the road. Walk back to the nearest trailhead, marked with a brown hiker' sign.

DISTANCE: 1 mile to the very top; elevation gain 1,000 feet; 2 to 3 miles of trails on top

LEVEL OF DIFFICULTY: moderate overall; difficult in a few steep spots

HISTORICAL HIGHLIGHTS: Steamboat Rock; view of the former Grand Coulee

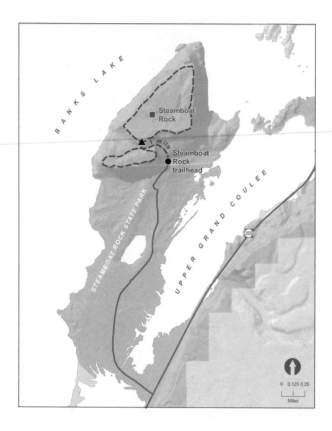

The peripatetic artist Paul Kane, who was traveling and painting the Pacific Northwest in 1847, had determined to go to Fort Colvile in north central Washington "by the Grand Coulet." Part of the coulee's allure was its mystery: no one could tell him anything about it, "nor could I hear of another, either Indian or White, who had penetrated any considerable distance up it; the place was, however, so much talked of as an abode of evil spirits and other strange things, that I could not resist the desire of trying to explore it." Unable to find an Indian guide, he enlisted a mixed-race man named Donny to go with him.

The Grand Coulee was created when an ice dam formed in the Columbia River during the age of glaciers. Water diverted from the

A John Mix Stanley lithograph depicts the Grand Coulee. Washington State Historical Society.

river by the dam ploughed a deep valley through lava beds on the Columbia Plateau. In subsequent centuries, the ice dam melted, and the water moved back into the course the Columbia River follows today, leaving the coulee dry.

Kane left the river near its confluence with the Snake and struck out overland to explore the coulee. Approaching its lower part, he crossed country that seemed like "a barren sandy desert, without a drop of water to drink, a tree to rest under, or a spot of grass to sit on." One narrow lake had the historical equivalent of a Canadian geese problem. It was "swarming with pelicans, whose dung had made the water green and thick." After accidentally setting fire to the grass at one campsite and getting separated for several hours from "my man Donny," Kane and his guide arrived together at the upper part of the coulee.

Kane described the "wonderful gully" as about 150 miles long and walled-in by twenty miles of basalt 1,000 feet high. During the

Steamboat Rock overlooks Banks Lake, created by the Grand Coulee Dam.

night, a thunderstorm came on. "In the whole course of my life I never heard anything so awfully sublime as the endless reverberations amongst the rocks of this grand and beautiful ravine," he recorded. "There is hardly another spot in the world that could produce so astounding an effect."

Then, the bottom of the coulee was covered with luxuriant grass; today, it is covered with water. Then, bases of enormous rocky islands studded the coulee's bottom, remnants of the lava the floods had swept away. Today, one large rock rises above the water—Steamboat Rock, the remaining lip of what was once a giant waterfall. To Kane, the rock loomed like a giant steamboat beached on a dry shore. He and Donny were running out of food and eating salmon that had to be well shaken before eating because it was alive with maggots, but the artist stopped long enough to sketch the rock.

Kane's sketch matches what today's hiker sees approaching Steamboat Rock. The rock rises above the flat plain and beaches of Steamboat Rock State Park, an island-peninsula reached by a causeway. The glacial water that fell 800 feet over the lip of the rock is long gone, and the dry shore is under the blue water of Banks Lake.

No longer mysterious after Kane's visit, the coulee became a nineteenth-century highway, as a nearby interpretive sign explains. Fur traders such as Alexander Ross and John Work traveled through it and passed by Steamboat Rock, as did botanist David Douglas. Even members of the U.S. Navy rode through in 1841 as part of the Wilkes Expedition exploring the Northwest interior. In 1879 Lieutenant Thomas Symons of the U.S. Army Corps of Engineers also noticed the tall, grand walls of the coulee. He was looking for a shorter way for the military to travel from Fort Walla Walla to posts on the northern bend of the Columbia. Striking out across country, like Kane, he went north through the coulee, "its perpendicular walls forming a vista like some grand old ruined, roofless hall, down which we traveled hour after hour."

That vista, which has been greatly altered by human engineering, is best seen from the top of Steamboat Rock. Three small sandy trails cross the sagebrush fields of the park and converge at the base of the rock. There's only way up: a one-lane scramble up a dirt trail with rocks that sometimes slip and slide (wear good shoes or boots). At the top of the plateau, in the middle of the rock, trails branch off in two directions, leading to higher plateaus and views both north and south. At an overlook on the south end of the rock, swallows flit around like the motorboats on the lake below. There is no shade, so this is a hike best done early or late in the season or early in the day, with plenty of carried water. The green watered lawns of the state park mock the barren heat from the top of the rock, but the views are worth the sweat.

After Symons's trip, the coulee lay quiet for many years before it again spurred the human imagination. Local promoters thought the coulee would be perfect for holding water again if the federal government would build a dam on the Columbia. In 1932 they caught the ear of a presidential candidate who was touring eastern Washington, Franklin D. Roosevelt. When elected, Roosevelt made good on his campaign promise to build the dam, and in 1939 the

Grand Coulee Dam put the waters of the Columbia River back into the coulee, forming Banks Lake. The lake flooded everything that earlier visitors had seen, except for Steamboat Rock.

28

Northrup Canyon

GETTING THERE: Take Highway 155 to mile marker 19 and turn east up a gravel road. Drive or walk uphill past a gravel pit .7 mile to the trailhead at the end of the road. The road to the left is gated; go around it for the trail to the homestead and the lake. Straight ahead and to the right is the wagon road, which is closed from November 15 through March 15 to protect the eagles.

DISTANCE: wagon road, 1 mile; 1.5 miles to homestead

LEVEL OF DIFFICULTY: moderate

HISTORICAL HIGHLIGHTS: wagon road; Northrup homestead; Grand Coulee construction debris

Before the Grand Coulee Dam filled the Grand Coulee with water, there were three places to cross the coulee's sandy bottom: at the northern end, "by a very bad wagon-road," as described by Lieutenant Thomas Symons; at the bottom, where Coulee City Stagecoach Road crossed; and in the middle, where a wagon road crossed at Northrup Canyon, just opposite Steamboat Rock, about seven miles south of the Columbia River.

To this crossing, in 1841, came Lieutenant Robert E. Johnson of the Wilkes Expedition, whose party descended Barker Canyon on the west and crossed the three-mile wide floor of the "chasm" by rounding Steamboat Rock on its north side. Leaving the coulee, the expedition went eastward up Northrup Canyon.

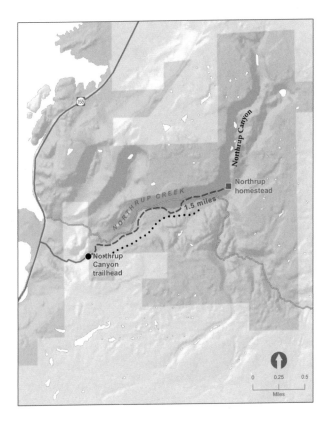

Northrup Canyon has long been cool and green amid the harsh, dry coulee country. There are two hikes, one along a wagon road, which is really a trail, and one into the canyon, to an old homestead. Both begin at the end of the dirt road from the highway. Cliffs along the road display yellow-stained earth, noticed by missionary Samuel Parker in 1836, and described as "much stained with sulphur" by the Wilkes Expedition.

The trail to the homestead goes off to the left at the gate. John W. Northrup settled in the canyon in 1874, then built a barn out of logs, filed a notice of water rights, started an irrigation program, and finally, in 1904, installed a water system. He planted the area's first orchard, and for a time all was well. Then Northrup died, and

An old barn remains from the Northrup homestead.

his widow and daughter ran the ranch from 1906 on. According to local writer Monty Hormel, at least one murder occurred on the homestead after that. A man leasing range land is thought to have killed both his wife and then the widow who lived on the ranch, but the alleged murderer was never caught.

The trail to the ranch is at first a pleasant hike through shady areas. A small rattlesnake slithered off the trail one July day as I hiked with a friend who was carrying her toddler in a backpack (locals had warned about the abundance of snakes). Northrup Creek runs alongside the trail at times as it heads east back into the canyon. The rusty tin cans along the trail happen to be protected state property. During the building of the Grand Coulee Dam in the 1930s, construction crews dumped an enormous heap of cans, stoves, and other artifacts of camping.

Stay to the left as a road goes off to the right. The canyon narrows, and the trail goes over a bridge and becomes grassier, among signs of human activity, such as beams and aluminum panels. The homestead consists of a seasonal park residence, a century-old cabin, and a collapsing barn. A trail to Northrup Lake at the head of the canyon winds to the left of the old chicken coop.

After the Northrups left and the ranch was used to range cattle, the canyon once again flourished as a farm when new owners brought in electric power and ran thirteen sprinklers to irrigate alfalfa in the 1970s. Washington State Parks took over the canyon as an adjunct to Steamboat Rock State Park in 1976.

Back at the gate, the wagon road goes straight ahead, beginning at barbed wire that is bent down to invite crossing. Local residents carved the road out of the hillside above the ranch with handpicks and teams of horses. The wagons carried wheat from the Columbia Plateau to markets. The road led from the small settlements of Almira and Hartline, descended Northrup Canyon, crossed the dry coulee, and ascended Barker Canyon—the same route Johnson had taken in 1841. The canyon led to the ports of Brewster and Bridgeport on the Columbia River. When the Northern Pacific and the Great Northern dueled for routes through the sagebrush in the early 1900s, the wagon road gradually lost importance and narrowed to a trail.

The trail follows two ruts but quickly becomes a mere path among rocks along a steep hillside—difficult to imagine as a road. The path parallels the canyon for a while, then turns away into sandy sagebrush and disintegrates into several faint trails that lead to downed barbed wire. From a high point, the shimmering blue of Banks Lake is visible in the distance.

You may be startled out of your historic cloud by the roar of supersonic jets, flying just high enough to clear the canyon walls. As you return toward Banks Lake, the sounds of speedboats and cars confirm that no one carves roads out of rock with a pickax any more.

If you want to pick up the stagecoach route on the other side of the once-dry coulee, drive all the way around on Highway 174 and come back along Foster Creek and through Barker Canyon. The reservoir water laps right up against the end of the road, drowning the old coulee walls.

29

Coulee City Stagecoach Road

GETTING THERE: From Sun Lakes State Park, past the campground and before the day-use area, turn left at the sign for Deep Lake. At a junction of roads, stay right. At 2.2 miles (.3 mile before the Deep Lake boat launch), a gravel/dirt road goes off across the canyon floor to the east. A white gate and rock cairn indicate the trail. Park in a small gravel pull-off on the north side of the road.

DISTANCE: about 1 mile one way

LEVEL OF DIFFICULTY: moderate

HISTORICAL HIGHLIGHTS: stagecoach road

Below Banks Lake, which filled the Upper Grand Coulee, the Lower Grand Coulee stretches south to Moses Lake. Steep walls rise above

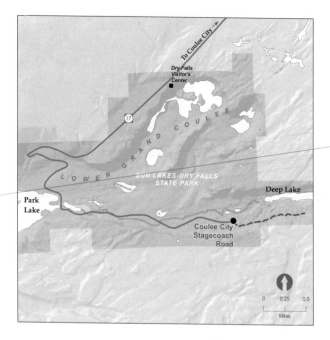

the coulee floor, which is dotted with lakes and ponds. Dry Falls, once ten times larger than Niagara Falls, is a magnificent reminder of the force of water along this channel. At the break between the upper and lower coulees was another way across, the Coulee City Stagecoach Road.

Coulee City, a watering hole on the Cariboo Trail, has long been a crossroads. In 1879 Lieutenant Thomas Symons camped here and named the area Middle Pass because it was roughly halfway up both coulees. An army engineer, Symons thought that this was the only place the coulee could be crossed by a railroad. The lower coulee could not be crossed, he said, "owing to the lakes and steep walls." Most of the upper coulee was "a deep chasm, with vertical, impass- able walls." Only about midway did the walls break down enough on both sides that a wagon could ascend them, and that's where Symons located a road.

Coulee City grew on rumors that the Northern Pacific would build a branch line, which it did. By 1890 the town was platted and soon boasted the Coulee City Hotel. The train arrived in Cou- lee City in the afternoon, but went no farther. Passengers wishing to continue to Bridgeport had to wait for the morning stagecoach departure, assuring the hotel some business. The stagecoach came to Coulee City from Ephrata, winding over the sagebrush steppes from the south and avoiding the lakes and steep walls Symons had mentioned.

The faint wavering path of the Coulee City Stagecoach Road still crosses the steppes above the lakes on land now leased for cattle ranges. Begin at Sun Lakes State Park, where Native Americans once caught fish jumping up a small waterfall. The road passes near Park Lake, where homesteaders irrigated the land from the stream that feeds the lake. They planted orchards and lilac bushes and con- structed a dance hall. The stagecoach brought mail, medicines, and contact with the larger world.

As you walk or drive along the road to Deep Lake, notice the course of Mirror Creek and then Meadow Creek, marked only by the path of vegetation. When this area burned in 1987, some of the old irrigation canals and patterns of settlement were more visible. Despite federal acts that increased claim sizes and supported irrigation, most homesteaders found the land impossible to farm and abandoned their claims. Among the plagues were grasshopper invasions that could turn the roads slippery with the bulk of their crushed bodies.

After finding the trace of the old stagecoach road that veers off over the sagebrush, walk around the white gate and follow the ruts over the canyon floor. Although some of the land is leased as cattle range, it is public, and you are free to walk. The gravel road changes to dirt and rises to a small saddle with a barbed wire fence. Either open the gates or squeeze through the wire. The trail soon becomes mostly depressions in the grass, but go up to the left (straight ahead leads to a pond). At the top of the rise, the trail joins another dirt road coming in from the left (west) on the ridge of the canyon. You may continue among the cattle toward Coulee City or ramble out to the edge of the canyon wall for a look down on a very green Deep Lake and a look back at the faint tracks marking the stagecoach road.

30

Lower Crab Creek

GETTING THERE: From the I-90 crossing of the Columbia River at Vantage, drive south on the east side of the river on Highway 243. At Beverly, Lower Crab Creek Road (dirt) heads east along the north side of the Saddle Mountains. The Milwaukee Road Corridor runs to the north of this road and may be accessed at several points, including Beverly, Fish and Wildlife parking areas, and Smyrna. A day-use permit

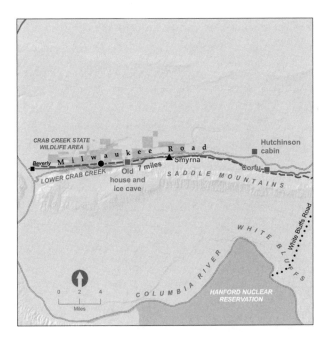

is required. Call the Department of Natural Resources Southeast Region, 509-925-8510.

DISTANCE: up to 14 miles one way

LEVEL OF DIFFICULTY: easy walking, but desert weather conditions

HISTORICAL HIGHLIGHTS: abandoned farmhouse and cabin; old schoolhouse in Smyrna; Taunton electrification plant for the Milwaukee Road

In 1879 Lieutenant Thomas Symons climbed to the top of White Bluffs, where the Columbia River bends south on a C-clamp curve. Looking east and northeast toward the Columbia Plateau, Symons described the country spread out before him as "gently rolling, as far as the eye could reach. . . . The country was covered with a luxuriant growth of bunch-grass. . . . Quite a large number of cattle were seen."

"We could gather fat cattle in winter and spring when they were poor in every other place," wrote A. J. Splawn, a cattleman and historian of the late 1800s. "I bought and drove thousands of cattle from the White Bluffs range to Portland and Puget Sound."

Farther inland from the river, the land dried out. "The country we had traveled was covered partly with sagebrush, bunch-grass, and weeds, and was utterly waterless and lifeless," Symons wrote. "Not even the cheerful coyote lived there, for not one lulled us to sleep."

White Bluffs Road crossed this lifeless country, connecting Portland, the biggest city in the Northwest, to Fort Colvile and the mines of Idaho and Montana. The route began at White Bluffs, went around the Saddle Mountains on the eastern end, through the potholes area and Moses Lake, past Odessa and Davenport, and on to Colville, Spokane, and the Pend Oreille region. The Hudson's Bay Company met boats at White Bluffs with horse-loads of furs. In the 1860s, the Oregon Steam Navigation Company ran steamboats up the river to the docks, then transferred freight to mule teams, which carried it overland to Pend Oreille Lake, where it was transferred to lake steamers and delivered to the Montana goldfields. The lake steamers themselves were hauled overland on White Bluffs Road. Cattleman Ben Hutchinson was on hand to push one such boat, sawed in two, over the crest of Saddle Mountain.

At the turn of the century, this sagebrush plateau became more than a cattle range or a freight route. Planning to make the desert bloom, the federal government offered land to homesteaders such as the Tice family, who moved from Missouri to 160 acres near Othello in 1906. They hoped to grow wheat in these shallow, sandy acres. Laura Tice Lage described their hopes in *Sagebrush Homesteads*. "If we just had water," settlers avowed, "this soil would grow anything." As they put up barbed wire fences and started plowing, the land itself began to change.

Because of overgrazing by cattle, sheep, and wild horses, much of the bunchgrass had been crowded out by sagebrush, which the homesteaders used as fuel. The movement of herds of cattle and horses, followed by plowing, raised a lot of dust. March was particularly dusty when the wind picked up the light soil from the newly plowed fields. As the Tice children walked home from school, they squinted to shield their eyes from the dirt, and often walked backward. "Hair, eyebrows, lashes, nostrils and clothing were filled with the powdery dust," Laura Lage recalled. One father plowed a three-mile furrow for his children to follow to school and told them never to veer from the furrow during a dust storm, for fear of becoming lost. Such dust did not bode well for sustainable farming.

White Bluffs Road flourished for a time as a route to water for homesteaders, but, as earlier travelers had discovered, the miles of loose sand slowed progress considerably. As more land was claimed, the road vanished behind fences and under plowed ground. The bluffs themselves were enclosed by the Hanford Nuclear Reservation.

The land is no longer waterless and lifeless. Fourteen miles of an old railroad grade along Lower Crab Creek lead past a string of abandoned homesteads, dusty settlements, and the long-awaited irrigation channels. The Milwaukee Road Corridor extends as a public trail from Beverly to Smyrna. In the western part of the state, this Milwaukee Road is a state park (see chapter 4), but east of the Columbia it is managed by the Department of Natural Resources, which requires a permit for hiking.

Begin where everyone else alighted—at the Columbia River. Instead of stepping off a steamboat at White Bluffs, however, drive to Beverly, where the railroad crossed the river on a magnificent trestle (which is closed but still standing). Just north of the trestle was the Indian village of Wanapum, one of many spread out along the banks of the Columbia between Wenatchee and White Bluffs. Symons counted nineteen lodges in just one fishing camp in 1879.

Indians moved through the Crab Creek area but did not establish permanent camps in the desert environment, staying instead in

This lodging house near Jericho sheltered workers on the Milwaukee Road.

Moses Coulee or on the river. On cattle drives, Wanapum Indians at Priest Rapids helped swim the herds across the river. Youth went on vision quests in the Saddle Mountains and found hemp for making fishnets and rope in the Crab Creek area. The Wanapum never moved to a reservation; they stayed on the river until the Wanapum Dam flooded their fishing sites in the 1950s.

The railroad grade and a dirt and gravel road head due east from Beverly, paralleling each other much of the way. The Saddle Mountains to the south and the lower Frenchman Hills to the north forced human and animal traffic into this east-west corridor that follows Lower Crab Creek. The mountains and hills were barriers, but the creek offered water, shade, and a direction to follow.

Less than ten years after the Tices moved to Washington, as they were struggling with dust and hauling water, stakes from a preliminary railroad survey appeared on their land. The Chicago, Milwaukee, St. Paul, and Pacific Railroad started negotiating with the homesteaders for a right-of-way. Railroad agents offered Laura's father twenty-five dollars an acre and paid her mother for noontime meals for the construction crew. The line, known as the Milwaukee Road, was completed in 1911.

Railroads eased the isolation of homestead families and shortened their daylong trips to town for supplies. A young woman like Laura could save the three-mile walk from Othello to her home near the Novarro stop with a ten-cent fare. The railroad and the development of towns also provided work for homesteaders whose farms went bankrupt when the crops failed for too many years.

Of the fourteen Milwaukee Road miles open to the public, one of the best stretches for hiking is from Jericho seven miles east to Smyrna. The railroad grade is built up above the surrounding land or dug through small bluffs that sometimes line it. It leads in a straight line that seldom varies. The trains stopped for farm products, mail, and an occasional passenger at Jericho, Smyrna, Corfu, Taunton, Novarro, and Othello.

Jericho was never a town; instead it served as a telephone call box to the dispatcher in Tacoma and as a loading dock for farmers shipping their wheat. A sturdily constructed log cabin near the site has three doors, indicating that it may have been a bunkhouse for railroad workers. Chinked with concrete, the construction is a mix of whatever scrap could be found: railroad ties, bridge timbers, drift logs from the river, and factory-made siding for the ceiling.

About two miles farther east is a roofless, two-story frame house tilting crazily toward an old road and the railroad bed. The house belonged to Terry Chambers, a farmer-rancher who came to Crab Creek in the 1890s. Not far from the house, near the foot of the Saddle Mountain slope, is an ice cave that has been cool for generations. A railroad worker, Jim Johnson, noticed the spot and bought the property. After he dug a ten-by-ten-foot room in the rock, residents hauled in ice to make the room even colder. They stored food and meat there and made ice cream in the summer. The cave functioned into the mid-1950s, according to local historian Gladys Para, but talus has since blocked the entry, which still emits cool air.

An old schoolhouse and bell tower mark the hamlet of Smyrna. Young women who lived in small settlements had an ingenious method of taking the train to dances in Othello. Passengers could flag the train to stop anywhere on the way to town, but the train only stopped for mail or freight on the way back. On the day after a social event, a resident of Smyrna or Corfu might receive a mysterious gunnysack full of straw. When the train stopped to deliver the freight, the socialites would alight.

The jackrabbits abounding in this area are descendants of the survivors of conflicts with the homesteaders. Jackrabbits invaded the potato crops and ate from the haystacks that provided winter food for the cattle. When haystacks "became the mecca for all the rabbits in the country," Lage said, a roundup was organized. In 1913 people came from as far away as Seattle to eat a large communal breakfast. Then they stretched out across the country for five miles in a great semicircle and drove the rabbits toward a V-shaped fence, shooting thousands.

For half of this stretch, the railroad grade is in sight of Crab Creek and the ponds it creates. Where Symons observed that the creek had no water to flow into the Columbia in September and October, on a contemporary September day the creek's current runs brown and strong, swollen with irrigation water runoff. Cattails, milkweed, and desert olives mark the wetter places on the generally shadeless walk.

The much-anticipated water came too late for the first generations of homesteaders. The Grand Coulee Dam drowned the Upper Grand Coulee in 1939, diverting water to the new Banks Lake. Power stanchions marched over bluffs high above the coulees and the lakes. Not until the 1950s, however, did water for irrigation come to the Columbia Basin from a series of dams and reservoirs, including O'Sullivan Dam near Othello. The Tice homestead reverted to the bank before World War I, and family members found other kinds of work. The Potholes Canal now runs through the Tice homestead land.

Parts of the Milwaukee Road between Smyrna and Warden belong to a working railroad or cross private land, and hikers must take detours. Before Corfu, out of sight of the road, is the cabin of Ben and Sam Hutchinson. After working for Ben Snipes, Ben Hutchinson and his brother Sam herded their own cattle. Then, with their nephew Cash McLeod, they built homesteads along Lower Crab Creek. The creek bottom here yielded good hay crops for their horses, especially when heavy snows covered the tall bunch grass. Ben and Sam, who were 6 feet 8 inches and 7 feet 4 inches tall, respectively, entertained homesteaders' children with their lariat skills and with stories of Indian life they had learned from native cowboys on the range.

All that remains of Corfu is the stone foundation of a school hidden in the grass. Near the eastern end of the Saddle Mountains, just down from Saddle Gap, where White Bluffs Road crossed the mountains, stands a brick power station. This was the Taunton substation, which provided electrical power to the trains.

To overcome the loneliness of isolated homesteads, families organized annual Fourth of July or Labor Day celebrations on Crab Creek, about a mile north of Deadman Lake. People came from as far away as Beverly, Quincy, Ephrata, and Moses Lake, and square dancing went on into the early morning. On their way to the outing, the Tice family traveled Morgan Lake Road, the same route used to drive cattle to market. The children would watch for the face outlined on the northern end of Deadman's Bluff, which runs along the west side of the road. Following roughly the same route and White Bluffs Road, cattlemen like Ben Snipes herded cattle onto the long, slanting bluff to hold them overnight before the morning drive.

There is indeed a dead man, or at least a dead boy, in the history of this bluff and lake. During the night, one or two cowboys would guard the cattle, riding around to keep them calm. Fifteen-year-old Edward O'Roarke, from Walla Walla, was on watch one April night in 1880. When his companions came looking for him in the morning, they found his body and that of his mule at the foot of the bluff, where he had fallen or been pushed by the milling cattle. The cowboys washed his body in the clean waters of Deadman Lake and sent it home. Deadman Lake is on private land, but a small portion of the wagon track is still visible north of the lake and south of the intersection of McMannamon and Morgan Lake roads. Just north of the intersection, a five-foot triangle of rocks marks the spot where O'Roarke's body was found. In the middle of land changed by railroads, irrigation, and industrial agriculture, the rocks form a simple memorial to the cowboy generation.

CHAPTER SEVEN

Northeastern Washington

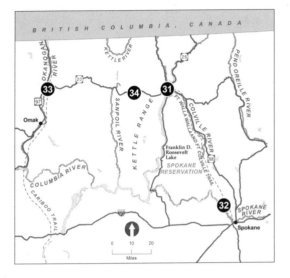

I n northeastern Washington, the rivers have sustained human
life for more than 9,000 years. Along the Columbia, Okanogan, and Spokane, Native Americans fished the falls, the fur-
trade expresses ran the rapids, and miners and cattle drives followed
the gold. The Columbia River is the main stem. It flows south
from Canada for more than 100 miles as the Colville, Kettle, and
Spokane rivers flow into it. Then it bends west for another hundred
miles, gathering water from the San Poil and Okanogan, before
turning south again. The ribbons of river defined the region and
determined settlement.

On its tumble from the Canadian Rockies, the Columbia rushed
over blocks of quartzite, and these falls created roiling cauldrons
or kettles. Thousands of salmon struggled up the falls in five runs

during the summer. Native Americans from many tribes gathered for centuries on two large islands to fish and dry the catch, then to trade, gamble, and dance. Kettle Falls was the most significant Indian fishery in Washington State, along with Celilo Falls, which is much lower on the river, near The Dalles.

Scotsman David Thompson came to Kettle Falls in June 1811. A mapmaker and fur trader, Thompson had spent ten years tracing the mighty river of the West. Once he discovered that the Columbia first flowed north from its origin and then turned south at Boat Encampment in Canada, he knew that the river could carry furs to the Pacific. That summer, with the help of Indians and French Canadian voyageurs, Thompson built canoes at Kettle Falls and traveled 700 miles more to the Columbia's mouth. His voyage opened up the Columbia's northern reaches to the fur trade. Soon trading posts were established at Spokane House, on the Spokane River, and Fort Colvile, at Kettle Falls. Priests and missionaries came to preach and teach to the Spokane, Colville, and Kettle Falls people and to the French Canadians settling in the Colville Valley.

In the 1850s and '60s, miners rushed north to the Cariboo gold fields in Canada. Herds of cattle soon followed, fattening on bunchgrass as they trailed through the Okanogan Valley. Miners crossed lands that had not been ceded through treaty negotiations, and military expeditions subjugated tribes that objected to the incursions. When the conflicts were over, most Indians in the region were relegated to the Colville reservation, west of the Columbia River, and to the Spokane reservation, north of the Spokane River.

Settlers moved into the river valleys to plant orchards, raise timothy for horses, quarry marble, harness hydropower, dig clay, mine magnesite, log yellow pine, and build railroads. In 1939 the federal government built Grand Coulee Dam, and the Columbia backed up for a hundred miles behind it. Lake Franklin Delano Roosevelt buried Kettle Falls and the foundations of Fort Colvile. Because the 350-foot dam was built without fish ladders, which were deemed too expensive and unworkable, salmon no longer ascended the upper Columbia.

Except for Spokane, the population of northeastern Washington is relatively sparse, and history still seems close. Ghost towns and mines dot the highlands between the river valleys. With the important exception of Lake Roosevelt, much of the landscape is relatively undisturbed. In this corner of the state, we'll hike along part of the portage road around Kettle Falls; along the Spokane River from Spokane House to Horse Slaughter Camp; through dusty canyons in the Okanogan Valley; and along the Kettle Range, named after the river and the falls, to the state's oldest standing lookout cabin.

31

Kettle Falls

GETTING THERE: Take Highway 395 west from the town of Kettle Falls. Just before the bridge over Franklin D. Roosevelt Lake, turn right onto a dirt road. The road leads to the Kettle Falls Historical Center and to St. Paul's Mission. Park in front of the old church.

DISTANCE: 1 mile one way

LEVEL OF DIFFICULTY: easy

HISTORICAL HIGHLIGHTS: St. Paul's Mission; grinding stone; portage road

Native Americans called Kettle Falls Shonitku, "roaring or noisy waters." When Father Pierre Jean De Smet performed a baptism at the falls in 1842, he said the "distant roar of the cataracts [broke] in on the religious silence." At the falls, "impetuous waters rush in fury and dash over a pile of rocks."

Mourning Dove, of the Colville tribe, described the falls passing on either side of a large central rock that created a smooth backwater

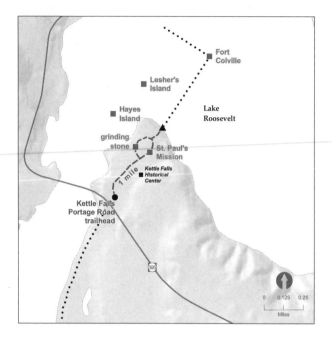

behind it. "It was a beautiful place to camp, with cliffs overhanging the falls on the west side and trails leading to the water between the high grayish-white rock formations that so often glistened in the sunlight." Campers could more easily get water on the east side, where flat rock slabs were much closer to the whirling pools. In the late 1800s, the area was "filled with mist, ribboned with many colors creating a faint rainbow on a summer evening."

The Colville camped at Kettle Falls in August to catch the king salmon, one of five salmon that ran up the Columbia and its tributaries in the summer. The Colville would be joined by the Kalispel, Spokane, Coeur d'Alene, Flathead, Okanogan, Sanpoil, Omak, and Wenatchi people. Large log scaffolds extended over the river, from which the Indian men speared or netted the fish. Some placed big baskets woven of red willow underneath the falls to catch the salmon that occasionally fell back into them. The daily catch could reach 3,000. Women cut and cured the fish, which were distributed by the Salmon Chief.

The falls are silent today, the large central rock, the kettles, and two large islands buried beneath the placid waters of Lake Roosevelt. A portion of the old portage road around the falls still rises from the water to the high terraces overlooking the ancient camp. A mission church stands where Father De Smet blessed it.

Begin at this mission, St. Paul's, but before opening the mission door, take the loop trail behind it to the grinding stone, a big rock made out of amphibolite, left by the last glacier. Here at the southern end of the fishery, Native Americans sharpened spear points and knives for fishing.

Look north from the whetstone and imagine a fort with many outbuildings under the water. When he passed the Indian fishery in 1811, the fur trader David Thompson marked Kettle Falls as a good location for a trading post. Fourteen years later, Fort Colvile was built on land donated by the chief of a local tribe under the condition that the traders would not interfere with the Indian fishery by taking more than they needed. For fifty years, the fort was a key post for the Hudson's Bay Company, which traded for the furs of badger, bear, beaver, fox, lynx, martin, mink, muskrat, otter, raccoon, and wolf. When the fur trade declined, the fort expanded into agriculture, claiming fields along the Colville River.

Every few years, when the U.S. Army Corps of Engineers decides to lower Lake Roosevelt, the outlines of Fort Colvile and the farmlands that surrounded it can be seen, most easily from the air. After an aerial reconnaissance in the late 1990s, local historian Lethene Parks donned long boots and rain gear to venture out over the mudflats. She saw remnants of a boathouse, stores, a cow and pig house, a forge, a shop, a hall, a stockade, a barn, coal kilns, an office, and gentlemen's quarters.

Return to the mission on the bluffs, where local Indians first built a chapel in 1845. The small frame church was pleasing to Father De Smet when he visited the next year. Over a period of thirty years, the mission served both Native Americans and the French Canadian

Catholics at Fort Colvile. Two more buildings replaced the first, the last a church of logs and shingle shakes. By the 1860s, the numbers of fish reaching the upper Columbia declined as the commercial catch on the lower Columbia rose. Reservation lines drawn for the Colville in 1872 eventually pushed the tribe to the west side of the river. The fishery at Kettle Falls fell into disuse, and the mission was abandoned.

Mourning Dove came by the old church one Sunday morning in 1888 with her family, after crossing above Kettle Falls in canoes from the west. They walked up a steep trail that switchbacked to the top of the bench, where it met the main north-south trail. After walking a mile, they were in full view of the abandoned chapel, just northeast of the fishery. "Mother stopped to rest and took this opportunity to tell me that she and Father had been married at that old church." By that time, the church "stood in ruins, overgrown by weeds and vines."

It still stood on the portage trail in 1921 when adventurer Madison J. Lorraine set out to row down the length of the Columbia, from source to mouth, with its 109 rapids and waterfalls. Like Thompson 120 years before him, Lorraine was able to run or line his seventeen-foot rowboat through all the rapids except Kettle Falls. Here he had to portage, and he passed the old church, which, he said, had "the most smoothly hewn logs I ever saw."

Open the door with the wooden lever to find one dark, empty room. In 1939, when the Grand Coulee Dam was constructed, the structure was restored to its original Hudson's Bay Red River style of construction, which used no nails. Horizontal logs on the walls have tongued ends that slid into the grooves of upright posts. The posts were joined to the floor with sills and then secured with wooden pegs.

A cemetery near the mission shelters the graves of hundreds of Indians and dozens of fur traders and their families, a fitting juxtaposition of supplier and buyer in the fur trade. Many more

Colville men fish from the rocks at Kettle Falls. Northwest Museum of Arts & Culture/Eastern Washington State Historical Society, Spokane, Washington. L93-75.31.

graves were moved from islands in the river when it was flooded in the 1930s. On the day the river rose over Kettle Falls, the Indians gathered on the bank and held a Ceremony of Tears. In 1989 the Colville were finally reimbursed for the loss of their traditional fishing grounds along the Columbia River. A museum interprets their history on this surviving bluff.

From the loop just to the northwest of the church, a grassy, weedy path with low pines growing on both sides leads down to the shores of the lake. This is a portion of the two-mile trail used by anyone who portaged around the falls, including the Hudson's Bay Company, which carried tons of furs and trade goods along the high terrace. Much as Mourning Dove described it, the road began north of the two large islands (Hayes Island and Lesher's Island), now submerged in the lake, headed due east to Fort Colvile, and then turned ninety degrees south, past the mission. Bateaux—thirty-foot boats that could carry three tons—could be parked at each end of the portage, one set near the fort and the other at a landing half a mile south of the falls. Wagons and draft animals from the fort carried the goods from boat to boat.

This old path was cleared of small trees a few years ago when Boy Scouts dragged canoes up the bluff in a historical reenactment. Besides this short walk, what remains of the portage road is the dirt road that leads to the mission from Highway 395. On the south side of 395, the road continues high on a bluff occupied by the Boise Cascade Timber and Wood Products Division. Boise Cascade is the largest employer in the region. On the west side of the river is national forest, and south of that the largest reservation in the state, where twelve tribes constitute the Confederated Tribes of the Colville Reservation. Five thousand residents, not all of them tribal members, live on the reservation, with income from the sale of lumber and wood products, and from tourism and casinos.

After the fur brigades portaged around Kettle Falls, they floated another 800 miles to the Hudson's Bay Company's headquarters at Fort Vancouver. Before pushing off, however, they often paid a visit to the "country club" of fur country—Spokane House, sited on the Spokane River, and the next hike.

32

Spokane Centennial Trail

GETTING THERE: From Spokane, drive northwest on Francis Avenue and Nine Mile Road (which becomes Highway 291) to the entrance on the south side of the road to Spokane House Interpretive Center in Riverside State Park.

DISTANCE: 36 miles from Spokane House to Horse Slaughter Camp

LEVEL OF DIFFICULTY: easy

HISTORICAL HIGHLIGHTS: Spokane House; Antoine Plante's ferry; Horse Slaughter Camp

Native American fisheries, British trading posts, American soldiers, and early settlers clustered on the banks of the Spokane River, from Fort Spokane, where the river flows into the Columbia, to Antoine Plante's ferry near the Idaho border. Right in the middle sat Spokane House, hub of the early fur trade.

Approaching Washington's centennial year of 1989, the city of Spokane fashioned a long trail that connects much of this history. The Spokane Centennial Trail, a bicycling and hiking trail, spans thirty-seven miles along the Spokane River. The trail is paved in most places but sometimes continues on streets. It remains near the river, crossing from one side to the other. Three sites along the trail—Spokane House, Antoine Plante's ferry, and Horse Slaughter Camp—trace fifty years that began in cooperation and ended in conflict. Trail miles are numbered starting from the Idaho border, but for the sake of chronology, begin at Spokane House, just west of the trail's western trailhead in Riverside State Park.

The early 1800s were a time of fierce corporate competition in the fur trade between the Hudson's Bay Company (HBC) and the Scottish-dominated North West Company, which was expanding ever westward in the search for furs. Northwester David Thompson had established trading posts from the company's headquarters on Lake Superior through 2,000 miles of present-day Canada, Idaho, and Montana. In 1810 he directed a Scotsman, Finan McDonald, and a French Canadian, Jacques (Jaco) Finlay, to establish Spokane House on the Spokane River. Americans from the Pacific Fur

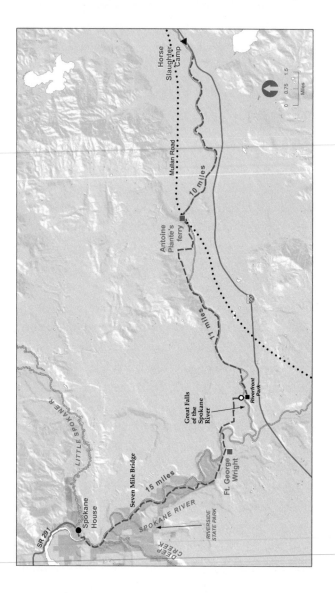

Company briefly set up camp next door, but they had to sell out during the War of 1812.

At the height of its operations, Spokane House was a community of Native Americans, French Canadians, Scotsmen, and Americans. Indeed, it became the country club of the interior trading posts, with its sturdy buildings, good food, relaxed atmosphere, dances, and friendly Spokane Indians. At various times, the post had a bakery, a library, a racetrack, a three-story house, and a warehouse that doubled as a dance hall.

A corporate merger handed over Spokane House to the English-dominated company in 1821, and the company saw problems with its location. The Spokane River was not navigable to the Columbia, and goods had to be transported sixty miles to the river by horses, which could be hard to find. The Spokane Indians were eager to acquire tobacco in trade for furs, but after fifteen years of trapping, the beaver had been depleted. During the winter of 1824–25, the HBC decided to build Fort Colvile at Kettle Falls and move operations there. They took everything of value with them.

No original buildings remain at the site, but the interpretive center provides a rich history (its hours fluctuate with state funding). Among the grasshoppers at the back is a display of metal posts in different colors. These mark the stockade walls and rectangular shapes of the three different fur companies—Scottish, American, and English—and the posts they operated here. The markers are the results of archaeological digs in 1950–53 and 1962–63, which found handwrought square nails, square washers, files, awl points, and enough evidence to mark the post's walls.

The digs also turned up a skeleton in the prone position characteristic of European burials. Of the several pipes buried with it, one had the letter "J" carved on it. After the HBC moved to Fort Colvile, Jaco Finlay stayed on at Spokane House with his Spokane wife Teshwentichina and many children (he had at least three wives and sixteen children). Before he died in 1828, he asked to be buried under the bastion.

Go down to the river to imagine what the site looked like nearly 200 years ago. The "red firs" or Ponderosa pines on its banks were the building material for bateaux, and the spruce roots laced planks together. This was probably the location of the post's boathouse, and it may have been an Indian burial site too. Spokane villages lay across a ford of the river.

A short walk west is the oldest log building in Spokane County, probably built in the 1850s or '60s. Its windows open onto a breezeway used to store grain, hay, and tools. Farther west along Nine-Mile Road, the Little Spokane River flows into the Spokane River. The North West Company built the first Spokane House on a small island at this confluence before it took over the American post upstream. The Little Spokane River Trail goes upstream through a freshwater marsh to Painted Rocks, the site of Indian pictographs. It follows the portage road used to carry goods northwest to the Pend Oreille River.

After exploring the Spokane House grounds, walk an old road east in Riverside State Park. The Centennial Trail officially begins at Nine-Mile Bridge. Early travelers followed several old trails through the Spokane Valley. From Spokane House, an Indian trail led downstream along the north bank of the river to join a trail to Kettle Falls. The Colville Road crossed the Spokane River where Long Lake is today, then continued along Chamokane Creek, past the Protestant mission at "the place of the springs," to Fort Colvile and Kettle Falls. The Centennial Trail passes Deep Creek, where the Palouse Road led to Fort Walla Walla, then Seven Mile Bridge (seven miles from the great falls of the Spokane River), and a bowl and pitcher formation that is popular with kayakers, who like to paddle through the swirls around the rocks.

In Spokane proper, the trail passes Fort George Wright and crosses the river over the falls (once the third-largest fishery in Washington, after Celilo Falls and Kettle Falls). It goes through Riverfront Park with its big red wagon and past statues marking the site of Sacred Heart, Spokane's first hospital, founded by the Sisters of Providence. Gonzaga University and Spokane Community College border the trail before it heads east out of town. A couple of miles past the Upriver Dam, teenagers dive from rocks where

Antoine Plante ferried passengers and freight on the Mullan Road at this crossing of the Spokane River.

Spokane and Coeur d'Alene Indians once fished as the trail crosses the river on a suspension bridge.

At Mile 12 is the site of Antoine Plante's ferry, the best place to cross the river between the falls and Coeur d'Alene. Like Jaco Finlay, Antoine Plante was a *meti*, of mixed race—the son of a French Canadian father and a Flathead woman. His father had been a voyageur who expertly navigated the rivers for the fur companies. Plante had been a fur trader for twenty-eight years when he settled in the Spokane Valley in the 1850s, well upstream of the abandoned Spokane House. He operated a cable ferry across the river, and his house became the stopping place for everyone traveling through the area.

A visiting scientist and physician, Dr. A. J. Thibodo, arrived at Plante's in November 1859 as part of an expedition scoping a wagon road. "The scenery about here is beautiful, we are within a few hundred yds. of the Spokane River," he wrote in his diary. "Plante told me that very little snow fell here during the winter and that he had all of his crops in before the end of March, he has a great many fat horses and cattle."

"About the fattest cattle I ever saw were at Antone Plant's place," wrote Elizabeth Ann Coonc, who came through in 1864.

"The ferry at the Spokane is a good one, consisting of a strong cable stretched across the river, and a boat forty feet long," wrote John Mullan, the builder of the Mullan Road, which crossed at Plante's ferry; "it is kept by a very worthy man, Antoine Plant . . . who speaks both French and English."

A monument explains the site's history, but the landscape tells the story too. Ruts from the old Mullan Road lead northeast from the ferry site. Literally beating the bushes with knowledgeable companions, I found a cement post that had replaced the old wooden ferry post marking the main landing. Here is where the forty-foot barge propelled by river current and guided by cable carried wagons, people, and animals.

Across the river, on the south side, the approach to the ferry is visible as an indentation between two trees, including one with a triple trunk. To the north is the corral area where remnants of fencing have been found. Down a dirt road off of Upriver Road, the original planks of Antoine Plante's home are visible in what looks like an old barn.

In December 1855, the new territorial governor, Isaac Stevens, convened a council of Colville, Spokane, and Isle des Pierres Indians at Plante's farm. Stevens had completed treaty signing conferences in Montana, which was then part of Washington Territory, and at Walla Walla, but the Yakama were at war, and tribes in northeastern Washington had not yet agreed to reservation lines. The governor gathered local leaders, including Catholic missionaries, Chief Spokane Garry, and Angus McDonald, the HBC factor at Fort Colvile. After a three-day council, the northern tribes agreed to remain peaceful but made it clear that Americans should stay south of the Snake River.

This agreement didn't last. In May 1858, miners flooded the Colville Valley, and Lieutenant Colonel Edward J. Steptoe of the U.S. Army crossed the Snake River and marched north in defense of the miners and in pursuit of horse raiders. Eighteen miles south of the Spokane River, Steptoe was forced by local tribes to retreat.

Avenging that defeat a few months later, Colonel George Wright engaged the Spokane Indians at the Battle of Four Lakes in which many were killed by the army's long-range repeating rifles. The next day, September 2, the two forces battled indecisively for fourteen miles on the Spokane Plains, moving north from the modern Fairchild Air Force Base to the river. Wright's men rested for a day on a flat plateau as the Indians withdrew. The next day, Wright's troops moved eastward up the Spokane Valley, burning winter storehouses of wheat, oats, vegetables, camas root, and dried berries.

Then, in the distance, Wright's men saw a huge cloud of dust. Young Indian herders were trying to move a large band of horses away from the army, toward an opening in the hills. Wright captured and corralled the horses in a natural bowl bounded on one side by the Spokane River and on two sides by bluffs. He encamped for two days, kept 100 of the horses for the army, and slaughtered the rest, about 690 horses. The destruction of the Indians' wealth and means of travel secured the Spokane Valley for American settlement.

Several years after this conflict, Plante's toll ferry stopped running when Isaac Kellogg built a free bridge over the river a short distance upstream. As Plante and his family moved back to Montana, the new bridge spawned a town, Spokane Bridge. Farther west, the settlement of Spokane Falls used water power from "the great falls," the site of a major Coeur d'Alene fishery, to propel the town's growth. In the late 1880s, the Northern Pacific Railroad made Spokane Falls into the city of Spokane, a railroad hub of the Inland Empire.

Near the end of the Centennial Trail in Washington, two miles from the Idaho border, is Horse Slaughter Camp. A commemorative marker at the west end of the Washington State Patrol weigh station marks the long flat area between I-90 and the Spokane River as the site of the slaughter. The bluff to the south formed the natural bowl that Wright's men used as a corral to fire volleys into the milling herd. One soldier called the shooting "the most repulsive duty" of his ten years in the army. Bone piles from the slaughter were noticeable for years. Here on this quiet, grassy spot, the wealth of the local Indians was destroyed. A different era of wealth began, as signaled by the never-ending traffic on I-90 as it cuts through the bowl.

33

Cariboo Trail

GETTING THERE: From Highway 97, just north of milepost 310 and the bridge over the Okanogan River, turn east on Janis Road, which becomes McLaughlin Canyon Road. In .3 mile, McLaughlin Canyon Road goes left. Two miles up the road is the marker. Before the marker is an old wagon road/trail on the south side of the road. Find the trail just east of a wooden corral and parking area on the north side.

DISTANCE: 1 mile one way

LEVEL OF DIFFICULTY: easy

HISTORICAL HIGHLIGHTS: McLoughlin Canyon, site of ambush

David McLoughlin stood six feet tall and weighed well over 200 pounds. He was one of three sons of Dr. John McLoughlin, the Hudson's Bay Company's chief factor at Fort Vancouver, and McLoughlin's *meti* wife Marguerite Wadin. Living on a cultural frontier, McLoughlin gave his son a European education and primed him for the fur trade. When he returned from abroad to trap furs, however, the younger McLoughlin developed a taste for gold, reportedly accumulating $20,000 in gold dust in just five months in California.

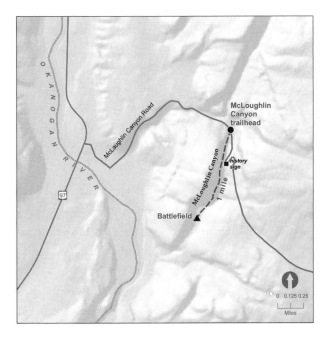

Then the gold frontier moved north to the Cariboo region of Canada. Eighteen thousand miners and camp followers streamed toward rumors of fantastic quantities of gold along the Fraser River. Most argonauts traveled across Canada by way of Victoria, but McLoughlin organized a party of 160 that would cross Indian lands in Washington Territory. Knowing that they might be challenged, McLoughlin sought safety in numbers; at least half of his group was armed.

About July 20, McLoughlin's party left old Fort Nez Perce, at the mouth of the Snake River, with 450 mules. They followed a corridor that had been used for centuries and was well known to his father's company. Fur brigades with 100 to 300 pack horses, carrying 180 to 200 pounds each, had traveled this stretch for twenty years, sometimes to the sound of the bagpipes. The trail crossed the Saddle Mountains, the Moses Coulee, and the Sun Lakes area and headed north.

The Colville and Spokane Indians had not yet signed the 1850s treaties or agreed to live on reservations. A U.S. Army force under Colonel Edward J. Steptoe had marched into the Colville Valley in May in an unsuccessful attempt to protect the miners. Two months later, tensions were high. A large wooden sign on a dirt road above McLoughlin Canyon acknowledges that tension: "Upset by an increasing flow of miners heading for British Columbia goldfields, Indians lay in ambush the length of this canyon."

For several days, McLoughlin's group knew that Indians were watching their progress. One man had the unfortunate habit of taking too long getting himself and his pack organized in the mornings. He had been warned several times about the folly of lingering behind. When the pack train left without him one morning, he never caught up. He was killed by Indians from the Wenatchee and Moses tribes at a place below Coulee City now known as Dead Man's Spring.

Continuing north, the miners crossed the Columbia River near present-day Bridgeport and passed Fort Okanogan, established by

McLoughlin Canyon on the Cariboo Trail.

American fur traders. This stretch of the trail was first known as the Okanogan Trail because it followed the flat valley of the Okanogan River, sometimes on the east side, sometimes on the west side. South of present-day Tonasket, however, steep rock walls come right down to the river's east side, and pack trains could not squeeze by.

When the miners' large party reached this narrow point in mid-morning, they stopped, noting many footprints in the sand and gravel. A James McLaughlin was then in charge of the group (which explains the spelling of the road), but an advance guard under David McLoughlin veered off from the river, looking for passage through a canyon that gradually ascended the highlands to the east.

From the sign at a curve in McLaughlin Canyon Road, look down on that canyon, a slit in the earth between two towering rock walls. Notice the canyon's rocky western walls, which are devoid of any natural camouflage. Notice any refrigerators or rusty cars tossed over the side; they will help locate the sign from the canyon below.

To walk through the canyon, walk or drive back down the road to a rare shady interlude with trees on both sides of the road. Here an old wagon road, blocked by a big stone, leads into the canyon. Stay in the ruts, and watch out for rattlesnakes and poison ivy along the sides and in the middle of the road. The walk through the canyon is cooled by the high rock walls on both sides and a lovely smell of pine. The path goes through some fenced areas, but the walkway itself is open; the point below the sign comes at about the second gate. The path comes out of the mouth of the canyon into an open area, with barbed wire and a closed gate blocking the south end, from which the miners approached.

On July 29 there were 200 of the Chelan, Okanagon, and Columbia tribes waiting throughout this mile-long canyon, armed with flintlock rifles. Chief Moses planned the attack to avenge the death of Quil-tin-e-nock, a Yakama warrior killed in a raid on other miners. The Indians had placed a barricade of trees along the north end of the canyon and hidden themselves behind rocks, on ledges, and along the canyon's rim. The ambush would begin when the miners were well into the trap.

The advance party rode slowly into the deepening canyon, past boulders and sparse tree cover on the sides, and one of the company, Francis Wolff, left an account of what happened next: "We entered the mouth with the guard in advance and had proceeded about 100 yards when one of the men noticed some wilted bushes and thinking strange of it went to examine them."

"The Indians . . . suspecting that we had noticed their ambush fired, then shots came from the sides and in rear of us, evidently trying to drive us into the canyon," Wolff recounted. An exchange of gunfire lasted several hours, but because the firing had started prematurely, only a few miners died. Three were killed in the canyon and buried the next day, their graves marked by cairns. Others were carried away as the miners backed out of the canyon.

The number of Indians killed is unknown, although Narcise Nicholson, Sr., the son of one of the attackers, said he had heard there were "many Indians killed. Nobody knows how many." Wolff wrote in his recollections, "We do not think we Killed any of the Indians," but he crossed out the sentence.

That night as the Indians set fire to the grass along the ridgelines, the miners built rafts. They crossed to the west side of the Okanagan at daybreak and continued with their wounded to the border, reaching the Fraser River after a journey of thirty days.

Later that summer, Colonel Wright won the Battle of Four Lakes near present-day Spokane, then executed two Indian leaders and slaughtered Indian horses. Major R. S. Garnett made a sweep through the Okanogan area, looking for any of the Indians who had attacked McLoughlin, but he found no one to punish. As miners and cattle drives pounded the path along the Okanogan River, it became known as the Cariboo Trail, after the goldfields it led to. Undeterred by the conflict or by Indian claims, miners and cattle poured north on the Cariboo Trail until the last drive in 1868.

The encounter in the Okanogan Valley is still remembered as an intended massacre. As I searched along railroad tracks for the point where the advance guard must have left the river, a local property owner warned me away. Almost 150 years later, he spoke with bitterness of the attack.

Now Highway 97 and a railroad follow the Okanogan River through the same land, which is still used for cattle ranching but is also dotted with orchards. A large wooden sign just past Malott claims that the 800-mile long Cariboo Trail was just as important as the better-known Chisholm Trail in Texas. There is little else to mark the route: no wagon ruts or hundred-year-old hoofprints, just a sense that many animals could pass this way if railroad tracks, highways, and barbed wire fences hadn't claimed the same path.

34

Columbia Peak

GETTING THERE: Take Highway 20 to Sherman Pass (28 miles east of Republic and 23 miles west of Kettle Falls). From the sign for the Kettle Crest Trail, drive north a short distance on a dirt road to the parking area. The trail crosses the road right before the parking area. A Forest Service trail pass is required.

DISTANCE: 3.5 miles one way

LEVEL OF DIFFICULTY: moderate

HISTORICAL HIGHLIGHTS: lookout cabin

In the early 1900s, devastating fires, such as the Yacolt Burn of 1902 (see chapter 5), convinced federal, state, and private timber companies to construct a vast network of fire lookout stations. At the system's peak, there were 5,000 lookouts nationwide, including 685 in

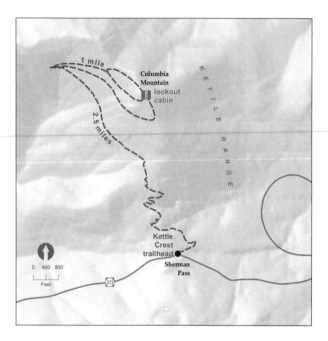

Washington. From Five Fingers in the North Cascades to Oregon Butte in the Blue Mountains of southeastern Washington, men and women in the lonely outposts were the first to spot fires. They were also the first line of defense, fighting fires with only a shovel, a pick, and their own strong backs. When fire detection methods switched to aerial reconnaissance, many of the lookouts were dismantled or burned to remove an attractive nuisance. Washington now has 105 lookouts still standing, with only thirty of those in active use. Columbia Peak in the Kettle range is the site of the oldest existing Forest Service cabin not still in use.

This Kettle Crest Trail begins high at Sherman Pass. Columbia Mountain is the first peak to the north. The trail winds along the west side of the mountain for about two miles to a junction with Trail 24, which cuts diagonally back along the shoulder of the mountain, forming a one-mile loop. A spur trail to the top comes three-quarters of the way around the loop going southeast, or one-

A lookout cabin outlasted the tower at Columbia Peak.

quarter of the way going northwest. It's marked only by a post with no sign.

From the spur trail, climb to reach the highest point. Just north of the summit are the remains of a stone wall shelter that served as the original lookout in 1912. The lookouts on Columbia and Mount Bonaparte, thirty miles away, were built in 1914. They were designed by forest supervisor C. C. Reed so that the live-in cabin was below the tower. Made out of hand-hewn logs, the cabin walls slanted inward at the top. The platform tower rose fifteen feet above the roof. When such cabins were replaced by live-in towers in the 1930s, the towers on Bonaparte and Columbia were simply sawed off at the roofline, and the cabins remained.

The cabin has a corrugated iron roof, a wood floor, a door, three windows, pine boughs on the floor, a rusted stovepipe venting through the roof, and names and dates carved inside. The remains of the tower lie a bit farther, on the highest knob. Relax here and scan the skies in all directions. In two centuries, the most valued resources in this northeastern region have changed from salmon and fur to bunchgrass and gold to electricity, lumber, and uranium. From this viewpoint, however, little has changed.

CHAPTER EIGHT

Southeastern Washington

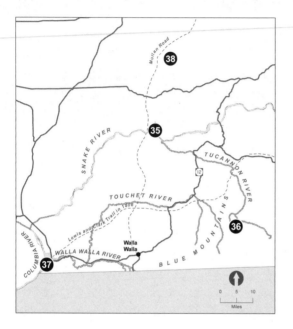

At Palouse Falls State Park, birds perch on the water spigots, waiting patiently for a drop. The breezy, watered camping and picnic areas and the sound of the falls are also a relief to the people who live in this dry corner of Washington. Travelers through this region etched trails that went from spring to spring along ancient channels, following the course of rivers: the Snake and Walla Walla flowing east to west, the Touchet and Tucannon providing respite along their banks. Travelers avoided, if they could, the coulees, the scablands, and the mountains—evidences of dramatic upheavals in the land.

For at least 10,000 years, ancestors of the Nez Perce, Palouse,

Cayuse, and Walla Walla people crossed the land. They moved freely, hunting, fishing, digging roots, and gathering berries. They used first dogs and then horses to carry their goods on the frame of a travois, a trailer with long poles extending from a harness or saddle. Several Nez Perce bands, including Chief Joseph's, had winter villages along the Snake and the Grande Ronde rivers. Beyond their homelands at the intersection of Washington, Idaho, and Oregon, they traded east and west, using the Chinook trade jargon with coastal tribes or sign language with the Plains Indians.

In their seasonal migrations, the Nez Perce carved three major trails. Two went across Idaho's Bitterroot Mountains into buffalo country. The third trail, in Washington, led west, down the rapids of the Snake to its mouth at the Columbia, and down the Columbia to Celilo Falls, the great fishing and trading emporium of the Northwest Indians. Coming back from the falls, the Nez Perce avoided the Snake's upstream currents by going overland. They followed the valleys of the Walla Walla and Touchet rivers, then went up Patit Creek, crossed a ridge, and descended to the Snake. After years of being pulled back and forth, the travois poles wore a wide, rutted swath.

When Lewis and Clark crossed the continent from 1804 to 1806, their Corps of Discovery followed the routes worn by the Nez Perce. They camped with Native Americans at the confluence of the Snake and Columbia rivers and followed their advice to take canoes down the rivers and return overland. Fur traders, missionaries, and settlers followed. The Oregon Trail channeled immigrants south of the Columbia River, but a branch came out of the Blue Mountains to the station established by Protestant missionaries Marcus and Narcissa Whitman at Waiilatpu near what is now Walla Walla.

As more settlers moved in, a weathered string of dusty towns spun out along the Nez Perce Trail between Walla Walla and Clarkston, along today's Highway 12. The U.S. military sent an expedition to build a road from the confluence of the Snake and Columbia rivers, through the Palouse country, into Idaho. Walla Walla became the prime city of Washington Territory in the 1860s.

Only remnants of the old Nez Perce Trail are visible today; highways have covered the paths, and farmers and ranchers have claimed and fenced the fields. This chapter finds figurative footprints in places reclaimed as public, such as the Wallowa-Tucannon Wilderness. It shadows Harlen Bretz, a geologist who wandered all over the Channeled Scablands; Paul Kane, an artist who traveled and sketched; Chief Joseph and his band as they crossed the Blue Mountains; and Lewis and Clark as they embarked down the Columbia. The last hike invokes the mule packers and stagecoach drivers who fanned out from Walla Walla along the Mullan Road, which still leads off over fields and scablands.

35

Palouse Canyon

GETTING THERE: Drive State Road 261 to the north side of the Snake River crossing and the day-use area of Lyons Ferry State Park. The trail is at the north end of the park. Palouse Falls State Park is farther north on Highway 261.

DISTANCE: .75 to 1 mile one way

LEVEL OF DIFFICULTY: a moderate climb

HISTORICAL HIGHLIGHTS: gravesite of Chief Old Bones; view of Marmes Man site and Palouse Canyon

The canyons and rolling hills of the Channeled Scablands, land that is healing from calamity, have attracted both artists and geologists. The Irish Canadian artist Paul Kane was inspired by George Caitlin

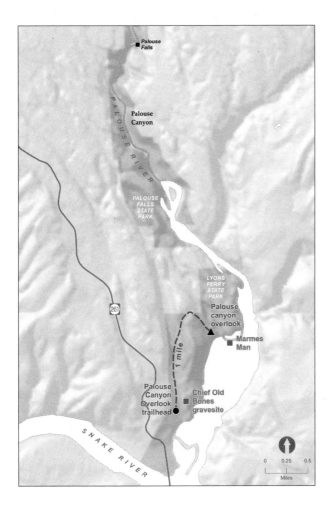

to document the life of Native Americans in the Pacific Northwest. He spent most of two years, from 1846 to 1847, sketching many different tribes, collecting artifacts, and recording his travels in a journal. Later Kane would use the pipe stems, masks, and other items to elaborate on his sketches in oil paintings.

On his travels from Walla Walla, Kane met Palouse chief Slo-ce-ac-cum where the Snake and Palouse rivers converge. Slo-ce-ac-cum sat for a portrait and was so pleased with the result that he told Kane about a falls on the Palouse that no white man had ever seen. The chief said he would conduct Kane up the bed of the river, as it was sufficiently shallow for horses.

"I accepted his proposal, and rode eight or ten miles through a wild and savage gorge, composed of dark brown basaltic rocks, heaped in confusion one upon another to the height of 1000 and 1500 feet, sometimes taking the appearance of immense ruins in the distance," Kane wrote.

Slo-ce-ac-cum left Kane at Palouse Falls, where Kane sketched and then spent two more days drawing "the surrounding magnificent scenes" farther up the river. He could have stayed longer. "I was anxious to have remained in this neighbourhood for a week or ten days longer, to have made some more sketches of the curious and strange region in which I found myself," Kane wrote, but his guide was eager to return to his wife, "of whom he was jealous."

The Lower Monumental Dam, built on the Snake River in 1968, has changed the contours of the landscape enough that riding a horse through shallow water up Palouse Canyon is no longer possible. However, both Palouse Falls State Park and Lyons Ferry State Park provide overlooks of this wild and savage gorge.

At Palouse Falls, trails lead off along railroad tracks and the steep cliffs of the Channeled Scablands, which mystified geologist J Harlen Bretz. While teaching at a Seattle high school, Bretz was intrigued by the potholes and the large Dry Falls he observed just south of Grand Coulee. He wondered why there were granite rocks, called glacial erratics, sitting in the middle of fields and looking nothing like the basalt rocks around them. When Bretz began teaching at the University of Chicago in the 1920s, he returned to eastern Washington in the summers. His wife and two children came along in a Dodge sedan with a grub box on the back, bedrolls strapped to the side, and an umbrella tent and poles on the front bumper. Bretz walked as many as forty miles a day, trying to understand the pattern of the strange rolling hills.

Water was the only force that could have carved the channels, he concluded. Bretz wrote papers on his theory that 3,000 square miles of the Columbia Plateau had been swept by a glacial flood. All he lacked was an explanation of where the sudden rush had come from. Not until 1940 did another geologist, Joseph T. Pardee, describe glacial Lake Missoula, with its tendency to burst through ice dams and cascade across the land west of it. These Spokane floods occurred a number of times, and the latest, 12,000 to 14,000 years ago, released more than 500 cubic miles of water in less than two weeks—in some places flowing more than seventy miles an hour. This last flood created the Channeled Scablands.

The size of the basalt curve over which the Palouse River falls provides more evidence of the floods. The reader board has a faded article about Bretz, but the Dry Falls Interpretive Center (south of Banks Lake) provides a more detailed account of his work. The board also relates an alternative explanation for the texture of the canyon's walls: Coyote chased Beaver down the canyon, and Beaver left his claw marks on the walls.

Return to the confluence of the Palouse, Snake, and Tucannon rivers at Lyons Ferry State Park, where Kane met Slo-ce-ac-cum. At the north end, a short hike climbs a lava rampart for 400 feet to an overlook of this historic crossroads. Everyone who was anyone in the nineteenth-century Northwest came to Palus, Slo-ce-ac-cum's village and the ancestral home of the Palouse Indians. Meriwether Lewis and William Clark's Corps of Discovery came down the Snake River in October 1805. A little below the mouth of the Palouse River they found "a large fishing-establishment, where are the scaffolds and timbers of several houses piled up against each other." The villagers were downriver that day, fishing and visiting other villages.

Spurred by Lewis and Clark's reports of beaver, members of the American-backed Pacific Fur Company came through in 1812 on their way to Spokane River country. Missionaries Elkanah Walker and Myron Eells bought potatoes and salmon from the villagers in 1838, and Henry Spalding and Marcus Whitman scouted the loca-

The Mullan Road approached the Snake River at Lyons Ferry.

tion as a possible mission site. An exploring party from the Wilkes Expedition crossed the river in 1841. Then Paul Kane sketched, John Mullan built a road, and Harlen Bretz explained the damaged land.

Follow the trail another 950 feet to the reburied remains of Palus people and remains recovered from a cemetery at the mouth of the Tucannon River. The most prominent grave is that of Chief Old Bones, who died in 1916 at the age of eighty-nine. During his boyhood, people in his village had talked about the visit of Lewis and Clark. The captains had given important Indian leaders Jefferson Peace Medals inscribed with the message "Peace and Friendship." One of the rare medals was discovered here in 1964. It had been buried with an unidentified adult male in a dugout canoe between 1900 and 1915, about the time of the Lewis and Clark centennial. The Nez Perce asked Washington State University for the medal and has now reburied it.

A quarter of a mile beyond the overlook, watch for the Marmes Man diggings. After the great floods, people lived in rock shelters along canyon walls. In the 1960s, WSU scientists found human remains in a small, shallow cave in the canyon walls of the Roland

Marmes ranch. Radiocarbon dating indicated that the remains went back more than 13,000 years—the oldest in the Western Hemisphere at the time of discovery. Seventeen burials were eventually revealed at the site, as well as weapon points, bone needles, olivella shells, and an amulet made from an owl's claw. Engineers building the Lower Monumental Dam on the Snake River tried to protect the diggings with a coffer dam, but the dam leaked, and most of the artifacts now lie deeply flooded.

Return to the river for more waves of change. Most early travelers crossed the river on horseback or by holding on to a horse's tail, but the Indians also used a canoe-and-rope technique to ferry goods. Then steamboats came up the Snake and unloaded goods in a large warehouse at the mouth of the Tucannon River. From this settlement freight wagons carried goods to towns along the Nez Perce Trail. Hub-deep ruts are visible where the wagons came down to the river. The Mullan Road and the Colville Road from Fort Walla Walla to Fort Colvile in northeastern Washington passed through here too.

Lyon's Ferry operated from 1944 to 1968 and took passengers and livestock across the Snake River, just downstream from the mouth of the Palouse, using the current to push the boat along a cable from one side to the other. Remains of this dock are still visible in the park. Today the Union Pacific crosses the river high above, on an impressive trestle (the Joso Bridge), but state parks have replaced commerce at this ancient confluence.

36

Chief Joseph's Summer Trail

GETTING THERE: To the Panjab trailhead: 13 miles east of Dayton, on Highway 12, turn south on the Tucannon River Road for 33 miles. Where

Tucannon and Panjab creeks flow together, take Road 4713 for 3 miles to the trailhead.

To the Mount Misery Trail: Take County Road 128 south from Pomeroy for approximately 10 miles. At the Y, continue straight on to Mountain Road 40, entering the Umatilla National Forest. Continue on Road 40 for 17 miles and turn right on Road 4030, following it a rugged 5 miles to the trailhead.

DISTANCE: Panjab Trail (3127), 5.6 miles to Indian Corral; Mount Misery Trail (3113), 13 miles to Indian Corral

LEVEL OF DIFFICULTY: difficult; 2,700-foot elevation gain on the Panjab Trail

HISTORICAL HIGHLIGHTS: Indian Corral; sheep camps

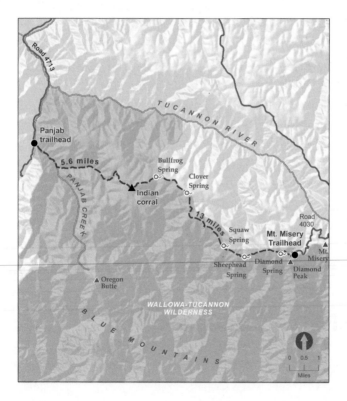

"Indian Corral"—these two words burned on a sign on a fir tree evoke the Nez Perces' use of the mountainous land along the Washington-Oregon border. I spent parts of three summers scouting this legendary place. In the remote Wenaha-Tucannon Wilderness, it is possible to walk Chief Joseph's Summer Trail in silence, admire the wildflowers, cool off at the springs, and encounter no one but elk and foxes. It's no wonder the Nez Perce cherished this land.

During the winter, Chief Joseph's Wallowa band stayed in the lower Grande Ronde Valley, but during the spring, summer, and fall, they roamed the Blue Mountains. In the spring, they gathered where Fields Spring State Park is now to dig kouse, the first root of the season. In June they moved livestock higher up the mountains to graze. Early in July, after the snow had melted, camas bloomed in the high country. As the camas matured for harvest in August, the Nez Perce moved to the ridges.

Joseph's band came up Smoothing Iron Ridge from the east. Reaching Wickiup Springs, they went around Mount Misery and on to the high prairies. What became known as Chief Joseph's Summer Trail passed through the best huckleberry country with wonderful deer and elk hunting and some of the best fishing streams. According to Gerald Tucker, a forest ranger of the 1930s, the Indians traveled from spring to spring, staying long enough for the women to gather the roots. As the men hunted elk and deer, the women tanned hides and dried the meat. At Indian Corral, they stayed to gossip, smoke, gamble, and race.

Two trails reach the corral today, one shorter, the other more historically authentic. The Panjab Trail comes from the west side of the wilderness, from the Tucannon River, and reaches the high meadows in 5.6 miles. The Mount Misery Trail follows the Nez Perce route from the east side, over Diamond Peak, reaches high country quickly, then stretches along the ridges twelve miles to Indian Corral.

Mount Misery was named by pioneers. Bishop Norbet Blanchet

noted that many American families coming over the Blue Mountains had "suffered dreadful miseries," traveling hundreds of miles on the Oregon Trail, crossing the Rockies, and then facing mountains like this one. The one-lane dirt road clinging to the mountainside was partially built by the Civilian Conservation Corps in 1933 and still drives like a partially built road.

The Mount Misery Trail climbs one mile to Diamond Peak, then follows ridgetops from spring to spring: Diamond, Basque, Sheephead, Squaw, Bear Wallow, Clover, and Bullfrog. Most are marked by signs. In the late 1800s, large herds of sheep grazed around these springs, driven from the small settlements of Pomeroy or Alpowa and up a sheep "driveway" to their summer ranges. A Frank Jackson grazed 2,000 ewes and uncounted lambs at Indian Corral and Squaw Spring. An R. A. Jackson kept 9,000 ewes in the Oregon Butte and Panjab areas. The men sold wool to buyers from as far away as Wyoming and shipped fat lambs to Chicago by rail.

Despite thousands of hooves in these meadows, Forest Service rangers report that arrowheads have been found at some of the springs. Plenty of other human evidence remains: remnants of wooden corrals, trampled grass, logs for sitting, old campfires, and even a couple of carved tree chairs, with both a seat and a back. At Clover Spring cold water flows out of a pipe into a trough for horses. On a hot, sunny day, it works for dipping bandanas too.

From these camps, Nez Perce women gathered camas bulbs "by dint of long and painful labor," according to Pierre Jean De Smet, an early Catholic missionary. "The women arm themselves with long, crooked sticks, to go in search of the camash," he wrote. He described the camas as "abundant, and, I may say . . . the queen root of this clime. It is a small, white, vapid onion, when removed from the earth, but becomes black and sweet when prepared for food." Gathering roots and berries required a knowledge of the seasons when each food source ripened and the ability to recognize what was edible.

The Nez Perce men were good horsemen and measured their wealth by the number of horses they owned. Wild horses roamed the area, including more than 500 on Smoothing Iron Ridge, until, beginning in 1901, an outbreak of mountain fever killed thousands of wild and domestic horses. Although the Indians also had some cattle, they were best at raising the horses that grazed on abundant fields of bunchgrass.

Without a horse, Indian Corral is a long slog from the Mount Misery trailhead, but the shorter Panjab Trail reaches the sign in about three hours. From the west, the trail climbs along Panjab Creek for three miles. (At the one-mile fork, follow the sign to Diamond Peak.) For two miles it heads away from the creek and up to the ridge, coming out of the woods and onto a mountain meadow for the last half mile.

On this high, vast meadow, with views south toward Oregon and the rolling ranges of the Blue Mountains, the Indians gathered in great numbers. Many trails come together here, marked by a wooden sign in the meadow. Chief Joseph's Trail led south three miles to Oregon Butte, where it split in two directions, one route going east toward Asotin on the Snake River, and one south along the Wenaha River to Wallowa.

Just beyond this weathered intersection stood the fir tree with the "Indian Corral" sign. To contain the horses, the Indians formed a rough corral of stones. Horses with unshod hooves tended to avoid the rocks and thus stay inside. Many of the scattered rocks here could be remnants of the corral, but the sign itself disappeared after the extensive fires of 2007, long after Nez Perce life had changed.

When settlers brought wagons over Mount Misery in 1859, they built homes along the shaded banks of creeks and rivers. Since the cottonwood trees that lined the creeks were of poor quality for building, settlers followed the ridges into what is now the Umatilla National Forest and cut the sturdier tamarack (western larch), which provided long, straight poles and rails for fencing. Levi

Watrous's sawmill on the North Touchet River, near the mouth of Jim Creek, turned the timber into a crop. He and his son Henry cut trees on the top of Cahill Mountain, which was covered with ponderosa pine, then sent the logs flying down the mountain in a deep trench they had dug. Henry walked thirty-five miles beside an ox team to transport the logs to Walla Walla, the early hub of commerce in the region.

The Nez Perce welcomed the newcomers and traded with them. When they traveled to the mountains, they stayed on Levi Waltrous's place. Chief Joseph (Tu-e-ka-kas) converted to Christianity and was given a Christian name by missionary Henry Spalding. Spalding once rode 100 miles from Lapwai to Alpowa to treat Joseph for a fever. The first treaty with the Nez Perce, in 1855, preserved the summer trail, but as more settlers moved in, the range where the Nez Perce ponies had grazed was overtaken by cattle and sheep. Gold discoveries in Idaho in the 1860s made cattle raising profitable and caused a clamor for more Nez Perce land. Old Joseph refused to sign a treaty that would have reduced the reservation to one tenth of its original size and ignored orders to move onto the new reservation.

Young Joseph, who succeeded his father, also did not want to leave his homelands in the Blue Mountains, but in 1877, young warriors who were angry at the pressure to move killed some white settlers, and the Nez Perce took flight, pursued by the cavalry. That journey ended in Montana, just miles from the Canadian border, where Young Joseph conceded, "I will fight no more forever." Thereafter, the Nez Perce were confined to reservations in Oregon, Idaho, and Oklahoma (where Joseph was sent). In 1895 the Nez Perce reservation in Asotin County was dissolved, then a series of government actions reclaimed the land for public use.

After heavy grazing on the prairies, the bunchgrass that "once clothed the hills with waving beauty" was gone by 1940, according to Tucker, who wrote a history of the forest. Wild animals on the slopes were also endangered. In 1806 Lewis and Clark had met an

Indian named Weahkoonut who wore the horn of a bighorn sheep on his arm. More than 100 years later, the hunting of deer, elk, and mountain sheep was still popular. When the population of elk dwindled, more were imported by train from Montana.

President Teddy Roosevelt, both a hunter and a conservationist, reserved the Wenaha Forest, in 1905, which eventually became part of the Umatilla National Forest. The state of Washington then created a state game range, which became a Wildlife Recreation Area and forced those living on the upper Tucannon River to sell their land. The Endangered American Wilderness Act designated the Wenaha-Tucannon Wilderness in 1978. A high meadow once teeming with people, horses, and sheep returned to wilderness, and so I once ate my lunch near the Indian Corral tree, witnessing only the bugling of elks and the flash of a fox.

37

Twin Sisters/Two Captains

GETTING THERE: The marker, rocks, and small parking area are on the south side of U.S. Highway 730. From the west, the parking area is at milepost 4. From the east, it is 1.9 miles from the intersection with U.S. Highway 12. Watch out for trucks coming around the bend as you exit the parking area.

DISTANCE: .25 to .5 mile one way

LEVEL OF DIFFICULTY: steep with loose footing, and sandy and flat

HISTORICAL HIGHLIGHTS: views of Wallula Gap, and Lewis and Clark camp sites

On October 18, 1805, Meriwether Lewis, William Clark, and the Corps of Discovery embarked on the last miles of their eighteen-

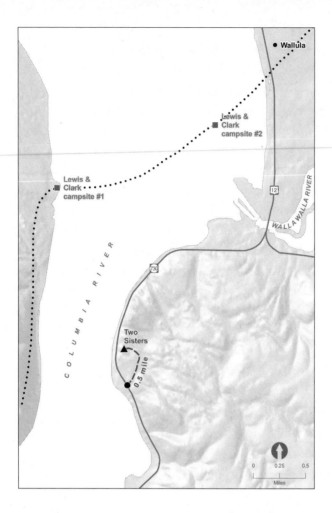

month journey to the Pacific. After crossing into present-day Washington, where Clarkston marks the spot, they had been making rapid time on the Snake River. For two days they had been camped with several hundred Indians gathered at the confluence of the Snake and Columbia rivers at the end of the annual salmon migration. After an exchange of smokes, the Corps and tribes traded dances into the night, with the Indians drumming and the Corps men jigging to tunes played on a violin. The Corps handed out Jefferson Peace Medals to the Wanapum and Yakama chiefs. Leaving the grand gathering refreshed and replenished, the Corps pushed off, hoping the Great River of the West would speed them to the Pacific.

Although brown and white signs mark the "Lewis and Clark Trail" on highways in southern Washington, and although there are state parks and markers for various campsites, there is no foot trail to follow. The expedition's 1805 journey was mainly on water; the Celilo trail they followed on the return trip in 1806 is now largely obscured on fenced, private property. The traveler wanting to follow Lewis and Clark must either book passage on a barge down the Snake and Columbia rivers or settle for an auto-stop tour. However, a short hike at Wallula Gap samples the journey.

Sixteen miles from the confluence of the Snake and Columbia rivers, after the Walla Walla River flows in from the east, the Corps canoed through water, "bordered with black rugid rocks." This was Wallula Gap, where cliffs forced the Columbia to bend west in its final run to the ocean. Along the eastern shore rose two basalt pillars, standing sentinel to the journey.

The artist Paul Kane noted the same pillars in his 1847 journey up the Columbia River. "As we approached the place where the Walla-Walla debouches into the Columbia river, we came in sight of two extraordinary rocks projecting from a high steep cone or mound about 700 feet above the level of the river. These are called by the voyageurs the Chimney Rocks. . . . The Walla-Walla Indians call these the 'Rocks of the Ki-use [Cayuse] girls.'"

Kane related a Walla Walla tradition that explains the pillars: The great medicine wolf of the Columbia River fell in love with three beautiful sisters who were carrying stones into the river to make a rapid, to catch the salmon when they leapt over it. For three days the wolf secretly watched their operations and destroyed their work each night. On the fourth morning, he saw the girls weeping on the bank, and on inquiring what was the matter, they told him that they were starving, as they could get no fish for want of a dam. He then proposed to erect a dam for them, if they would consent to

Two Sisters stand sentinel above the Columbia River at Wallula Gap.

become his wives, to which they consented sooner than perish from want of food. For a long time he lived happily with the three sisters, but at length the wolf became jealous of his wives, and, using his supernatural power, changed two of them into basalt pillars on the south side of the river, and then changed himself into a large rock on the north side, so that he might watch them ever afterward. The third wife he turned into a cave downstream.

In geological terms, the pillars are remnants of a lava flood more than 15 million years earlier. For a view of the gap and the sweep of the land leading west, climb the short trails to the rocks. You must clamber over a barbed wire fence on a wooden stile, then ascend to a fork in the trail. Two trails to the left climb steeply to a point between the rocks from which you can see the Columbia reaching north and southwest before you, much wider than it was in the early 1800s because of the river's many dams. Islands in the river where the Corps saw Indian lodges are now under water.

The other trail leads around the back and through sand dunes to a small mesa. The sand is geographically disorienting. Where did it come from? Kane said the sand was "a frightful feature of this barren waste. . . . the salmon also becomes filled with sand to such an extent as to wear away the teeth of the Indians, and an Indian is seldom met with over 40 years of age whose teeth are not worn quite to the gums." The wind coming through the Wallula Gap was also hard on the Indians' eyes. Lewis and Clark tried to treat them with eye water, a combination of zinc sulfate and lead acetate. When the river was undammed, wind blew the sand from its many islands, creating sand and gravel bars across the land, but that sand no longer blows, and the dunes are revegetating.

In the evening, the Corps camped three miles below the two pillars, in "a range of high Countrey at which place the rocks project into the river from the high cliffs." In recording the day's travels, Lewis and Clark made no mention of the formations, but later chroniclers called the pillars the Two Captains. The official name is the Twin Sisters, according to the U.S. Board of Geographic Names.

When they returned from the coast in May 1806, the expedition came down from the Horse Heaven Hills on horseback and crossed the Columbia just north of Wallula Gap. Camping on both sides of the now wider river, they stopped again to enjoy the hospitality of the Indians. Chief Yelleppit of the Walla Walla presented Clark with a white horse. He also recommended that the corps take the Nez Perce overland trail to save eighty miles and to avoid the tough upstream currents of the Snake.

Following the trail made by travois ruts, Lewis and Clark went northeast along the Walla Walla River, west of Ninemile Canyon, and followed the Touchet River. They crossed the river opposite the mouth of Patit Creek, at a place called "the Crossing" (which later became Dayton). Here they found "considerable quantities of quamish [camas]," which they did not know how to cook, and "killed nothing but a duck" to feed the thirty-three people in the party.

Going upstream, they followed Patit Creek, whose name may come from the French *petit,* "small." They crossed the Tucannon River near the cabin of Louis Raboin, a French fur trapper who married an Indian woman. Continuing across the southeastern corner of today's Washington, Lewis and Clark crossed high plains and followed Pataha Creek in foul weather "for a disagreeable journey of 28 miles." They ate the last of their provisions during a snow-storm, then reached the Snake the next day, May 4, at the mouth of Alpowa Creek, not far from where they had first camped in Washington. The next day they crossed over into what is now Idaho, and within a few months they were home, rich with tales of the resources of the West.

The land near Wallula Gap has not been one of those resources. The nineteenth-century traveler Caroline Leighton described in her book *Life at Puget Sound* the "cheerless little settlement" of Umatilla City just beyond the bend: "In the midst of a bleak, dreary waste of sand and sage-brush, without a sign of a tree in any direction, a perfect whirlwind blowing all the time. What could induce people to live there, I could not imagine." Few people do. There is no longer a reason to travel this way to reach the great fishing grounds of Celilo Falls, which have been drowned by the Bonneville Dam. Instead of sisters doing the ancient work of trapping salmon, sailboats tack to the wind on the river, trucks roar past the rocks, and industry camps on the shores.

38

Mullan Road

GETTING THERE: From Highway 261, take Washtucna-Benge Road northeast for 17.5 miles; as the road comes into Benge, park near the water tower; the trail is visible nearby.

DISTANCE: 3.5 miles from Benge to Cow Creek overlook

LEVEL OF DIFFICULTY: easy, except for lack of shade and crushed rock surface

HISTORICAL HIGHLIGHTS: Cow Creek Valley, where Colville Road and Mullan Road diverged; stone corral; Mullan campsite

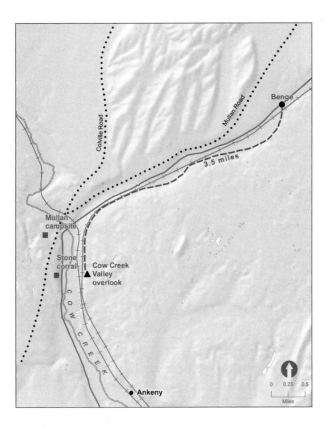

Lieutenant John Mullan, an army engineer, had already discovered a pass through the Rocky Mountains in Idaho, but he had more ambitious goals. Like Lewis and Clark before him, he envisioned an easy connection between waterways across the North American continent, a 600-mile "land bridge" between the head of the Missouri River and Wallula Gap, where the Columbia River lunged to the ocean. Mullan had surveyed for a transcontinental railroad in Washington Territory, so he had a route in mind. The first two hundred miles would cut a diagonal across southeastern Washington, from Walla Walla to Spokane.

Walla Walla was the largest town in the territory in the mid-1800s. When gold was discovered in Idaho, miners rushed over the

Nez Perce Trail. At the height of the mining rushes in the 1860s, 6,000 mules left the Columbia River and Walla Walla in one year, loaded with freight. "There is nothing imaginable, from a bag of oats to a load of crockery, that cannot be securely fastened on the mule's back," wrote one mule packer, James W. Watt. Another packer transported a piano to a "sporting house" in the Coeur d'Alene mining camps, using four mules.

Paths stretched out in all directions from Walla Walla: east to the growing settlements of Dayton, Pomeroy, Almota, Colfax, Lewiston, Fort Hall, Boise, and Salt Lake City; northeast to Colville, Cheney, and Spokane; and west to Wallula, The Dalles, and Portland. The roads were hardly more than ruts. Felix Warren ran a stagecoach line from Almota to Colfax over roads that were "unimproved and almost impossible . . . , ruts deep with dust in midsummer and the same depth of mud in the winter and spring, very few bridges, all streams possible being forded with innumerable . . . dangerous places to overcome."

The region's economy needed better roads, and Mullan had a plan, but funding was scarce, and some tribes in eastern Washington did not want a road through their homeland. A potential boundary dispute with Great Britain provided a military excuse for the road; the army's engagement of Spokane and Palouse Indians at Four Lakes and Spokane Plains dampened native resistance. Mullan left The Dalles in June 1859 with more than 200 men, intent on road building.

Mullan's method was to send out individuals or small parties to select the best route—avoiding swamps, weaving through outcroppings or rocks, finding the best waterway fords, and always choosing the easiest route, which was often the path of ancient floodwaters. Since most of the country was rolling prairie, little actual construction was required—all the men had to do was build the log bridges, blast the rocky stretches, grade, side-hill, and corduroy portions of the road. The route went north from Fort Walla Walla along the road to the Colville gold mines, staying within reach of water for pack animals. The road crossed the Touchet River Valley and then the Snake River. From the mouth of the Palouse, the road continued north along the river, past Palouse Falls, to Cow Creek, twenty-five miles north of the Snake.

Of the 200 miles of the military road that Mullan's crew constructed, only remnants ramble through eastern Washington—on segments of roads, maps, roadside signs, and the stone markers that replaced the cedar posts his crew pounded into the dry soil. The most accessible stretches for hiking are part of the Columbia Plateau Trail. They follow the grade of the Spokane, Portland, and Seattle Railroad, which coincided with parts of the original Mullan Road. One of the richest historical stretches is along the Cow Creek Valley, between Washtucna and Benge.

The Cow Creek Valley has long attracted visitors, some of whom lost themselves in its charms. In August 1812, a trading party from John Jacob Astor's fur company found respite after traveling from 4 a.m. until noon with no water. Arriving "in a small valley of the most delightful verdure, through which ran a clear stream over a pebbly bottom [Cow Creek]," they enjoyed a hearty breakfast. An eighteen-year-old clerk with the company, Ross Cox, wandered some distance along the rivulet. He came to "a sweet little arbor formed by sumach and cherry trees" and fell asleep. When he awoke some time later, the Astorians had left without him.

"All was calm and silent as the grave. . . . Not a vestige of man or horse appeared in the valley. My senses almost failed me. I called out in vain in every direction until I became hoarse. I could no longer conceal from myself the dreadful truth that I was alone in a wild, uninhabited country." Luckily the country was not uninhabited. The Palouse traditionally gathered camas in Washtucna Coulee, southwest of Cow Creek Valley. Cox wandered for thirteen days, eating cherries and searching constantly for water, until two Indian women found him and reunited him with his party.

Mullan camped along Cow Creek on June 6, 1859. He described it in his journal as carrying a small volume of water, "which runs in a very irregular bed with respect to its width. The creek is scantily lined with brushwood intermixed only now and then with a grove of white thorn and cottonwood trees." The road through the valley, he wrote, was much obstructed by little ravines and rocky elevations with steep ascents and descents. Rocky, bare bluffs enclose the valley.

The next day, at Cow Creek's junction with Twelve Mile Creek, Mullan turned away from the Colville road and climbed a bluff 400 feet high, "with great exertions to the animals," and continued on a northeasterly route across high prairies toward Spokane. The road crossed the Spokane River at Plante's Ferry (see Chapter 7) and continued east toward the south end of Lake Coeur d'Alene.

A marker on Washtucna-Benge Road marks Mullan's campsite and more, but to experience Cow Creek Valley on foot, begin in Benge—a small town with a park, grocery store, and water tower— and hike southwest. The Mullan Road was used as a farm-to-market road as late as the 1960s and here runs parallel to Highway 261 as part of the Columbia Plateau Trail.

The trail itself is a wide, level grade, with a crushed rock surface. It straight-lines through pastures, patches of low trees, and surprising wetlands. Sometimes it is elevated above the surrounding fields; sometimes it goes through small rock bluffs; much of the route is through hot, shadeless terrain. Early on a September Sunday, amid the stares of the white-faced cattle, only a distant rooster and birds broke the silence.

After three and a half miles, the active railroad line that runs on a bridge over Washtucna-Benge Road comes into view. Spread below is the north-south expanse of the fertile Cow Creek Valley, still rich with cattle, horses, coyotes, deer, and pheasant in irrigated fields and pastures that rest the eyes today, much as they did for Ross Cox. Traveler and writer Caroline Leighton passed through here on the

Colville/Mullan road in 1884: "To wake up in the clear air, with the bright sky above us, when it was pleasant; and to reach at night the little oases of willows and birches and running streams where we camped,—was enough to repay us for a good deal of discomfort. At one of the camping-grounds—Cow Creek,—a beautiful bird sang all night; it sounded like bubbling water."

Cox heard other sounds, which we experienced too. "The rattlesnakes were very numerous this day, with horned lizards and grasshoppers. The latter kept me in a constant state of feverish alarm from the similarity of the noise made by their wings to the sound of the rattles of the snake when preparing to dart on its prey."

From above, one can see Cow Creek and Twelve-Mile Creek divide, on a farm below, the same place the Mullan Road turned east as Colville Road went north. (A marker on Ralston-Benge Road identifies where Colville Road crossed it.) The marker on Washtuchna-Benge Road is also visible from the trail—but not the fine print, which describes the nearby rock corral, built by George Lucas more than 120 years ago. He had a "stopping place" that was used by travelers. Today, maybe two pickup trucks in one hour barrel along without stopping.

In six months of 1859, Mullan's crew plotted the miles from Fort Walla Walla to their winter headquarters in Montana; the next year they reworked the road on the way back to Walla Walla. Mullan worked on the road again in 1861. Three years in the finishing, the Mullan military road never became the connection Mullan had envisioned. It was used once by a military expedition, then became a stampede trail for miners rushing to the Montana gold fields. Mule packer James Watt made one trip over the road to Montana in 1865. It took thirty-five days to travel from fort to fort with pack strings, fifty days by wagon. Some called it a $200,000 fiasco. Pioneer Joe Meek called it "a hard road over Jordan."

Pioneers and ranchers did use it, sometimes as a cattle trail. A farmer such as Charles Farnsworth could haul his wheat from the Palouse country over the trail to Spokane, a distance of about seventy-five miles, which took four or five days round-trip. There was no money for upkeep during the Civil War, and the route was abandoned in 1872, when railroads began to provide faster transportation.

The Spokane, Portland, and Seattle Railroad was constructed over this east-west part of the Mullan Road in 1908. The Union Pacific still runs north and south through the valley. Where Snyder farm buildings now dot the valley below was the phantom railroad station of Ankeny, still included on detailed maps. Levi Ankeny owned land along Cow Creek and would not give a right-of-way to the railroad to cross his ranch unless they put a station there with his name on it. He also negotiated the right to use the railroad free of charge and to make trains stop in Ankeny.

While surveying along Washtucna-Benge Road in 1933, Walter Athey, the county engineer of Adams County, discovered a weather-worn cedar post bearing the Roman numerals XXI. Mullan liked to mark his progress. "When we finished the first mile I happened to think of the way the old Roman roads in Europe were marked. We had an old branding iron with us, with the letters 'M', 'R' [for "military road"], so I had a young tree cut down, the bark stripped off, then the wood was branded and there was our first mile post." The marker Athey found was almost exactly twenty-one miles from Lyon's Ferry on the Snake River.

Although the cedar posts are gone, newer stone markers for the historic road pepper eastern Washington. They tend to be in towns such as Lamont and Prescott and on roads where people driving cars can see them, such as on Highway 26, three and a half miles east of Washtucna.[1] A gravel road still named the Mullan Road follows the original route between Highway 26 and Gray Road. In this vast landscape, these remnants remind the lonesome traveler of another generation's discoveries and struggles.

CHAPTER NINE

The Lower Columbia River

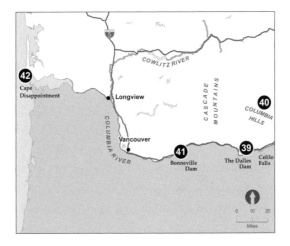

L ong before the Columbia River was charted on maps, it was known by its great reputation. Mid-Columbia Indians called it Nchi'-Wana, "the Big River." Early explorers and fur traders called it "the mighty river of the West" and hoped that it would lead them across the continent. American captain Robert Gray discovered the river from the coast in 1792 and named it after his ship, the *Columbia*. Not until 1811 did David Thompson, of the fur-trading North West Company, canoe the Columbia's length from source to mouth. He discovered that the river flows north and south as far as it flows east and west.

After seventeen months on the trail, Meriwether Lewis and William Clark found the mighty river too—but not a smooth ride to the coast. The Corps of Discovery embarked on the Columbia on October 18, 1805, after two days of smoking and feasting at its confluence with the Snake. They would arrive at its mouth a month later, greatly relieved at reaching the ocean.

This chapter follows the expedition down the lower Columbia: past the great trading emporium of Plains and Coastal Indians at Wishram and Celilo Falls; past the Columbia Hills, where thousands of cattle and horses would graze; past cascades where the U.S. Army built forts to protect the passage; past the mouth of the Cowlitz River, where thousands of emigrants would turn north toward Puget Sound, and on to the big mouth of the Columbia at the Pacific Ocean. Even though highways 4, 12, 14, and 124 tout themselves as the Lewis and Clark Trail, you can't hike them. Traveling by water, the early explorers left few footprints on land, but captains' journals lead to the shores they visited and the trails along those sites. Grand dams such as the Bonneville and Dalles have smoothed the once-mighty rapids, and windsurfers and ocean-going freighters ride the Gorge between cascade ridges, but the ancient rocks and the course of the Columbia remain much the same. The biggest changes came for Native Americans as related in the Yakama Nation Museum:

> One day downriver from the east came strangers,
> White men and a black man in canoes.
> We received them as honored guests
> As tradition would have us do.
> In a few days, they departed downstream to the west.
> Life for our people
> Would never be the same again.

39

Horsethief Lake

GETTING THERE: The park is off of Highway 14, 28 miles west of Goldendale and 2 miles east of the intersection with Highway 197. In summer, call (509) 767-1159 for reservations for the pictograph tour.

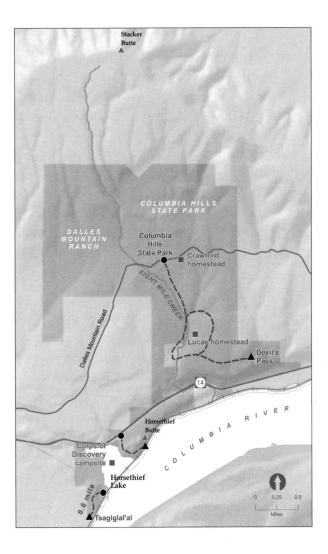

DISTANCE: .6 mile to Tsagigla'lal; about 1 mile of wanderings around Horsethief Butte

LEVEL OF DIFFICULTY: moderate

HISTORICAL HIGHLIGHTS: petroglyphs

Horsethief Lake State Park claims the shore where the Columbia River once rushed through treacherous rapids between hills and mountains. William Clark described a place where "the water of this great river is compressed into a Chanel between two rocks." Indians explaining the Columbia Gorge said that in ancient times the people upriver had been hoarding the fish in a lake created by a dam. Coyote came and saw that the people downriver were starving and needed fish, so he destroyed the dam. The water rushed downstream and carved the gorge through the mountains so fish would come.

Celilo Falls was a natural fishing site where thousands of salmon jumped the rapids each year on their return upstream. The rocks on both sides were lined with platforms built of poles and planks reaching out over the water. Some fishermen tied ropes around their waists, their only means of rescue if they fell in. A good fishing station could net a ton of fish a day. For centuries the Wishram people on the north side of the river and the Wasco on the south side fished at Celilo Falls and controlled commerce at the narrows.

The rapids are known as the Long and Short Narrows, five and ten miles east of The Dalles, respectively. The Corps of Discovery decided to run the rapids instead of portaging their canoes over the high rocks at the head of the first narrows. "I thought . . . by good Stearing we could pass down Safe, accordingly I deturmined to pass through this place notwithstanding the horrid appearance of this agitated gut Swelling, boiling & whorling in every direction," Clark wrote. He admitted that once they were in it, the water was worse than it had appeared from the top of the rock. "However, he said, we passed Saf to the astonishment of all the Inds," who were watching from the high rock.

A Wishram village, Nixluidix, meaning "trading place," squatted at the head of the Long Narrows; it contained the first wooden houses the corps had seen since Illinois. Nearby, Clark saw a mound of earth about thirty feet high, called Wakemap Mound. When the railroad cut through the north end of Wakemap, excavators uncovered evidence of extensive trading in the mound: pipestones from

Minnestoa, turquoise from the Southwest, copper from Michigan or Alaska, graphite and galena from Montana, and dentalium from Vancouver Island. Columbia River Indians, generally those of the lower and upper Chinook tribes, traded salmon for buffalo hides from the Plains. Coastal peoples brought dried seal meat, dogfish oil, and whale blubber. The trade language used here, Chinook jargon, originated from Chinook words but later added vocabulary from European traders.

Today the river is placid, bordered by highways and railroad lines on both sides as barges roll by. Burlington Northern trains come around a rocky bend often, surprising walkers with their whistles. Swallows flit in and out of the rock buttes from which the Indians watched the corps run the river. People come to this park for recreation but also to find the history preserved on pictographs.

Joseph Drayton, an artist traveling with the Hudson's Bay Company, was the first European-American to notice the rock art, in 1841. What he called the Hieroglyphic Rocks were about twenty feet high, "and on them are supposed to be recorded the deeds of some former tribe." The fur brigade passed so quickly that Drayton could make only two hasty sketches.

Perhaps that was a blessing. The rock art at Horsethief Lake State Park has suffered from too much attention, and the trail along the river has been closed to protect the carvings from vandalism. They may be seen only on guided tours given by docents on Fridays and Saturdays in the summer. The sun is often bright, even early in the morning. Hats are recommended, not only as sunscreen but also to create shade for seeing the pictographs.

The pictograph artists used red, white, and black paint—the red normally coming from iron pigment and the white probably from volcanic ash. The pictographs reflect the influence of both Coastal and Plateau cultures. The ladder image of the human body, for example, showing ribs like a ladder, is a Plateau image.

The last, biggest, and most famous art on the trail is Tsagigla'lal, or She Who Watches, a face with distinct ears, mouth, nose, and eyes peering out above fallen rocks. Such masklike faces also appeared on small stones and bone carvings that date from 200 to 300 years ago, when smallpox and other diseases decimated people along the river. Tsagigla'lal was a powerful guardian spirit used by shamans trying to ward off the epidemics.

There are other explanations for the image. One oral tradition attributes the bearlike features of this face to a tribal woman's liaison with animals. The daughter born from the relationship was an outcast. She lived alone in the hills until one day she saw stick people, big men on horses, approaching the village to steal food and belongings. As the younger people were off hunting or gathering huckleberries, she ran down to warn the older people and to hold off the stick people. They laughed at her, but she began doing a dance. Soon it began to thunder and lightning, and then an earthquake struck. The stick people were vanquished, but the daughter was buried in the rubble. The returning villagers worked all night to uncover her from beneath the fallen rocks but could not find her. In the morning, her face appeared on the rock.

Another story connects the picture to the transition of power from women chiefs to men. Tsagigla'lal refused to give up power, so Coyote changed her into a face on a rock, where she could watch over her people even as changes came.

Tsagigla'lal is a combination petroglyph/pictograph, lightly carved and painted with red paint. There are bullet holes on her face that were also visible in a 1911 photograph. One explanation for the holes is that whites desecrated the painting for sport, and another is that Indians desecrated it because too many people were coming to this sacred spot thus diluting its power.

To the east of the pictographs, footpaths wind through the rocks of Horsethief Butte, a vision quest area for native people. Signs ask hikers to stay out of some areas, but it is possible to wander in and out of other rock faces, taking in the expanse of the river and feeling on top of the world.

The Wishram placed platforms for the dead at the top of Horsethief Butte. A burial site at the bottom was named Colowesh Bottom. Smallpox and measles epidemics brought by white traders spread along the Columbia in the late 1700s; malaria devastated 90 percent of the people in lower Columbia villages between 1830 and 1833. During the 1855 treaty negotiations, the Wishram exchanged their land for inclusion in the Yakama Reservation, but they came back to the river to fish. In the early 1900s, 1,500 permanent residents still lived in the village of Spedis, west of Colowesh Bottom. A woman in the Spedis family told her son that she remembered Lewis and Clark.

Construction of the Bonneville Dam in the 1930s drowned many of the pictographs. The lakes created behind The Dalles Dam in 1957 buried Celilo Falls. Native American tribes still have fishing rights here, with a major access on the Oregon side of the river, but the wild salmon have greatly declined. The name Horsethief is completely fictional, made up in a contest sponsored by the Army Corps of Engineers. The town of Wishram (or Spedis), no longer a trade emporium, stretches along the railroad tracks, still close to the river.

40

Columbia Hills

GETTING THERE: Dalles Mountain Road leads to the park. From the southwest, on Highway 14, take the first left beyond the intersection with Highway 197. From the southeast, take the first right beyond Horsethief Lake State Park, at milepost 84.5. The ranch is 3.5 miles northeast along this road. Approaching from the north, take 142 west from Goldendale, then go south on Esler Road, which becomes Simcoe Mountain Road and then Dalles Mountain Road after Centerville. The ranch is approximately 14.3 miles from Centerville.

DISTANCE: 3 miles to Stacker Butte; a 2-mile ramble south along Eight-Mile Creek

LEVEL OF DIFFICULTY: moderate; 1,200-foot elevation gain to Stacker Butte

HISTORICAL HIGHLIGHTS: old farm wagon; yellow rose bush; cemetery; Crawford home

Above the pictograph and vision quest sites at Horsethief Butte loom the Columbia Hills. The bunchgrass growing here caught the attention of artist Joseph Drayton in 1841. As he traveled up the Columbia with a fur expedition, Drayton noticed that the trees ended, and in their place were "rolling, barren, and arid hills. These hills, as well as the country nearer at hand, were covered with a natural hay or bunchgrass, which affords very nutritious food for cattle."

Indeed it did. When Lewis and Clark returned east in April 1806, the Indians were in these hills tending their horses, which were a source of wealth and mobility. Decades later, the first Cattle King of Washington, Ben Snipes, used much of the land as a range, employing Yakama cowboys to tend the herds (see chapter 6). Also profiting from the hills, Charles Newell of Goldendale became the biggest horse dealer in the world. He bought and sold Indian ponies, shipping 1,350 by train to New York in 1885. Henry Stacker ran sheep in the same hills.

Sheep still graze on these rugged highlands above the Columbia River. As we approached from the north and east in 2001, following a maze of paved then dirt and gravel roads, my husband and I stopped at the intersection of Dalles Mountain Road and Uecker Road, where a blanket-clad horseman herded a large flock of sheep and a few goats. Whistling commands to his five working dogs, the

A wagon pastures at Dalles Mountain Ranch.

herder controlled the amoeba flow of sheep across the road in front of us, a wondrous sight to Puget Sound eyes.

Besides the cattle and sheep, the hills are only lightly inhabited and still feel lonesome. Homesteads that began hopefully in the late 1800s have been abandoned, leaving only a few permanent markers. The few ranch buildings remaining, clustered on both sides of the road, provide the only shade on a hot day. This is an undeveloped park—no campground, no concession stand, no paved parking, and one lone port-a-potty—which makes it ideal for solitary exploring.

Begin at the old ranch wagon that marks the Crawford homestead. Two families that stuck it out for three generations were the Crawfords and the Lucases. The two-story Victorian house was the second home of John Crawford and Mary Lucas, son and daughter of the homestead families. They married in 1898 and built this home in 1906.

The homesteaders were attracted to this western land by the provisions of congressional acts offering land for settlement. The Homestead Act of 1862, for example, gave a 160-acre plot to a homesteader willing to live on the land for five years. The Timber Culture Act of 1877 envisioned new forests to replace those cut down in the Midwest and offered another 160 acres if the homesteader would plant forty acres of trees. Nobody could do that, especially on arid land, so the acreage was reduced to ten, and the whole act was soon repealed—but not before settlers in the Columbia Hills planted a few trees.

William Crawford claimed land here in 1877, leaving his ten-year-old son John in a rock dugout that first winter to tend a small herd of sheep. William's wife Julia, their younger son, and their newborn daughter stayed with relatives in the Willamette Valley until father and son built a cabin up the hill on the flat east side of Eight-Mile Creek. The first grave in the small family cemetery was dug in 1880 when their youngest child, a seven-month-old son, died in an epidemic.

The Crawfords put in a garden and started a family orchard. A red apple tree still produces there. Across the road, the large barn

Stacker Butte overlooks the Columbia Hills to the north.

may include parts of the small barn originally built by the Crawfords to pen their first sheep.

Eight-Mile Creek bisects the park, burbling through a gully of green running south of the road. There is no clear trail, but the old pastures gradually give way to faint paths that follow the creek and sometimes climb the ridge on the west side. There is some shade among the scrub oak trees that shelter the creek—and the welcome sound of water.

About a half mile south, on the east side of the creek, is the homestead site of John and Emma Lucas, Mary's parents. They arrived a year after the Crawfords and claimed 160 acres south of them along the creek. John, a blacksmith and stock man, had also been a buffalo rider, providing meat to railroad crews laying track across the country. He claimed additional land through the Timber Culture Acts and planted osage orange and black locust trees to fulfill his contract. The Lucas site is marked by locust trees, a chestnut tree, a grapevine, and rock fences. A yellow rose bush, called Harrison's Yellow, brought by the settlers, still blooms on the homestead.

Stay alert for both ticks and rattlesnakes. The Crawfords once killed seventy-six rattlesnakes in a single hour in one den of rocks.

Despite the comforts homesteaders created, it was hard to sustain life on this land. The Black Cricket Plague of 1864–70 swept the hills bare of greenery, and some early settlers left then. John Crawford gradually consolidated land parcels into one big ranch of 2,000 acres, but he had to borrow money during the hard times of the Depression. Two years after his death in 1933, Mary and their son Malcolm were unable to make payments and lost the land in foreclosure. Forty years later, the ranch had grown to 6,000 acres—two miles wide and five miles long, from the river up over Stacker Butte to the Lyle-Centerville road. The new owner went bankrupt, and the ranch was sold at a sheriff's auction. Yakima Valley ranchers Darlene and Pat Bleakney bought it, maintained it, loved it, and wrote a book called *Dalles Mountain Ranch*. They sold the land in

1990 to the Trust for Public Land, which finalized a sale in 1993 to the Washington State Department of Natural Resources.

There is much more to explore in this park. Also east of the creek, an old road leads over the hills—the cattle drive route of Ben Snipes and the stagecoach road that went from Fort Dalles to Fort Simcoe in the late 1800s. South of here is Devil's Pass, an unmarked opening behind a huge frontage rock where native people started on a trail from the river to the huckleberry fields on Mount Adams.

The Columbia Hills Natural Area Preserve above the park has 2,833 acres. Because it is a preserve, roaming the hills is discouraged, but a road leads uphill 1.4 miles to a gate. Park there and walk the road to the top of Stacker Butte, named after the sheepherder. Beyond the intimidating FAA VORTAC (Very High Frequency Omni and Tactical Air Navigation) station is a knoll with a view of six mountains: Mount Adams, most prominent on the skyline; Mount Rainier hiding a bit behind it; the Goat Rocks to the right of Adams; the gray cone of Mount St. Helens barely emerging to the left; and mounts Hood and Jefferson visible to the south. In the near distance is rangeland. The Dalles, a hub of commerce in the 1800s, spreads out on the southern bank of the Columbia.

Use of the land has varied, from cattle grazing to nature preserve, from homesteading to wineries, from sheepherding to defense installations, but rock walls and rock fence corrals constructed by both homesteaders and natives still line the hills. Wild balsamroot and desert parsley return in force every spring, tenaciously holding on alongside the apple trees, grapevines, and rosebushes.

41

The Cascades

GETTING THERE: The trail begins off Highway 14, 1 mile west of the Bonneville Dam powerhouse, just east of North Bonneville.

DISTANCE: 1.5-mile loop

LEVEL OF DIFFICULTY: easy

HISTORICAL HIGHLIGHTS: portage route; Cascades townsite; Fort Cascades

After passing through the narrows below the Columbia Hills, the Corps of Discovery camped for three days at The Dalles, named for the flat stones in the Columbia River. Continuing on downstream, they passed through another narrowing of the river, which was later called the Cascades. Here William Clark described a curious phenomenon with his usual erratic spelling: "The rocks project into the river in maney places and have the appearance of haveing fallen from the highe hills," and so they had.

Several hundred years previously, perhaps as few as 300, Table Mountain had caved and fallen to the river from the north side. This Bonneville Landslide created a land bridge 200 feet high over the Columbia River, which a Klickitat legend called the Bridge of the Gods. The bridge collapsed, the legend says, during an explosive fight between warring volcanoes that hurled rocks into the river. Scientists say that the river may have undermined the bridge in just a few years.

The dumped rocks created rapids and a navigation hazard for all who wanted to travel up or down the Columbia. Clark said he could "plainly hear the roreing of the grand shutes below." Instead of trying to run them, the men slipped their four large canoes over poles placed between rocks. Three of the canoes received "injuries,"

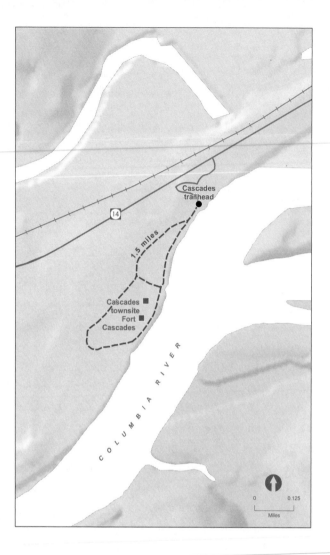

which obliged the corps to delay and repair them. As they camped, the corps noted eight Indian villages, which belonged to bands that became known as the Cascades Indians.

In addition to the physical hazards of passing through the cascades, fur traders described the necessity of dealing carefully with the tribes that controlled the passage. One method later employed by the fur trade was to hire the natives. "The weather being exceedingly warm, many of the Indians were employed to transport articles on their horses, of which they have a large number," wrote Joseph Drayton as he traveled with the Hudson's Bay Company brigade in 1841. "It required seventy men to transport the boats, which were carried over bottom upwards."

The cascades spread over three main sites a few miles apart: upper, middle, and lower. Early settlers rafted down the river from The Dalles, then reassembled and portaged their wagons at the upper cascades before continuing on more placid waters downstream. A few decided not to bother with the portage and stayed put. George W. Johnson filed the area's first land claim in 1850, and the Cascades townsite was platted at the lower cascades, not far from a seasonal Indian fishing site. To secure settlers' land claims, Fort Rains was built at the middle cascades, named after the man who invented landmines. This permanent settlement challenged control of the river passage.

The Cascades portage and settlement can be walked today without a canoe on your shoulders or a wagon to reassemble. A one-and-a-half-mile trail loops along the lower cascades. Numbered markers and an explanatory brochure detail the site's history, from ancient petroglyphs to the flood of 1894, when the Columbia reached its highest recorded level and destroyed every building in town. That act of nature restored this one spot to an undeveloped state, making a historic trail possible.

The loop starts at the site of a fish wheel, follows the river along its 1894 floodplain, and reaches the Cascades townsite. In response to American incursions, Cascades and Yakama Indians attacked this hamlet at the lower cascades on March 26, 1856, burned every structure to the ground, and killed three people; other residents took refuge upstream. Two days later, Colonel George Wright forced the Indians out, and the U.S. Army ordered construction of more blockhouses—Fort Cascades at the townsite, and Fort Lugenbeel at the upper cascades.

Julia Gilliss, wife of an army quartermaster, mentioned in her letters the "terrible Cascades Massacre." When she came for a visit more than ten years later, she found the place a relief from The Dalles, where her husband was stationed. "'Tis the tiniest little mite of a place you can imagine, boasting only one store and no hotel," she commented, and "a few poor little deserted houses, but "the wild entanglement of flowers, trees, everything green, flowery and beautiful made poor rocky, sandy Dalles suffer by comparison."

The trail passes the Johnson land claim and a replica of a petroglyph near the site of a Cascades Indians village. Looping back east, the trail follows remnants of portage routes from the earliest canoes to a steam railroad. The first portage railway in 1851 was a wooden cart pulled by mules on wooden rails. Gillis found a somewhat improved portage when she visited: steam cars for five miles around the falls. When her party went ashore, however, they found that only a locomotive had been sent, minus the passenger cars. "So the only alternative was to ride on an iron horseback." The seven passengers packed themselves into the tender, and Gillis sat in the engine proper. They went on "charmingly" until within a mile of their stopping place, where the track was covered with snow, rocks, and loose dirt that had slid down the mountainside. They walked the rest of the way, rolling carpet bags, portmanteaux, and baskets ahead of them.

The Oregon Steam Navigation Company operated this Cascade Portage Railway for more than forty years, but in 1896, the Cascades Canal and Locks smoothed the river and made the portage obsolete. When the Spokane, Portland, and Seattle Railway was completed in 1908, and a transcontinental railroad ran along the Oregon shore, land transportation overtook water transportation.

The Gorge continued to be an economic center along the river. Capitalizing on the narrowness of the river's course, fish wheels scooped large quantities of fish out of the water for 50 years, from the 1880s until they were outlawed in 1934. The biggest change of all came in 1934 when the construction of the Bonneville Dam completely buried the cascades, causing a decline in the fish runs. With the river's flow now controlled by engineers, and fish runs limited to concrete ladders, this contested vortex of commerce became a mere curiosity.

42

Cape Disappointment

GETTING THERE: From Ilwaco, take the 100 loop south to Cape Disappointment State Park. Past the information station, turn right on the campground road. The McKenzie and North Head Lighthouse trails leave from this road, with limited parking at McKenzie. Other access points are at Beard's Hollow, the Port of Ilwaco, and Long Beach—10th Avenue (Sid Snyder Drive) or Bolstad Avenue.

DISTANCE: .5 mile to McKenzie Head; 1.6 miles to North Head Lighthouse; 1 mile on the Westwind Trail to Beard's Hollow; about 6 miles from Beard's Hollow to Long Beach and the end of Clark's walk. Return on the Discovery Trail for a full circuit, 8 miles from North Long Beach to Ilwaco

LEVEL OF DIFFICULTY: moderate in headlands, easy along beach

HISTORICAL HIGHLIGHTS: McKenzie Head; Clark party campsite; whale skeleton; Clark's tree

The day after leaving the Cascades, Lewis and Clark first noticed the rise and fall of ocean tides in the Columbia River's currents. As they hurried on down the river, they saw prairies that offered good spots for settlement, such as the bluff on which the Hudson's Bay Company would build Fort Vancouver; the mouth of the Willamette River, where Portland would grow; and the mouth of the Cowlitz River, which led to Puget Sound.

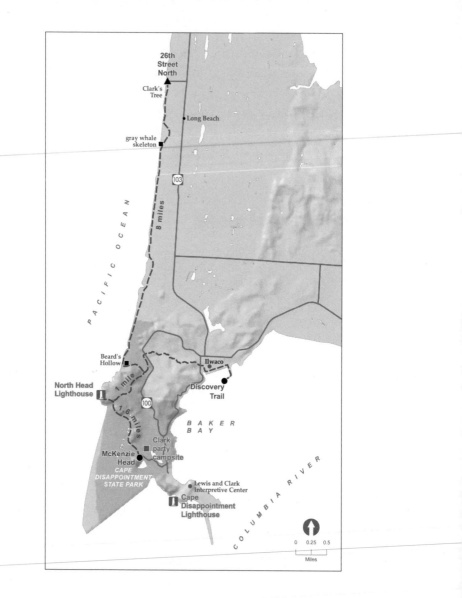

On November 7, 1805, they camped at Pillar Rock, just west of Skamokawa. Here the river broadened greatly. "Great joy in camp we are in View of the Ocian," wrote Clark, "this great Pacific Octean which we been So long anxious to See."

In view, but not there yet. After the next day's travel, the expedition was pinned to the rocky shore at the western edge of Gray's Bay in a "dismal nitch. . . . Scerce of Provisions, and torents of rain poreing on us all the time." Their bedding was soaked and their clothes were rotting off their backs. The river's current was so strong that for six days they could not launch the canoes to move on. Only a canoeload of Cathlamet Indians relieved their misery. The locals crossed the Columbia, "through the highest waves I ever Saw a Small vestles ride," to trade thirteen sockeye salmon to the famished corps.

When the storm subsided, the corps ventured around rocky Point Ellice, which they called Blustering Point or Point Distress. On the west side of the point they found a beautiful sand beach onto which they pulled their canoes. Calling this Station Camp, the "end of our Voyage," they camped for ten days near a Chinook village.

Within sight and sound of the ocean, the wet, tired group still had a sense of adventure. Early Sunday morning, November 17, Meriwether Lewis hiked over the headlands for a better view of the ocean. When he returned to camp, William Clark decided he would go too. He "directed all the men who wished to See more of the main Ocian to prepare themselves to Set out with me early on tomorrow morning." At daylight, ten went with him "and my man York to the Ocian by land."[1] When they returned to Station Camp, Clark drew a map with a dotted line showing where he had been.

Cape Disappointment and the Long Beach peninsula provide the only trails in Washington that follow Lewis and Clark on land, from Station Camp, over the headlands and along the beach to the point where he carved his initials on a tree. Let "all who wish" follow Clark's dotted line.

From Station Camp, in the vicinity of today's McGowan, Clark's crew first climbed a point of rock, the present site of Fort Columbia, then went north and west along Baker Bay on a sandy beach. Crossing inlets and the Chinook River with the help of native women paid in fishhooks, they found and killed a "remarkably large buzzard" near the remains of a whale. With a sense of friendly competition, Clark found Captain Lewis's name branded on a tree and engraved his own. These trees are long gone, but a sculpted condor at the Port of Ilwaco recalls the rare California condor, which is no longer present on the river.

From the beach, "I crossed the neck of Land low and ½ of a mile wide to the main Ocian." After climbing to the top of a "high open hill projecting into the ocian," they camped on a log-strewn beach, having hiked nineteen miles that day. A shower of rain soaked their blankets during the night.

There is no trail yet for this first day's hike, but a short hike leads to McKenzie Head, the hill Lewis and Clark each climbed on successive days. The land has changed but not the wide panorama of the Columbia River meeting the ocean, gray upon gray. From here Clark could see Cape Disappointment, now marked by a black and

The North Head Lighthouse signals the Columbia bar at Cape Disappointment.

white lighthouse. (British trader John Meares named the cape in 1788 when he could not see the mouth of the Mighty River of the West even though he expected it to be there.) In 1805 McKenzie Head was a rock almost surrounded by water and reached by a narrow spit; Clark would not have seen the two jetties reaching into the ocean and the land that has filled behind them. The remnants of World War II battlements witness to the more recent history of this strategic entry to the Pacific Northwest.

The approximate site of the wet campsite is across the road from McKenzie Head, marked on the trail to the North Head Lighthouse. Early the next day Clark arose from his blanket and gave instructions for breakfast: "Sent two men on a head with directions to proceed on near the Sea Coast and Kill Something for brackfast." After three miles of hiking, Clark caught up with the hunters, and they ate a small deer for the first meal of the day. (Deer are still visible on these trails, but a power bar should suffice.)

The trail to the North Head Lighthouse follows the direction Clark traveled the second day, through "rugged Country of high hills and Steep hollers." At 1.6 miles, the trail connects with the Westwind Trail, which fills in Clark's dotted line one mile to Beard's Hollow. At Beard's Hollow, Clark's eleven men reached the sandy shore of Long Beach Peninsula and turned north.

The Discovery Trail picks up the day's hike here, proceeding approximately five miles, as Clark did. It goes through dune grass at a safe distance from the fluctuating tides, but I'm sure Clark found easier walking on the beach. The trail is paved at first, then graveled, then becomes a grassy track.

If you do nothing else, walk the last mile of Clark's exploration of north Long Beach. In the town of Long Beach, the paved trail crosses under the boardwalk and passes the rearticulated skeleton of a whale. This whale beached in May 2000 and was buried before it began to smell. Two years later, students, city employees, and biologists dug up the skeleton, cleaned and preserved the bones, and

A fish-cleaning table designed by Maya Lin frames the mouth of the Columbia River.

rearticulated them into this skeleton, as a reminder of what Clark saw: "Several joints of the back bone of a Whale which must have foundered on this part of the Coast."

Just north of Bolstad Avenue is a nine-foot etched basalt rock that marks the true end of Clark's journey. Here Clark turned inland and found another tree on which to carve his name and the date, replicated by a bronze tree now on the beach trail. After leaving his mark, Clark and the eleven returned over the headlands to Station Camp, finding a ten-foot sturgeon at Beard's Hollow. In 2009 contemporary fishermen were allowed only a few days in July when they could catch and retain a white surgeon.

From Beard's Hollow, the Discovery Trail east follows Clark's return route to Baker Bay. The trail is wide, graveled (to discourage bicycling), evenly graded, and steeply uphill for the first .4 mile, then fully paved for the last mile to Ilwaco.

Thirty-five years after Lewis and Clark, another American expedition, led by Charles Wilkes, arrived by sea at Cape Disappointment. Wilkes's ships could not cross the Columbia's bar because there were breakers extending across the river's mouth "in one unbroken line." A walk to the Cape Disappointment lighthouse from the Lewis and Clark Interpretive Center invokes this fearful history.

"Mere description can give little idea of the terrors of the bar of the Columbia," Wilkes wrote in his diary; "all who have seen it have spoken of the wildness of the scene, and the incessant roar of the waters, representing it as one of the most fearful sites that can possibly meet the eye of the sailor." Indeed, the ship *Peacock*, carrying supplies for the expedition, wrecked on a sandbar at the Columbia's mouth. More than 2,000 vessels have met the same fate.

Although Clark, too, was impressed with the waves' "tremendous force," breaking in every direction, he noted that his men appeared "much Satisfied with their trip beholding with estonishment the high waves dashing against the rocks & this emence Ocian."

The Pacific's roar and its beckoning sweep to the horizon also end this hiker's tour. My exploration began with young children at Cape Flattery and ends with Maya Lin's work at Cape Disappointment. Lin has inscribed the words of a Chinook praise song to the elders on a pathway: "We ask that they teach us and show us the way." From the Olympic Mountains to the Blue Mountains, from Kettle Falls to the mouth of the Columbia, the contours of the land and the flow of the water evoke Washington's richly textured history and show us the way.

Notes

Preface

1   Ivan Doig, *Winter Brothers* (New York: Harcourt Brace, 1980), 132.

CHAPTER ONE: The Olympic Peninsula

1   What he saw was Mukkaw Bay and Waatch Valley, a wetlands area between Cape Flattery and the mainland.
2   One man dropped out early when his wife became ill; one mule fell down a cliff, and the other was set free to fend for itself; one dog was killed by an elk.
3   The expedition called a lake here Lake of the Holy Cross, after the shape of a waterfall; the name became LaCrosse.
4   Alison Gass.

CHAPTER TWO: Puget Sound

1   The Cowlitz Trail has been well documented by Chuck and Suzanne Hornbuckle of the Oregon-California Trails Association. Most of it has been paved, however, into military roads—the Jackson Highway, the Pacific Highway (Old 99), and I-5.
2   Leschi's "X" appears on the treaty, but there is doubt that he signed it.
3   The other two were Forts Worden and Flagler on the Olympic Peninsula.
4   Most of the coal at Newcastle was classified as "sub-bituminous," not as valuable as anthracite.

CHAPTER THREE: The North Cascades

1 The National Park Service does not recommend hiking the old road bed beyond Bridge Creek.

2 In 2007 Congressman Doc Hastings introduced a bill to give the National Park Service authority to rebuild the road by adjusting the wilderness boundary.

3 Florence Lake is Upper Florence Lake. Lower Florence Lake was named between 1949 and 1957.

CHAPTER FIVE: The South Cascades

1 Cooper also saw Mount Jefferson, even farther to the south.

CHAPTER EIGHT: Southeastern Washington

1 Don Popejoy, of the Northwest Oregon-California Trails Organization, has plotted Mullan's route and all of the remaining markers in Washington.

CHAPTER NINE: The Lower Columbia River

1 York was Clark's slave, the only slave on the expedition.

Source Notes

The information in this book came from walking the trails, talking to people, and reading books of local history, diaries, journals, ships' logs, government reports, and letters. Many accomplished writers, historians, and hikers before me have written about trails, including the patriarchs Harvey Manning and Ira Spring; Harry M. Majors, whose *Exploring Washington* includes more than 2000 historic sites (Holland, MI: Van Winkle, 1975); and Ruth Kirk and Carmela Alexander, *Exploring Washington's Past* (Seattle: University of Washington Press, 1995).

United States Geographical Survey topographical maps were essential to these hikes. They are available online at http://topomaps.usgs.gov/. Other maps and more detailed trail descriptions and updates are available in the *Washington Atlas & Gazetteer*, 4th ed. (Yarmouth, ME: DeLorme, 1998); in hiking guidebooks published by the Mountaineers; at History Link (www.historylink.org); and at the Washington Trails Association Web site (www.wta.org).

For an overview of Washington history or for books on subjects that cross chapters in this book, refer to the list below. Additional reading and sources are listed by chapter.

Barkan, Frances B. ed. *The Wilkes Expedition: Puget Sound and the Oregon Country*. Olympia: Washington State Capital Museum, 1987.

Beckey, Fred. *Range of Glaciers*. Portland: Oregon Historical Society Press, 2003.

Clark, Norman H. *Washington: A Bicentennial History*. New York: Norton, 1976.

Dietrich, William. *Final Forest: The Battle for the Last Great Trees of the Pacific Northwest.* New York: Simon and Schuster, 1992.

Ficken, Robert E. *The Forested Land: A History of Lumbering in Western Washington.* Seattle: University of Washington Press, 1987.

———. *Washington Territory.* Pullman: Washington State University Press, 2002.

Kirk, Ruth, with Richard Daughtery. *Exploring Washington Archaeology.* Seattle: University of Washington Press, 1978.

Kresek, Ray. *Fire Lookouts of the Northwest.* Rev. 3rd ed. Spokane, WA: Historic Lookout Project, 1998.

LeWarne, Charles P. *Washington State.* Rev. ed. Seattle: University of Washington Press, 1993.

Schwantes, Carlos A. *The Pacific Northwest: An Interpretive History.* Lincoln: University of Nebraska Press, 1989, 1996.

Utley, Robert. *After Lewis and Clark: Mountain Men and the Paths to the Pacific.* Lincoln: University of Nebraska Press, 1997.

CHAPTER ONE: The Olympic Peninsula

Dalton, Russ. Interview with Julian McCabe, Sr., October 9, 1981.

Doig, Ivan. *Winter Brothers.* New York: Harcourt Brace, 1980.

Howay, Frederic W. *Voyages of the Columbia to the Northwest Coast, 1787–1790 and 1790–1793.* Portland: Oregon Historical Society, 1990.

Kirk, Ruth, with Richard D. Daugherty. *Hunters of the Whale: An Adventure in Northwest Coast Archaeology.* New York: Morrow, 1974.

"Lake Ozette History." *The Lost Resort at Lake Ozette.* www.lostresort.net. January 18, 2010.

Lien, Carsten. *Exploring the Olympic Mountains: Accounts of the Earliest Expeditions, 1878–1890.* Seattle: Mountaineers Books, 2001.

The Makah Cultural and Research Center. *Voices of a Thousand People.* Lincoln: University of Nebraska Press, 2002.

Meares, John. *Voyages Made in the Years 1788 and 1789.* London: Logographic Press, 1790. Reprint, New York: Da Capo Press, 1967.

Parratt, Smitty. *Gods & Goblins: A Field Guide to Place Names of Olympic National Park.* Port Angeles, WA: CP Publications, 1984.

Semple, E. "Report of the Governor of Washington Territory." In *Reports to the U.S. Secretary of the Interior for 1888*. Washington, D.C., 1889.

Snyder, Gary. *No Nature*. New York: Pantheon, 1992.

Swan, James G. *Almost Out of the World: Scenes in Washington Territory*. Tacoma: Washington State Historical Society, 1971.

Webber, Bert. *Retaliation: Japanese Attacks and Allied Countermeasures on the Pacific Coast in World War II*. Corvallis: Oregon State University Press, 1975.

Wood, Robert L. *Across the Olympic Mountains: The Press Expedition, 1889–90*. Seattle: The Mountaineers; Seattle: University of Washington Press, 1967.

———. *Men, Mules and Mountains: Lt. O'Neil's Olympic Expeditions*. Seattle: The Mountaineers, 1976.

CHAPTER TWO: Puget Sound

Badger-Doyle, Susan, and Fred W. Dykes, eds. *The 1854 Oregon Trail Diary of Winfield Scott Ebey*. OCTA Emigrant Trails Historical Studies Series 2. Independence, MO: Oregon-California Trails Association, 2002.

Ballard, Arthur C. *Mythology of South Puget Sound*. Seattle: University of Washington Press, 1929.

Ebey, Isaac N. "A Visit to Lake Washington in 1850." *Oregon Spectator*, October 17, 1850.

Farrar, Victor J. "Diary of Colonel and Mrs. I. N. Ebey." *The Washington Historical Quarterly* 7, no. 3 (July 1916): 240–41.

Gibbs, George. "Report on Niskwalli Nation." *Contributions to North American Ethnology*. Washington, D.C.: Government Printing Office, 1877.

"The Green-Duwamish River: Connecting People with a Diverse Environment." Seattle: Duwamish River Cleanup Coalition, 2008.

Harmon, Alexandra. *Indians in the Making: Ethnic Relations and Indian Identities around Puget Sound*. Berkeley: University of California Press, 1998.

Hartman, Sarah McAllister. "Memoirs." Sarah McAllister papers, 1893.

University of Washington Special Collections Manuscript and Archives Division.

Klingle, Matthew. *Emerald City: An Environmental History of Seattle.* New Haven: Yale University Press, 2007.

Manning, Harvey, and Ralph Owen. *Hiking and Strolling Trails of Cougar Mountain.* Issaquah, WA: Issaquah Alps Trails Club, 1981, 1991.

McDonald, Lucile and Richard. *The Coals of Newcastle: A Hundred Years of Hidden History.* Issaquah, WA: Issaquah Alps Trails Club, 1987.

Pascualy, Maria, and Cecilia Carpenter. *Remembering Medicine Creek.* N.p.: Fireweed Press, 2005.

Reinartz, Kay F. *Tukwila: Community at the Crossroads.* Tukwila, WA: City of Tukwila, 1991.

Thrush, Coll. *Native Seattle.* Seattle: University of Washington Press, 2008.

Warren, James R. *Where Mountains Meet the Sea: An Illustrated History of Puget Sound.* Northridge, CA: Windsor Publications, 1986.

Washington Department of Health. "Lower Duwamish Waterway Superfund Site Fact Sheet." November 2007.

Waterman, T. T. [Thomas Talbot]. "The Geographical Names Used by the Indians of the Pacific Coast." *Geographical Review* 12 (April 1922): 175–94.

White, Richard. *Land Use, Environment and Social Change: The Shaping of Island County, Washington.* Seattle: University of Washington Press, 1991.

CHAPTER THREE: The North Cascades

Agee, James, et al. *Fire History of Desolation Peak.* Seattle: NPS Cooperative Unit, College of Forest Resources, University of Washington, 1986.

Darville, Fred T., Jr. *Stehekin: A Guide to the Enchanted Valley.* Mount Vernon, WA: Darvill Outdoor Publications, 1996.

Ito, Kazuo. *Issei: A History of Japanese Immigrants in North America.* Translated by Shinichiro Nakamura and Jean S. Gerard. Seattle: Japanese Community Service, 1973.

Kerouac, Jack. "Alone on a Mountaintop." In *Lonesome Traveler.* New York: Grove, 1960.

Krist, Gary. *The White Cascade*. New York: Henry Holt, 2007.

Martin, Albro. *James J. Hill and the Opening of the Northwest*. With a new introduction by W. Thomas White. Saint Paul: Minnesota Historical Society Press, 1991.

Pierce, Henry H. "Report of an Expedition from Fort Colville to Puget Sound, Washington Territory, by Way of Lake Chelan & Skagit River." Fairfield, WA: Ye Galleon Press, 1973.

Roe, Jo Ann. *The North Cascadians*. Seattle: Madrona, 1980.

Schwantes, Carlos. *Railroad Signatures across the Northwest*. Seattle: University of Washington Press, 1993.

Snyder, Gary. *Mountains and Rivers without End*. Washington, D.C.: Counterpoint, 1993.

Suiter, John. *Poets on the Peaks: Gary Snyder, Philip Whalen, and Jack Kerouac in the North Cascades*. Washington, D.C.: Counterpoint, 2002.

Sylvester, Albert H. "Place-Naming in the Northwest." Albert H. Sylvester Papers, University of Washington Manuscripts and Archives Division. Accession number 1518+ 1, box T518a.

Wandell, Becky. Written for Volunteers for Outdoor Washington. *The Iron Goat Trail: A Guidebook*. Seattle: The Mountaineers, 1999.

Woodhouse, Philip. *Monte Cristo*. Seattle: The Mountaineers, 1979.

CHAPTER FOUR: Central Cascades

McClellan, George B. *Journal*. May 20-December 15, 1853. Microfilm A228. Suzzallo Newspapers and Microfilm Room. University of Washington Libraries.

Overmeyer, Philip H. "George B. McClellan and the PNW." *PNW Quarterly* 32, no. 1 (1941): 3–60

Prater, Yvonne. "Memories of Hyak before freeways and ski lifts." *The Daily Record,* December 10, 1997, p. 11.

———. *Snoqualmie Pass: From Indian Trail to Interstate*. Seattle: The Mountaineers, Mountains to Sound Greenway Trust, 1995.

Ridge, Alice A., and John Wm. *Introducing the Yellowstone Trail: A Good Road from Plymouth Rock to Puget Sound, 1912–1930*. Altoona, WI: Yellowstone Trail Association, 2000.

Shideler, John C. *Coal Towns in the Cascades: A Centennial History of Roslyn and Cle Elum, Washington*. Spokane, WA: Melior, 1986.

"Snoqualmie Pass Wagon Road." United States Department of Agriculture, Forest Service, Pacific Northwest Region, Snoqualmie National Forest Government Printing Office, n.d.

U.S. Government. *Reports of Explorations and Surveys from the Mississippi River to the Pacific Ocean*. Vol. 1, "Explorations and Surveys for the Pacific Railroad." Washington, D.C.: 1855.

Wood, Charles R., and Dorothy M. *Milwaukee Road West*. Seattle: Superior Publishing Co., 1972.

CHAPTER FIVE: The South Cascades

Allworth, Louise McKay. *Battleground, In and Around: A Pictorial Drama of Early Northwest Pioneer Life*. Vancouver, WA: The Write Stuff, 1984.

Bolduc, Jean Baptiste Zacharie. *Mission of the Columbia*. Edited and translated by Edward J. Kowrach. Fairfield, WA: Ye Galleon Press, 1979.

Cooper, J. G. "Report upon the Botany of the Route." In *The Natural History of Washington Territory*. New York: H. Baillie, 1859.

Douglas, William O. *My Wilderness: The Pacific West*. New York: Doubleday, 1960.

Egan, Timothy. *The Big Burn: Teddy Roosevelt and the Fire that Saved America*. Seattle: Sasquatch, 2009.

Gloss, Molly. *Into the Wild*. Boston: Houghton-Mifflin, 2000.

Haines, Aubrey L. *Mountain Fever: Historic Conquests of Rainier*. Portland: Oregon Historical Society, 1962. Reprint, Seattle: University of Washington Press, 1999.

Harris, Stephen L. *Fire and Ice: The Cascade Volcanoes*. Seattle: The Mountaineers; Seattle: Pacific Search Press, 1976.

Hill, Edwin G. *In the Shadow of the Mountain: The Spirit of the CCC*. Pullman: Washington State University Press, 1990.

Himes, George. "An Account of Crossing the Plains in 1853. . . ." In *Transactions of the Thirty-Fifth Annual Reunion of the Oregon Pioneers Association*, 19 June 1907, p. 145. Portland: Chausse-Prudhomme Co., 1908.

Holbrook, Stewart H. *Burning an Empire: The Story of American Forest Fires*. New York: Macmillan, 1943.

Kautz, A. V. "Ascent of Mt. Rainier." *Overland Monthly* 14 (May 1875): 393–403.

Kirk, Ruth. *Sunrise to Paradise: The Story of Mount Rainier National Park.* Seattle: University of Washington Press, 1999.

"The Legend of Sleeping Beauty Mountain." A handout at Trout Lake U.S. Forest Service Ranger Station.

Magnusson, Elsa C. "Naches Pass." *Washington Historical Quarterly* 25, no. 3 (1934): 174–75.

McClure, Rick, and Cheryl Mack. *For the Greatest Good: Early History of the Gifford Pinchot National Forest.* Seattle: Northwest Interpretive Association, 1999.

Nisbet, Jack. *The Collector.* Seattle: Sasquatch, 2009.

Pyle, Michael. *Where Bigfoot Walks: Crossing the Dark Divide.* Boston: Houghton Mifflin, 1995.

Rice, Marie Bauer. *James Longmire: His Life, His Family.* Printed by the Longmire family of Tacoma, Washington, 1982.

Rosen, Shirley. *Truman of St. Helens: The Man and His Mountain.* Seattle: Madrona, 1981.

Winthrop, Theodore. *Canoe and Saddle.* Portland, OR: Binfords & Mort, 1981.

Work, John. *The Snake Country Expedition of 1830–1831.* Edited by F. D. Haines, Jr. Norman: University of Oklahoma Press, 1923.

CHAPTER SIX: Central Washington

Anglin, Ron. *Forgotten Trails: Historical Sources of the Columbia's Big Bend Country.* Pullman: Washington State University Press, 1995.

Dow, Edson. *Adventure in the Northwest.* Wenatchee, WA: Outdoor Publishing Co., 1964.

———. *Passes to the North.* Wenatchee, WA: Outdoor Publishing Co., 1964.

Harris, Mary Powell. *Goodbye, White Bluffs.* Yakima, WA: Franklin Press, 1972.

Helland, Maurice. *They Knew Our Valley.* Yakima, WA: Maurice Helland, 1975.

Hormel, Monty. *Old West in Grant County*. Ephrata, WA: Tamanawahs Publications, 1992.

Lage, Laura Tice. *Sagebrush Homesteads*. Pullman: Washington State University Press, 1999.

Linsley, Daniel C. "Lake Chelan and Agnes Creek in 1870." *Northwest Discovery* 2, no. 6 (June 1981): 382.

Parker, Martha. *Tales of Richland, White Bluffs and Hanford, 1805–1943*. Fairfield, WA: YeGalleon Press, 1986.

Ross, Alexander. *Fur Hunters of the Far West*. Edited by Kenneth A. Spaulding. Norman: University of Oklahoma Press, 1956.

Sneller, Roscoe. *Ben Snipes: Northwest Cattle King*. Portland, OR: Binford & Mort, 1957.

Splawn, A. J. *Kamiakin*. Portland, OR: Binfords & Mort, 1944.

CHAPTER SEVEN: Northeastern Washington

Chance, David H. *People of the Falls*. Kettle Falls, WA: Kettle Falls Historical Center, n.d.

Cochran, Barbara Fleischman. *Exploring Spokane's Past*. Fairfield, WA: Ye Galleon Press, 1984.

Fahey, James. "The Spokane River: Its Miles and Its History." Spokane, WA: Spokane Centennial Trail Committee, 1988.

Kip, Lawrence. *Indian War in the Pacific Northwest*. Lincoln: University of Nebraska Press, 1999.

Miller, Jay, ed. *Mourning Dove: A Salishan Autobiography*. Lincoln: University of Nebraska Press, 1990.

Nisbet, Jack. *Mapmaker's Eye: David Thompson on the Columbia Plateau*. Pullman: Washington State University Press, 2005.

———. *Sources of the River*. Seattle: Sasquatch, 1994.

Peltier, Jerome. *Antoine Plante: Man, Rancher, Miner, Guide, Hostler, and Ferryman*. Fairfield, WA: Ye Galleon Press, 1983.

Scheuerman, Richard D., and Michael O. Finley. *Finding Chief Kamiakin: The Life and Legacy of a Northwest Patriot*. Pullman: Washington State University Press, 2008.

Wilson, Bruce A. *Late Frontier: A History of Okanogan County, Washington, 1800–1941*. Okanagon, WA: Okanogan County Historical Society, 1990.

Babcock, Scott, and Robert J. Carson. *Hiking Washington's Geology*. Seattle: Mountaineers Books, 2000.

Coleman, Louis C., and Leo Rieman. *Captain John Mullan: His Life, Building the Mullan Road*. Montreal: Payette Radio, 1968.

Cox, Ross. *Adventures on the Columbia*. Portland, OR: Binfords & Mort, 1975.

Gulick. Bill. *Chief Joseph Country*. Caldwell, ID: Caxton, 1981.

Gunselman, Cheryl and Roderick Sprague. "A Buried Promise: The Palus Jefferson Peace Medal." *Journal of Northwest Anthropology* 37, no. 1, 53–88. NARN, Inc., 2003. See http://www.wsulibs.wsu.edu/holland/masc/temp/buriedpromise.htm#palus.

Harper, J. Russell, ed. *Paul Kane's Frontier*. Includes "Wanderings of an Artist among the Indians of North America," by Paul Kane. Austin: University of Texas Press, 1971.

Kingston, Ceylon S. *Inland Empire in the Pacific Northwest*. Montreal: Payette Radio, 1968.

John Mullan's Report on the Construction of a Military Road from Fort Walla Walla to Fort Benton. Fairfield, WA: Ye Galleon Press.

Leighton, Caroline C. *Life at Puget Sound*. Boston: Lee and Shephard; New York: Dillingham, 1884.

Peltier, Jerome. *Felix Warren: Pioneer Stage Driver*. Fairfield, WA: Ye Galleon Press, 1988.

Soennichsen, John. *Bretz's Flood: The Remarkable Story of a Rebel Geologist and the World's Greatest Flood*. Seattle: Sasquatch, 2008.

Tucker, Gerald J. "History of the Northern Blue Mountains." 1940. Typescript. Available at the Pomeroy Ranger Station, Umatilla National Forest.

Watt, James W. *Journal of Mule Train Packing in Eastern Washington in the 1860s*. Fairfield, WA: Ye Galleon Press, 1978.

CHAPTER NINE: The Lower Columbia

Barkan, Frances. *The Wilkes Expedition*. Olympia: Washington State Capital Museum, 1987.

Bleakney, Darlene Highsmith. *Dalles Mountain Ranch: Museum of Natural & Cultural Heritage of the East Columbia River Gorge.* Salem, OR: Lynx Communication Group, Inc., 1992.

Gilliss, Julia. *So Far from Home: An Army Bride on the Western Frontier 1865–1869.* Edited by Priscilla Knuth. Portland: Oregon Historical Society Press, 1993.

Hunn, Eugene S., with James Selam and Family. *Nch'i Wana: "The Big River": Mid-Columbia Indians and Their Land.* Seattle: University of Washington Press, 1990.

The Journals of the Lewis and Clark Expedition. University of Nebraska Press / University of Nebraska-Lincoln Libraries-Electronic Text Center, October 5, 2005. www.lewisandclarkjournals.unl.edu (accessed 24 February 2010).

The Lewis and Clark Journals: The Abridgement of the Definitive Nebraska Edition. Edited by Gary E. Moulton. Lincoln: University of Nebraska Press, 2003.

Ramsey, Jerold Ramsey, ed. *Coyote Was Going There.* Seattle: University of Washington Press, 1977.

Index